SUMMARY OF GREG[G]

FORWARD STR[OKES]

K	G	R	L	N	

DOWNWARD STROKES

P	B	F	V	SH	CH	J	S	NG	NK	H

VOWELS AND DIPHTHONGS

a		came		calm		can	
e		meet		met		mit	
o		low		law		lot	
oo		to		tuck		took	

ū		unit		oi		toy		ow		out		i		tie	

ĭa, ēa		piano		create		īa		science		diet	

BLENDS

nt, nd		print		planned		mt, md		prompt		blamed	
ten, den		written		obtain		sudden					
rd		feared		ld		filled		ses		faces		races	
men, min		mend		minute		minimum					
ted, ded		greeted		needed							

WORD BEGINNINGS

be-		beneath		des-		describe		over-		overcome	
com-		comply		dis-		display		re-		receive	
con-		consider		ex-		example		sub-		subscribe	
de-		delay				explain				sublet	
di-		direct		for-		forgive		trans		transfer	
				in-		income		under		underneath	

WORD ENDINGS

-ble		table		-ings		readings		-rity		majority	
-cal		chemical		-lity		facility		-tion		nation	
-cle		article		-lty		faculty		-ual		mutual	
-ful		careful		-ly		namely		-ure		nature	
-ing		going		-ment		moment		-ward		forward	
-ingly		accordingly									

LOUIS A. LESLIE

is coauthor of *Gregg Shorthand Simplified* (a series of over 20 textbooks and supplementary books), and is author of many other textbooks in shorthand and reporting. An eminent authority in Gregg Shorthand, Mr. Leslie has lectured widely on Gregg Shorthand and methods of teaching the system. He originated and developed the "Functional Method" of teaching Gregg Shorthand and for over thirty years was associated with the publishers of the system. Mr. Leslie is a Certified Shorthand Reporter (C.S.R.).

CHARLES E. ZOUBEK

is Shorthand Editor, Gregg Publishing Division, McGraw-Hill Book Company, Inc., a coauthor of the *Gregg Shorthand Simplified* series, and is author of many other textbooks and professional books in shorthand and reporting. He taught classes in shorthand for many years in New York City. A popular lecturer, Mr. Zoubek has given methods courses for shorthand teachers in nearly every state and on many college campuses. Mr. Zoubek is also a Certified Shorthand Reporter (C.S.R.).

JAMES DEESE

is Professor of Psychology at The Johns Hopkins University. He is the author of *The Psychology of Learning*, now in its second edition, a coauthor (with Clifford T. Morgan) of *How to Study*, and a contributor to the widely used college textbook, *An Introduction to Psychology*, by C. T. Morgan. Dr. Deese is a recognized authority in the psychology of learning and has made many contributions to the field in his books, articles, and lectures.

Gregg Notehand

A Personal-Use Shorthand with Integrated Instruction in How to Make Notes

Gregg Notehand

A Personal-Use Shorthand with Integrated
Instruction in How to Make Notes

LOUIS A. LESLIE, C.S.R.

CHARLES E. ZOUBEK, C.S.R.

JAMES DEESE, Ph.D.

SHORTHAND WRITTEN BY CHARLES RADER

GREGG PUBLISHING DIVISION

McGraw-Hill Book Company, Inc.

NEW YORK   CHICAGO   SAN FRANCISCO   DALLAS   TORONTO   LONDON

GREGG NOTEHAND

A Personal-Use Shorthand with Integrated Instruction in How to Make Notes

August 1960-RD-1

Library of Congress Catalog Card No. 60-14223

Illustration on Part One by
David W. Corson from A. Devaney, N. Y.

Published by GREGG PUBLISHING DIVISION
McGraw-Hill Book Company, Inc.
Printed in the United States of America

Preface

Gregg Notehand, A Personal-Use Shorthand with Integrated Instruction in How to Make Notes, was written to meet a student need that educators have long recognized — instruction in making intelligent, meaningful notes from reading and from listening. Psychologists have long known that the process of making notes contributes greatly to learning and remembering. Many books dealing with study habits and techniques have been written in which the importance of making good notes is emphasized. However, these books provide little or no help in the actual processes and procedures of notemaking. It is the purpose of this volume to provide this help.

In addition to providing instruction in notemaking processes and procedures, this book equips the notemaker with a brief, easy-to-learn writing method — Gregg Notehand — with which to make notes much more rapidly and easily than he could with longhand.

ORGANIZATION OF THE TEXT

Gregg Notehand is organized in two parts:

Part I: Fundamentals of Gregg Notehand and Notemaking — Theory and Practice. This part presents all the theory of Gregg Notehand as well as the basic fundamentals of good notemaking. It contains 42 units (or lessons), of which 30 are devoted to presentation of the theory of Gregg Notehand; 6, to review of Gregg Notehand; and 6, to presentation of notemaking fundamentals.

The units in Part I follow this pattern: 1 unit on the fundamentals of notemaking; 5 units on Gregg Notehand theory; 1 unit on review of Gregg Notehand. This pattern is repeated six times in the 42 units of Part I.

Part II: Applications of Gregg Notehand and Notemaking — Extended Practice. This part is designed to extend and refine the notemaker's ability to use Gregg Notehand and to make good notes. It contains 28 units, 24 of which are devoted to Gregg Notehand and 4 to notemaking.

ORGANIZATION OF THE UNITS

The units in this book are basically of two types: notemaking and Gregg Notehand.

Notemaking. A typical notemaking unit contains:

1. A presentation of the fundamentals of notemaking
2. Exercises that apply these fundamentals
3. Practical tips and suggestions for notemaking
4. Exercises in which the student puts these tips and suggestions into practice

Gregg Notehand. A typical Gregg Notehand unit in Part I, which completes the theory of Gregg Notehand, contains a number of principles followed by a list of words or phrases in Gregg Notehand illustrating those principles. This list in turn is followed by a reading and writing practice exercise into which several illustrations of the principles have been woven.

A typical Gregg Notehand unit in Part II, which is devoted to the development of greater writing facility, contains drills in the form of word lists designed to strengthen the student's knowledge of the theory of Gregg Notehand. These drills are followed by reading and writing practice exercises that will help the student develop the ability to construct outlines rapidly for an ever-expanding vocabulary.

OTHER FEATURES

Illustrations. The book is illustrated generously with photographs, line drawings, and cartoons especially prepared for Gregg Notehand. These illustrations, many of them in color, do much to brighten the appearance of the pages and to make the book fun to work with.

Practice Suggestions. To be sure that the student derives the greatest benefit from the time that he invests in Gregg Notehand, the authors have provided specific suggestions to guide him in every phase of his practice. The student who follows these suggestions faithfully will not only absorb more, but he will also complete each unit in the shortest possible time.

Key. The key to the reading and writing exercises and illustrations of notemaking techniques appears in type in the back of the book, thereby enabling the Gregg Notehand student to make the most rapid progress, especially in the early stages. The student should be urged to follow the suggestions given in Unit 2 for the use of this key.

Practice Material. The practice material in the reading and writing exercises consists largely of short articles that are inspirational, informational, or entertaining. The material is on an adult level and will appeal equally to masculine or feminine interests.

In the early units, some of the words in the reading and writing exercises are given in longhand. This makes it possible to provide meaningful sentences and paragraphs for practice before the student has completed the theory of Gregg Notehand.

The publishers are confident that the authors of Gregg Notehand have made a unique and valuable contribution to general education, a contribution that will have a profound effect on the success that students enjoy not only in their pursuit of education, but in their later business or professional life as well.

The Publishers

Contents

PART ONE

Fundamentals of Gregg Notehand and Notemaking — Theory and Practice

What Good Notemaking Can Do for You

Making good notes can accomplish three things for you:

1. It can help you learn more and faster.

2. It can help you remember more and remember it longer.

3. It can help you study and work more efficiently.

MAKING NOTES CAN HELP YOU LEARN MORE AND FASTER

It is a well-known fact that you learn more and you learn faster through *doing*. "Doing" doesn't mean merely the physical act of being occupied at something. It means actively participating *with your mind* while you are engaged in the learning process.

Trying to learn without actively participating mentally is wasteful of time. But when you participate actively in the learning process, your time can be meaningful and productive. Let's put it this way: Learning will be meaningful and productive in proportion to the degree to which you actively participate mentally in the process.

What does this have to do with making notes? The very process of making notes as you listen, read, or observe will stimulate and guide your mental participation in the activity. In fact, the process of making notes actually forces you to participate actively. You can't help but learn more and learn it faster.

MAKING NOTES CAN HELP YOU REMEMBER MORE AND LONGER

The act of making notes will also help you to remember more of what you learn and remember it longer. Active mental participation helps fix important ideas and facts in your mind so that they become a part of you. As a result, you can remember them better. Good notes serve as a "memory storehouse" for you; that is, a reference source, just as does a dictionary or an encyclopedia, for the review and recall of facts and information. In addition, the notes trigger your memory of other facts, information, and ideas not recorded in your notes.

Learning and Forgetting. It is virtually impossible to remember everything one learns. Herman V. Ebbinghaus, a famous German psychologist, proved this in his experimental studies of verbal learning and retention. Among other things, Ebbinghaus was interested in how much of what he personally had learned he could remember after various periods of time. By finding out how much he could remember a week after learning compared with, say, four hours after learning, Ebbinghaus was able to construct a "curve of forgetting." That is, he could show by means of a curve graph when most forgetting takes place.

In his experiment Ebbinghaus learned — and this may surprise you — that he did most of his forgetting immediately after learning! Thus, based on the results of Ebbinghaus's studies and other later studies, a psychological rule of considerable importance has been formulated: *we forget most of what we are going to forget immediately after we learn it.*

Relearning Comes More Quickly. After Ebbinghaus had measured how well he could remember, he resorted to a test, which is called the "savings method." In this method, the person whose memory is being tested *relearns* something he learned previously. The measure of retention is the difference in time it takes between original learning and relearning. Suppose, for example, Ebbinghaus took five minutes to learn a list of 16 nonsense syllables. If, twenty-four hours later when he relearned the same list, he took only two minutes, he obtained a savings of three minutes, or 60 per cent.

The significance of this experiment is that, if you have learned something and then forgotten it, you can relearn it much more quickly than if you had to learn it "from scratch." In the relearning process good notes are especially useful. They con-

You'll study more efficiently if you make notes.

tain only the essential facts and ideas and will save a great deal of time and effort in relearning, such as reviewing for an examination. After all, reviewing is essentially a process of relearning.

MAKING NOTES CAN HELP YOU STUDY AND WORK MORE EFFICIENTLY

The process of making notes induces active mental participation in studying just as it does in any other form of learning activity. Every student needs a workable procedure for studying. Making notes is an important part of this procedure. What is more, participation by making notes helps you organize study effort.

In addition, the notes themselves provide material for subsequent study — the memory storehouse mentioned earlier. Naturally, the better the notes the more useful they are in studying.

Notes may be made over a period of time or immediately preceding or at the time of studying. They may come from many sources — lectures, discussions, textbooks, experiments, library research, and so on. They can be used for reference and for review, or they may be used to get ready for examinations or in preparing papers and reports.

NOTEMAKING IS A COMBINATION OF ABILITIES

Notemaking consists of more than simply writing things down on paper. There are definite techniques to learn about notemaking. *What* you record and *how* you record it are important. You need to know how to listen with concentration, how to read effectively when studying, how to grasp and record essential ideas, how to outline as you make notes, how to make notes for research papers, and so on. All these techniques are discussed fully in this book.

In addition to mastering the techniques for making notes, you need a simple, easy-to-use writing system — a system so quick and easy to use that it will permit you to give more attention to what is being heard or read. Gregg Notehand meets this need. Gregg Notehand, a simple adaptation of Gregg Shorthand, is expressly designed for notemaking. It is simple and easy to learn. It is simple and easy to write. It is simple and easy to read.

Good notemaking requires concentration, and you are not likely to give conscious attention to a book or a speaker if you have to bend every effort to record the barest essentials, such as is the case with longhand. Concentration leads to good notes — notes that are full enough to be useful, but that contain only really important ideas and information. Gregg Notehand requires less time to write than longhand; therefore, you have more time to concentrate, to select, to evaluate, to organize, and to record.

Gregg Notehand consists essentially of the alphabet of Gregg Shorthand, which utilizes the strokes, linear directions, and other characteristics of longhand. This alphabet was originally published in 1888 and has been in continuous use since that time as the basis of the Gregg system of shorthand. As you probably know, Gregg Shorthand has been learned and put to vocational use by millions of men and women — stenographers, secretaries, court reporters, and executives. Your notemaking can be efficient and effective with the use of Gregg Notehand.

In addition to the alphabet of Gregg Shorthand, Gregg Notehand uses 42 "brief forms" for words that occur very frequently, such as *a*, *what*, *with*, *and*, *about*; a single phrasing principle; and a few other abbreviating devices.

FOR DISCUSSION AND PARTICIPATION

1. Think of ways in which you have, or could have, used notes in your daily activities. See if you can make a list of fifteen different situations where notemaking is involved.

2. Why do you think the act of making notes helps you to remember more and longer? Discuss.

3. As an experiment, have someone read a brief paragraph to you. Listen carefully, but do not make notes. Try to give the important points aloud.

4. Now try another experiment. Have the same person read another brief paragraph to you on the same subject. This time make a few notes of the important points. Then reconstruct in your own words the gist of the paragraph.

A NOTEMAKING AND STUDYING INVENTORY

Size up your present notemaking and studying abilities by completing the inventory on the following page. Then after you have finished your study of Gregg Notehand, complete the inventory again to discover the improvement you have made. Chances are, at the start, that most of your answers will be "True." However, you should have very few "True" answers, if any, at the end.

A NOTEMAKING AND STUDYING INVENTORY

Directions: On a sheet of paper write the heading NOTEMAKING AND STUDYING INVENTORY. Then list the following statements by number. Opposite the numbers place "Before" and "After" boxes or spaces. Date each inventory first when you began your study of Gregg Notehand, and then when you finish it. Mark each statement "True" or "False" in each inventory. If your Gregg Notehand text is your personal property, you may record your answers in the spaces provided on this page.

BEFORE   AFTER

DATE _____ _____

☐ ☐   1. I do not have a plan for studying; I study on a "hit-or-miss" basis.

☐ ☐   2. I have trouble getting down to work and sustaining my effort in studying.

☐ ☐   3. I find it so hard to concentrate on what I am reading that I get very little out of it.

☐ ☐   4. When I make notes from reading, I always copy the author's words just as he wrote them.

☐ ☐   5. When I make notes, I put down too much; and later I have difficulty in sifting the important from the unimportant.

☐ ☐   6. My notes are too brief — they don't make sense to me when I come back to them for study and review.

☐ ☐   7. My notes lack organization and continuity; I can't seem to relate similar topics.

☐ ☐   8. The personality, voice, and mannerisms of speakers frequently disturb me and hinder my concentration.

☐ ☐   9. I miss important things in lectures and discussions because I am too pushed in getting down notes on what has gone before.

☐ ☐   10. It's difficult for me to grasp and organize ideas and information conveyed by a speaker and make notes at the same time.

☐ ☐   11. I don't know what to put down when I am making notes from reading—that is, I can't find the important ideas.

☐ ☐   12. I don't know how to use my notes efficiently once I have made them.

☐ ☐   13. I am so pressed for time when making notes that I can't read them later — they're too sloppy.

☐ ☐   14. When writing a term paper or a report, I have difficulty knowing how to go about making notes and then using them in writing my paper.

☐ ☐   15. Composition is hard for me because it is so laborious and time-consuming to write and rewrite in longhand.

☐ ☐   16. I put off too long reviewing my notes and preparing for examinations.

☐ ☐   17. I find it virtually impossible to make useful notes when participating in or listening to group discussions.

☐ ☐   18. I do not know the best tools for notemaking in various situations — notebooks or cards or what.

☐ ☐   19. My mind wanders so much when I listen to a lecturer or speaker that I get very little out of what he says.

☐ ☐   20. Essay examinations are a problem for me because I can't quickly draft answers before writing them.

UNIT 2

Gregg Notehand Is Easy to Learn

If you can write longhand with any fluency, you will have no difficulty learning to write Gregg Notehand. The strokes you will use in Gregg Notehand are the same ones that you are accustomed to writing in your everyday longhand.

Gregg Notehand is actually easier to learn than longhand. Why? In longhand, there are many different ways of writing a given letter; in Gregg Notehand, *there is only one way*. For example, here are six different ways in which the longhand r may be expressed:

$$Rr \mathcal{R} \mathcal{R} \mathcal{R} \imath r$$

In Gregg Notehand, there is only one way to express r.

The facility with which you will eventually write Gregg Notehand will depend, of course, on how well and how regularly you practice. If you follow carefully the practice suggestions given in this unit, your writing facility will develop rapidly and with each unit your study of Gregg Notehand will become more and more fascinating.

Group A

1. **S-Z.** Perhaps the most frequent consonant in the English language is s. In Notehand, s is a very small downward curve resembling the longhand comma. Notice how the s is derived from the longhand form of s.

In longhand, s often has the sound of z as in saves; therefore, in Notehand the s stroke also represents the sound of z.

2. **A.** The Notehand a is a large circle. Once again, notice how a is derived from the longhand form.

3. **Silent Letters Omitted.** In the English language many words contain letters that are not pronounced. In Notehand these silent letters are omitted, and only

those sounds in a word are written that are actually pronounced. For example, in the word say, the y would not be written because it is not pronounced; say would be written s-a. The word face would be written f-a-s; the final e would be omitted because it is not pronounced, and the c would be represented by the s stroke because it is pronounced s.

What letters in the following words would not be written in Notehand because they are not pronounced?

day   eat   main

mean   save   steam

Check your answers with the key to Paragraph 3 in the back of this book.

4.   **S-A Words.**   With the letters s and a, you can form two words.

say, s-a   ∂ℓ   ace, a-s   ☌

Practice these words, following the suggestions in Paragraph 5.

5.   **Practice Procedures for Word Lists.**   *You will learn the words in Paragraph 4—and all the other words that are given to illustrate the Notehand principles you will study—more quickly and remember them longer if you will practice them in this way:*

1. With the type key exposed, pronounce and spell aloud—if possible—each word and Notehand outline in the list, thus: say, s-a; ace, a-s. By reading aloud you will be sure that you are concentrating on each word as you study it. Repeat this

The student studies the word lists by placing a card or slip of paper over the key and reading the Notehand words aloud.

procedure with all the words in the list until you feel you can read the Notehand outlines without referring to the type key.

2. Cover up the type key with a card or slip of paper. Then spell and pronounce aloud, thus: s-a, say.

3. If the meaning of a Notehand outline does not come to you after you have spelled it, remove the card or slip of paper and refer to the type key. Do not spend more than a few seconds trying to decipher an outline. Reread the list of words in this way until you can read the entire list without referring to the type key.

4. In your notebook* write the entire list once in Notehand, saying each word aloud as you write it. Repeat this procedure two or three times until you feel you can write the words easily.

Caution: Under no circumstances write a full line or more of each word; this type of repetitious practice is not only monotonous, but it is also the least efficient way to learn the words.

6.   F.   The Notehand character for f is the same shape as s except that it is about three time as big. It is also written downward.

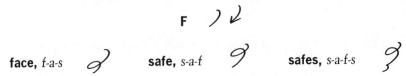

Did you notice that the c in *face* has the s sound and is, therefore, represented by s?

7.   V.   The Notehand character for v is the same shape as f except that it is about twice as big as f. It is also written downward.

Note the difference in the sizes of s, f, and v.

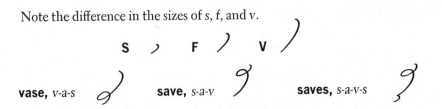

Did you notice that the final s in *saves* has the z sound, which is represented by the s stroke?

---

*A regular spiral-bound stenographic notebook will do nicely for your Notehand practice. The best writing instrument for your course in Notehand is a good ball-point pen. A ball point is easier to write with than a pencil; and the notes you make will be legible almost indefinitely, while pencil notes may become blurred and difficult to read.

8.   E.   The Notehand stroke for e is a small circle. Notice how it is derived from the longhand e.

E   *e*   ✓o

Always make the e circle small—tiny, in fact—and the a circle large.

Compare: E ₒ   A ◯

| see, s-e | ∂ | fee, f-e | ⟩ | ease, e-s | 9 |
| sees, s-e-s | 9⟩ | fees, f-e-s | 9⟩ | easy, e-s-e | ∂9 |

Did you notice that the y in easy is pronounced e and is, therefore, represented by the e circle?
Be sure to practice the e words as suggested in Paragraph 5.

Group B

9.   N.   The Notehand character for n is a very short forward straight line.

N   ⇁

| see, s-e | ∂ | say, s-a | ∂ | knee, n-e | —o |
| seen, s-e-n | ⌐ | sane, s-a-n | ⌐ | vain, v-a-n | ⌐ |

Did you notice that the k in *knee* is not written because it is not pronounced?

10.   M.   The Notehand character for m is a longer forward straight line, about three times as long as n.

M   →

Compare: N –   M —

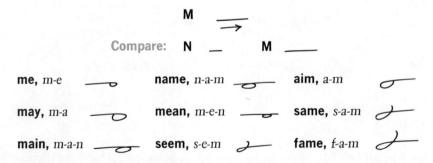

me, m-e	—o	name, n-a-m	—o—	aim, a-m	⌐—
may, m-a	—o	mean, m-e-n	—o—	same, s-a-m	⌐—
main, m-a-n	—o—	seem, s-e-m	⌐—	fame, f-a-m	⌐—

Remember, you will learn these words most effectively if you follow the practice procedures suggested in Paragraph 5.

11.   **T.** The Notehand character for *t* is a very short upward straight line.

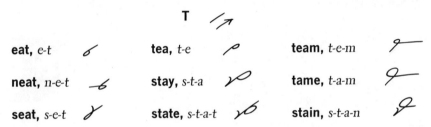

eat, *e-t* **tea,** *t-e* **team,** *t-e-m*

neat, *n-e-t* **stay,** *s-t-a* **tame,** *t-a-m*

seat, *s-e-t* **state,** *s-t-a-t* **stain,** *s-t-a-n*

12.   **D.** The Notehand character for *d* is a longer upward straight stroke, about three times as long as *t*.

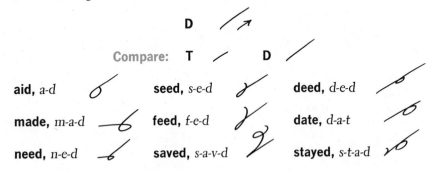

Compare: **T** **D**

aid, *a-d* **seed,** *s-e-d* **deed,** *d-e-d*

made, *m-a-d* **feed,** *f-e-d* **date,** *d-a-t*

need, *n-e-d* **saved,** *s-a-v-d* **stayed,** *s-t-a-d*

13.   **Capitalization.** Capitalization is indicated by two short upward dashes underneath the item to be capitalized.

Dave **Fay** **Amy**

14.   **Punctuation.** In Notehand the following marks of punctuation are used.

Period ﹨ **Paragraph** > **Parentheses**

Question × **Dash** ⹀ **Hyphen** =

For all other punctuation marks, the regular longhand forms are used.

15.   **READING AND WRITING PRACTICE**

With the aid of a few longhand words, you can already read complete sentences. These sentences contain only the following Notehand characters, which you have studied thus far:

S   A   F   V   E   N   M   T   D

To get the most out of each Reading and Writing Practice, follow the procedure suggested in Paragraph 16.

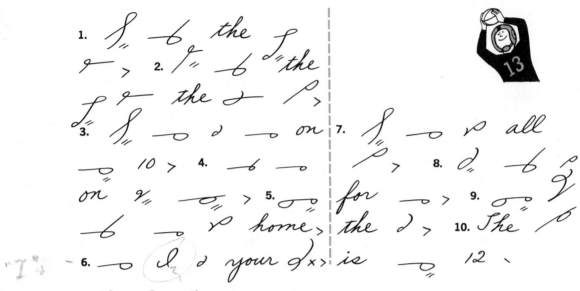

16. Suggestions

a. For Reading the Reading and Writing Practice Exercises.

1. Place your left index finger under the Notehand outline that you are about to read.

2. Place your right index finger on the type key to that Notehand outline. The key begins on page 280.

The student refers to the key whenever he cannot read an outline. Notice how the left index finger is anchored on the place in the Notehand; the right index finger, on the corresponding place in the key.

When copying, the student reads a convenient group of words aloud and then writes that group in his notebook. Notice how he keeps his place in the Notehand with his left index finger.

3. Read the Notehand, aloud if possible, until you come to an outline you cannot read. Spell the Notehand characters in the outline. If this spelling does not *immediately* give you the meaning, anchor your left index finger on that outline and turn to the key in the back, where your right index finger is resting near the point at which you are reading.

4. Determine the meaning of the outline that you cannot read, and then place your right index finger on it.

5. Turn back to the Notehand page from which you are reading, where your left index finger has kept your place for you, and continue reading.

This procedure is very important, as it will enable you to save much precious time that you might otherwise waste finding your place in the Reading and Writing Practice and in the key.

6. If time permits, read the Reading and Writing Practice a second time, perhaps even a third time.

You must keep in mind that during the early stages your reading may not be very rapid. That is only natural, as you are, in a sense, learning a new language. With faithful practice from day to day, however, your reading speed will increase rapidly.

b. For Writing the Reading and Writing Practice Exercises.

After you have read each Reading and Writing Practice, follow this procedure:

1. Read a convenient group of words aloud; then write that group in your notebook.

2. Keep your place in the Reading and Writing Practice with your left index finger if you are right-handed; with your right index finger if you are left-handed.

3. After you have made one complete copy of the Reading and Writing Practice, make a second copy if time permits. You will find that this second writing will go more smoothly than the first.

Of course, your early writing efforts will not be very rapid nor will your outlines look as pretty as those in the book. However, from day to day, as you use your Notehand in class and for your personal notes, your outlines will become noticeably smoother and more accurate.

UNIT 3

In Unit 3 you will study three new alphabetic characters, as well as two devices that will help you to write Notehand more rapidly. Be sure to follow the procedure recommended in Paragraph 5 when you practice the words in the lists.

17.   O.   The Notehand character for o is a small, deep hook. Notice how it is derived from the longhand form.

O

no, *n-o*		**so,** *s-o*		**own,** *o-n*	
toe, *t-o*		**phone,** *f-o-n*		**tone,** *t-o-n*	
dough, *d-o*		**vote,** *v-o-t*		**stone,** *s-t-o-n*	
snow, *s-n-o*		**note,** *n-o-t*		**dome,** *d-o-m*	

Did you notice that in the words in the last column the o is turned on its side? This enables us to obtain an easier joining.

18.   R.   The Notehand character for r is a short forward curve. Notice how it is derived from its longhand form.

R

air, *a-r*		**rain,** *r-a-n*		**more,** *m-o-r*	
ear, *e-r*		**read,** *r-e-d*		**tore,** *t-o-r*	
near, *n-e-r*		**free,** *f-r-e*		**door,** *d-o-r*	
dear, *d-e-r*		**freight,** *f-r-a-t*		**store,** *s-t-o-r*	

Did you notice that *fr*, as in *free* and *freight*, is written with one smooth motion, without an angle between the *f* and the *r*?

19. **L.** The Notehand character for *l* is the same shape as the Notehand *r* except that it is about three times as long. Notice how it is derived from its longhand form.

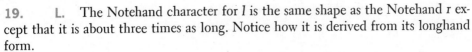

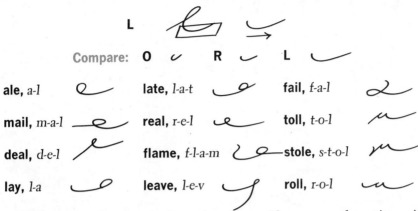

Compare: **O** ↄ **R** ↄ **L** ↄ

ale, *a-l*		**late,** *l-a-t*		**fail,** *f-a-l*		
mail, *m-a-l*		**real,** *r-e-l*		**toll,** *t-o-l*		
deal, *d-e-l*		**flame,** *f-l-a-m*		stole, *s-t-o-l*		
lay, *l-a*		**leave,** *l-e-v*		**roll,** *r-o-l*		

Did you notice that *fl*, as in *flame*, is written with one smooth motion, without an angle between the *f* and the *l?*

20. **Brief Forms.** In the English language there are certain words that are used so frequently that we can save a great deal of writing time by providing abbreviations for them. This is a common practice in longhand. In Notehand these abbreviations are called "brief forms." In your Notehand course you will study 42 brief forms for very common words. In this unit you will take up six of them.

Because of the frequency of these words, you will be wise to learn them well.

I	*O*	**a, an**	·	**for**	)
is	）	**have**	/	**am**	—

21. **Phrasing.** As you learned in Paragraph 20, we save writing time by providing short, easily written outlines for common words. Another device for saving time is called "phrasing," or the writing of two or more words together as one outline. See how easily and quickly the following phrases can be written.

I am		**for me**		**I may**	
I have		**I know**		**I feel**	

22. **READING AND WRITING PRACTICE**

Your progress has been so rapid that in the sentences of the following Reading and Writing Practice only a few words are written in longhand. To be sure that you get the most benefit from this Reading and Writing Practice, take a moment to reread the suggestions given in Paragraph 16. If you use the key correctly, you will be able to complete your work with these sentences in a matter of minutes.

Here are the Notehand characters you have studied thus far. All of them are used in the sentences. Review these characters now quickly.

S	A	F	V	E	N	M	T	D
,	O	)	)	∘	—	—	/	/

O	R	L
ᴜ	⌣	⌣

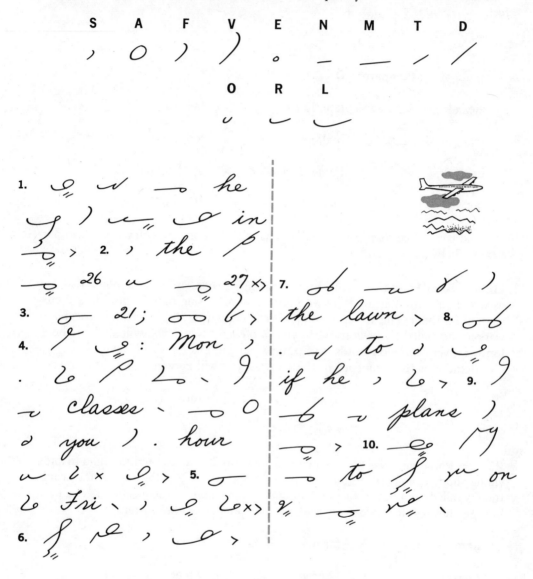

1.

2. the

26 27

3. 21;

7. the lawn 8.

4. Mon

to if he 9.

classes plans

you . hour

10. to on

Fri 5.

6.

In Unit 4 you will take up two new characters and a principle that enables us to save time by omitting vowels that are silent or only slightly sounded.

Reminder: See Paragraph 5 for suggestions on how to practice the word lists in this unit.

23.   H, -ing.   The letter *h* is simply a dot placed above the vowel. The letter *h*, with few exceptions, occurs at the beginning of a word.

Ing, which almost always occurs at the end of a word, is also expressed by a dot.

H

he		hair		whole	
hay		hate		heat	

-ing

Spell: **hearing,** *h-e-r-ing*

hearing		heeding		rowing	

24.   Omission of Minor Vowels.   Some words contain a vowel that is either omitted or slurred in ordinary speech. For example, *even* is pronounced *ev'n; motor, mot'r.* As these vowels are hardly heard in speech, they are not written in Notehand.

reader		motoring		hasten	
nearer		even		total	
dealer		season		favor	

25.   READING AND WRITING PRACTICE

You will notice that the number of words in longhand is getting smaller—a sign of the rapid progress you are making!

Reminder: See Paragraph 16 for practice suggestions.

1. ⟨shorthand⟩

ill, 2. ⟨shorthand⟩ my ⟨shorthand⟩ buy ⟨shorthand⟩

3. ⟨shorthand⟩ in ⟨shorthand⟩ cars, 4. ⟨shorthand⟩

with ⟨shorthand⟩ Sun,

5. ⟨shorthand⟩ 30 min ⟨shorthand⟩, 6. ⟨shorthand⟩ purchased ⟨shorthand⟩ our ⟨shorthand⟩,

7. Do ⟨shorthand⟩

to ⟨shorthand⟩ Sat ⟨shorthand⟩ at 8, 8. ⟨shorthand⟩ bought ⟨shorthand⟩ Fri, 9. ⟨shorthand⟩ Sat ⟨shorthand⟩ rest ⟨shorthand⟩

week ⟨shorthand⟩, 10. ⟨shorthand⟩ tho it, ⟨shorthand⟩ to ⟨shorthand⟩

UNIT 5

In this unit you will learn two more alphabetic characters, as well as a second form for s and z.

Beginning with this unit, you will find a Reading and Writing Practice after each new Notehand character or word-building principle has been introduced.

26.   Left S and Z.   The first Notehand stroke you learned was the small downward curve for s and z. Because these sounds are so frequent, a second form has been provided to represent them—a "backward" comma, written downward. The use of the two forms for s and z makes it possible to obtain an easy joining in any combination of strokes. Use whichever s makes the easier joining in a word. For convenience, this stroke is called the "left s."

Left S

seal	teams	fears
sailing	owns	seats
meals	days	seems
eats	stores	most

READING AND WRITING PRACTICE

27.   P.   The Notehand character for *p* is the same shape as the left *s* except that it is about three times as long.

P ⌇⌇

pay	𝟼	hope	⌇	praise	⌇
pair	𝟼	opening	⌇	paper	𝟼
spare	𝟼	paid	𝟪	plate	⌇
peel	𝟼	rope	⌇	please	⌇

Did you notice in the words in the third column how *p* joins to *r* or *l* with one smooth motion, without an angle between the *p* and the *r* or *l*?

READING AND WRITING PRACTICE

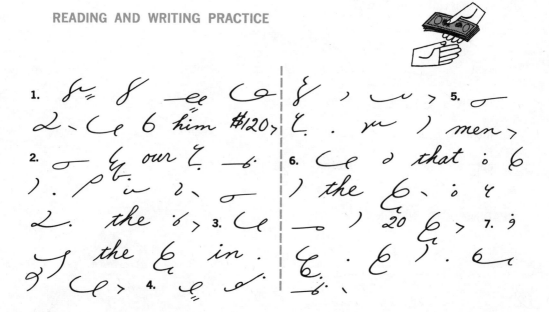

1. ... him $120, ...
2. ... our ... the ... the ... in. ...
3. ...
4. ...
5. ... men,
6. ... that ... the ... 20 ...
7. ...

28.   B.   The Notehand character for *b* is the same shape as the character for *p* except that it is about twice as long.

B ⌇⌇

Compare: **Left S** ⌇   **P** ⌇   **B** ⌇

bay	𝟼	bone	⌇	brief	⌇

base	*(shorthand)*	obey	*(shorthand)*	labor	*(shorthand)*
bearing	*(shorthand)*	beat	*(shorthand)*	blame	*(shorthand)*
boats	*(shorthand)*	beans	*(shorthand)*	label	*(shorthand)*

Did you notice in the words in the last column that *b* joins to *r* or *l* with one smooth motion, without an angle?

READING AND WRITING PRACTICE

1. *(shorthand)* first *(shorthand)* *(shorthand)*

2. *(shorthand)* on *(shorthand)* on Sat,

3. *(shorthand)* order) 1,500 *(shorthand)* 1,200 *(shorthand)* cards *(shorthand)* 100 *(shorthand)* of

4. *(shorthand)*

5. *(shorthand)*

6. *(shorthand)*

7. *(shorthand)*

UNIT 6

In this unit you will study six more brief forms for commonly used words and a number of useful phrases that are made up of those brief forms.

29.   Brief Forms.   These six brief forms will come up again and again in all the writing that you will do. Practice them, following the procedure suggested in Paragraph 5, until you know them well.

it	/	of	⌣	will	⌣
in	—	are, our	⌣	*the	⌐

*The word *the* is represented by a short upward curve. This curve represents the sound of *th*, which you will study later.

Did you notice that the Notehand *r* stands for two words? Perhaps you have already discovered that a few Notehand characters represent more than one word. You will never have any difficulty selecting the correct word in a sentence; the sense of the sentence will always give you the answer.

30.   Phrasing.   The brief forms in Paragraph 29 enable us to form additional useful, timesaving phrases.

of the	⌒	in the	⌒	it will	⌒
of our	⌒	is the	⋎	it is	⌒
in our	⌒	I will	⌒	for it	⌒

Phrasing, in addition to saving writing time, gives us another advantage—a phrase is easier to read than the parts of a phrase written separately. You are less likely to misread ⌒ than the separate parts — and ⌐ .

READING AND WRITING PRACTICE

The brief forms and phrases you studied in Paragraphs 29 and 30 are used many times in the sentences in the following Reading and Writing Practice to help impress them on your mind. If you follow faithfully the practice suggestions in Paragraph 16, you should be able to complete your work on this Reading and Writing Practice in 20 minutes or less. Can you do it?

Group A

1. _____ shape _____ 25, 2. _____ car at _____ end _____ 6 _____

$450 _____ 3. _____ _____ $50, 4. _____ $50 _____

Group B

5. _____ election _____ 6. _____ no, _____ 4-1414, 7. _____

_____ car _____ old, 8. _____ take _____ $10. _____ worth _____

Group C

9. bought _____ 10. _____ 11. _____ that _____

_____ 12. _____ end _____ off.

RECALL

There are no new alphabetic strokes for you to learn in this unit. You will simply review the strokes and principles you studied in Units 2-6. You will do this through a helpful recall chart and a Reading and Writing Practice consisting of complete sentences.

Here are the Notehand strokes you studied in Units 2-6. Review them quickly before you start your work on the recall chart and the Reading and Writing Practice.

F	V	Comma S	E	A	T	N	M	D

H	L	R	O	B	P	Left S

31. Recall Chart. The following chart contains one or more illustrations of every alphabetic stroke you have studied in Units 2-6. Spell and say each word aloud as you practice it, thus: s-a-v, save. If the spelling does not immediately give you the meaning of the outline, refer to the key in the back of the book.

There are 108 words and phrases in the chart. Can you complete your first reading of the chart in 12 minutes or less? If you can, you are making good progress indeed!

Words

1						
2						
3						
4						
5						

6						
7						
8						
9						
10						
11						
12						
13						
14						

Brief Forms

15						
16						

Phrases

17						
18						

32.   READING AND WRITING PRACTICE

Group A

1. *(shorthand outlines)*
2. *(shorthand outlines)*
3. drives . 1960
4. *(shorthand outlines)*
5. *(shorthand outlines)*

bought

ing

$50

Group B

6. *(shorthand)* tho *(shorthand)* Mon *(shorthand)* 7. *(shorthand)* $100 *(shorthand)* 8. *(shorthand)* to *(shorthand)*

9. *(shorthand)* living room *(shorthand)* 10. *(shorthand)* Sat.

Group C

11. *(shorthand)* at *(shorthand)* 12. *(shorthand)* 13. *(shorthand)* to *(shorthand)* error *(shorthand)* 14. *(shorthand)* 60 *(shorthand)* 15. *(shorthand)*

Group D

16. *(shorthand)* $180 *(shorthand)* $180 *(shorthand)* price *(shorthand)* 17. *(shorthand)* job *(shorthand)* 18. *(shorthand)* 19. *(shorthand)* 20. *(shorthand)*

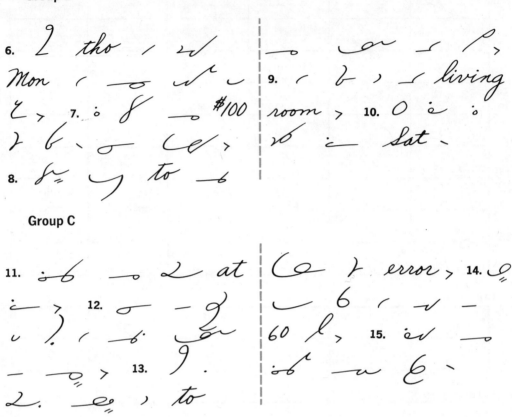

Effective Study and Notemaking

Studying is almost a full-time occupation for a high school or college student. And it doesn't stop upon graduation. Long after they have left school, many people continue to be students. They keep up with their business or profession by reading magazines, books, reports, and the like. The typical business executive, doctor, teacher, or lawyer today can't afford *not* to keep up to date on the latest developments in his field. In fact, education is a continuing process for almost everyone.

Knowing how to study efficiently is fundamental to making the most of one's educational experience. Many people have failed to benefit from much of their education because they never learned how to study. Let's consider some general techniques and procedures that will help you to study more efficiently.

EVALUATE YOUR GOALS AND AMBITIONS

First, take a look at yourself and see where you want to go. What do you want to achieve? Are your goals and ambitions worth the study efforts required to reach them?

Whether or not you have established your long-range goals, you will have immediate goals, such as high school graduation or admission to the college of your choice or even college graduation. On the other hand, your goal may be admission to graduate study or to a professional school, such as medicine, dentistry, or law. Effective study techniques will be invaluable to you in achieving these goals as well as personal-improvement goals. And they will be useful to you throughout your active life.

Studying is basically a matter of self-discipline. It takes time. It takes effort and concentration. It means sacrificing other activities that might be more pleasant and entertaining. But if you wish to accomplish your goals and ambitions, effective studying is worth any self-discipline. If you wish to make the most of your talent, your time, and your effort, if you genuinely and sincerely want to succeed, it is worth the self-discipline.

STUDY IN AN ENVIRONMENT THAT ENCOURAGES CONCENTRATION

Where is the best place for you to study? This is a pertinent question, and the answer to it will have a direct bearing on the productivity of your time and effort; that is, the *quality* and *quantity* of the results.

Studying is most effective when it is done in an environment that offers quiet, privacy, and freedom from distractions, whether in the home, in school, or elsewhere. In these days of crowding, both at home and at school, it is not always possible to find the ideal environment for study. At any rate, make every effort to study in a place that offers as much quiet and freedom from distractions as possible.

Once you select or arrange a good place to study, use it regularly rather than studying in a different place each day. A person tends to become adjusted to a particular study environment, and he will find it helpful to continue to use it once it has proved effective.

Adequate light is important, as are a comfortable temperature and suitable equipment and supplies. For writing purposes, a good firm surface, such as that offered by a desk or a table, is essential. Without good working environment, equipment, and supplies, it's easy to dissipate time and energy.

When you study, *study*, and do it in a place that is suitable for the purpose.

PLAN YOUR STUDYING

Planning is important in everything that you do — and studying is no exception. Advance planning will make the time and effort you put into studying more productive.

A first step in planning your study is to prepare a *schedule for studying*. Here are some suggestions.

1. Set aside a block of time for studying, allowing enough time to get your studying done. Don't plan more time for studying than you will actually use for the purpose. Allowing too much time may ac-

Effective study is achieved in surroundings that encourage concentration.

Harold M. Lambert

tually encourage poor study habits, for you will probably fritter away time and energy even though you have a schedule.

The right amount of time for studying will vary with the subject and with the student. Preparing a workable, realistic schedule requires your best judgment. Your objective is to study efficiently and effectively, and doing so isn't measured by *time* but by *results*. What you're after is getting the desired results as quickly and with as little effort as possible.

2. Some subjects will require more time than others. Allot to the study of each subject the amount of time required to do it well — enough time, but not too much.

3. Schedule your toughest subjects for study first. If you put off your hardest subjects until last, you will dissipate your energy by worrying about the difficult task ahead. You will also run the risk of not allowing sufficient time for the difficult subjects.

Long-range assignments, such as term papers and research reports, should be scheduled well in advance of the deadline. These assignments should be planned to utilize longer stretches of time, such as weekends and vacations.

4. Study for a particular subject or an assignment promptly after the related instruction, such as a class meeting or lecture.

5. Establish a regular time for studying. If possible, study at the same time each day.

6. Allow time in your study schedule for some relaxation. If you don't, you probably won't stick to your schedule.

7. Revise your study schedule according to your study requirements.

GET DOWN TO WORK

No matter how good your intentions are, or how well you have planned your schedule, results come only as you get down to work. Here is the real problem for most people. It is so easy to fritter away time.

Dribbling away time can be eliminated only by deliberate effort. If you are really a time waster, make your study periods short at the beginning. You will find it easier to get down to work if you know you have only a half hour or even fifteen minutes to go. It is better to work hard for only fifteen minutes than to spend a couple of hours intermittently studying, daydreaming, studying, talking, studying, and entertaining yourself. Once you actually adjust to the hard fact of working when you study, you can make your scheduled study periods longer, with fewer breaks.

GOOD NOTEMAKING CONTRIBUTES TO STUDYING EFFICIENTLY

Many factors contribute to effective studying: the individual's urge to achieve; his self-discipline; the environment for study, including equipment, materials, and supplies; the schedule for studying; and the habit of "getting down to work." Then there is notemaking — a tool of learning, a technique and procedure for studying, and a source of notes or materials for study.

The very process of making notes focuses attention on what is being studied, motivates and guides effort, and yields essential materials for further study and use.

Making notes in class discussions, in doing experiments, in listening to lectures, and so on, yields materials for studying. These materials, or *notes*, usually contain the essentials grasped from listening, from reading, from observing, and from other learning activities. The notes are particularly valuable in reviewing, relearning, preparing assignments, preparing for examinations, and preparing research papers.

Gregg Notehand will also be a great help to you in studying. Easier and quicker to use than longhand, it will save you time and effort, whether you're making notes, jotting down ideas, or writing a research paper or report.

FOR DISCUSSION AND PARTICIPATION

1. Why is it important for you to look at your goals and ambitions as a step toward improving your studying efficiency?

2. "Learning how to study efficiently and effectively is a matter of self-discipline." Explain this statement.

3. Examine your own study environment. In what ways might it not offer the best atmosphere for studying?

4. Why do you think it is important to establish a regular place for studying?

5. It is recommended that you study for a particular subject or assignment promptly after the related instruction, such as a class meeting or lecture. Relate this to the findings of Ebbinghaus discussed in Unit 1.

6. Prepare a study schedule for yourself. Use the form below as a guide.

Hour	Mon	Tues	Wed	Thurs	Fri	Sat

PRACTICAL TIPS AND SUGGESTIONS
FOR NOTEMAKING

COMBINE LONGHAND AND GREGG NOTEHAND

At this stage of your learning you will naturally have to write in longhand most of the words in any notes you make. If the longhand word comes to you more readily than the Gregg Notehand outline for the word, use the longhand. But even at this stage it will be to your advantage to make the extra effort to use Gregg Notehand outlines. As you progress, you will gradually find more Gregg Notehand outlines in your notes and fewer and fewer longhand words.

CONCENTRATE ON MOST-USED GREGG NOTEHAND FORMS

One helpful device that will enable you to increase the percentage of Gregg Notehand outlines in your notes is based on scientific research that has been done in the

field of word frequency. This research has shown that the ten most frequent words in the English language and their repetitions account for approximately 25 per cent of all the writing you will ever do.

MOST-USED GREGG NOTEHAND FORMS

In general, you should attempt to write as many words as you can in Gregg Notehand. Make a special effort, however, in everything you write to use the Gregg Notehand forms for at least these words:

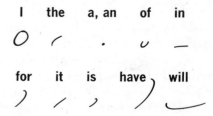

You have already learned all these words as brief forms. They were given special abbreviations in Gregg Notehand because of the high frequency with which they occur. They are called to your attention again here so that you may concentrate on them.

<u>Suggestion:</u> Write these ten Gregg Notehand outlines on a card and keep it before you whenever you are writing anything for your own use. Use the Gregg Notehand form every time you have occasion to write one of the words. Soon you will find yourself using these Gregg Notehand forms automatically.

The fact that these frequently used words are all brief forms does not mean that most of the words you write will be abbreviated. On the contrary, most of them will be written in full. There are only 42 brief forms in Gregg Notehand, and you have

Alternately daydreaming and studying produces little in the way of worthwhile results.

A. Devaney

already learned twelve of them. You can already write in full many frequently used words, such as *so, me, he, no, day, made, same, here, see, say, may,* and many others. Use as many of these as you can in your notes, but by all means use the ten outlines that you will keep with you on the card that you are going to write.

PUTTING GREGG NOTEHAND INTO PRACTICE

Read and copy the diary entries shown below, referring to the key on page 282 when necessary. Then write a few more real or fictitious diary entries, using as many Gregg Notehand forms as you can.

UNIT 9

In this unit you will study three new alphabetic characters. After you have completed Unit 9, you will have covered more than half the alphabetic characters of Notehand.

Suggestion: Reread Paragraphs 5 and 16 to be sure that you are practicing each word list and Reading and Writing Practice correctly.

33.   OO. The sound of $\overline{oo}$, as in *to*, is represented by a small hook. It is called the *oo hook*.

OO   ⌐ ∩

Spell: **to,** *t-oo*

to, too, two	/	true	⌐⌐	soon	₂
who	⌐	drew	/	pool	⌐
whom	⌐	room	⌐⌐	noon	⌐
do	/	rule	⌐⌐	move	⌐

Did you notice that the oo hook is placed on its side in *noon* and *move*? The oo hook joins more easily to the end of *n* and *m* if it is placed on its side than if it were written in the normal manner.

READING AND WRITING PRACTICE

1.

2.

repaired

3.

4.

5.

from

that

38

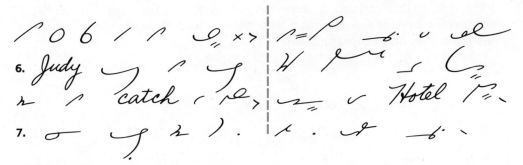

6. Judy ... catch ...

7. ...

34. **K.** The Notehand character for *k* is a short forward curve. Notice how it is derived from its longhand form.

K

ache		.care		baker	
take		came		cream	
make		scale		clear	
lake		keep		claim	

Did you notice:

    a. That *k* and *r*, as in *baker* and *cream*, join with one smooth, wavelike motion?

    b. That *k* and *l*, as in *clear* and *claim*, join with a "hump" between the *k* and the *l*?

READING AND WRITING PRACTICE

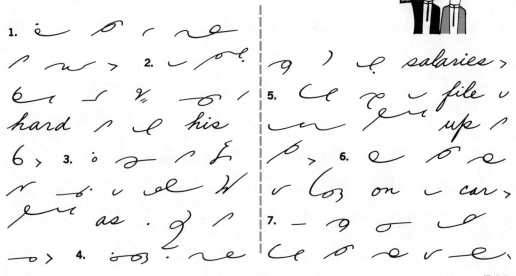

1. ... 2. ... salaries, 5. ... file ... hard ... his up ... 6. ... 3. ... on ... car, as ... 7. ... 4. ...

35.   **G.**   The Notehand character for *g*, as in *gate*, is the same shape as the character for *k* except that it is about three times as long. It is called "gay." Notice how it is derived from its longhand form.

Compare: **OO** ⌒   **K** ⌒   **G** ⌒

Spell: **gate,** *gay-a-t;* **gave,** *gay-a-v*

gate		**go**		**great**	
gave		**goal**		**grade**	
gain		**glare**		**grow**	
game		**gleam**		**girl**	

Did you notice that:

    a. When *g* joins to *l*, as in *glare* and *gleam*, it is written with one smooth, wave-like motion?

    b. When *g* joins to *r*, as in *great* and *grade*, it is written with a hump between the *g* and the *r*?

READING AND WRITING PRACTICE

1. *(shorthand)* ... ago ,

2. *(shorthand)*

3. If ... Sat ... box ,

4. *(shorthand)*

5. ... Miss ... on ... ,

6. *(shorthand)*

In this unit you will study four alphabetic characters—easy ones!

Are you practicing the words in each unit as suggested in Paragraph 5; the Reading and Writing Practice as suggested in Paragraph 16?

36.   Sh.   The Notehand character for the sound of *sh*, as in *she*, is a very short downward straight line. It is called "ish."

Sh   ／

Spell: **she,** *ish-e*; **share,** *ish-a-r*

she	shame	show
share	shape	shown
shades	shoes	showed

Did you notice that the *oo* hook and the *s* in *shoes* join without an angle?

READING AND WRITING PRACTICE

1. ⟋ ⟍ ⟋ . ⟋
ᵕ ⟋ ⟋ bought 〉 2. ⟋
⟋ 5 ⟋ ᵕ
stock 〉 Xmas 〉
3. ⟋ ⟋ Mrs ⟋
ᵕ line ᵕ ⟋
ᵕ visit ᵕ ⟋
⟋ 〉 4. ⟋ ᵕ sell
20 ⟋ ᵕ ⟋ stock

5. ⟋ ⟋ cash ⟍
ᵕ ⟋ ⟍ 〉
5. ⟋ ᵕ
that ⟋ ⟋
⟋ on ⟋ 10 〉
6. By ⟋ . 10,000 ⟋
ᵕ ⟋ ⟋ ᵕ ⟋
⟋ ⟋ 〉

37. **Ch.** The Notehand character for the sound of *ch*, as in *each*, is a downward straight stroke about three times as long as *sh*. It is called "chay."

Ch / ↓

Spell: **each,** e-chay; **reach,** r-e-chay

each	𝑔	chain	⌿	cheer	𝑏
reach	⌿	chairs	𝑏𝑟	chamber	𝜙
teach	⌿	speech	𝜙	chose	𝑏

READING AND WRITING PRACTICE

1. _e_ ... _from_ 7 ... on ... book on ... we ... 4. ...

2. ...

3. ... 5. ... _at_ ...

38. **J.** The Notehand character for the sound of *j*, as in *age*, is a long downward straight stroke, somewhat longer than *ch*.

J / ↓

Compare: **Sh** / **Ch** / **J** /

Spell: **age,** a-jay; **cage,** k-a-jay

age	/	pages	𝜙	jail	𝑏
cage	𝑔	stage	𝑦	strange	𝑟𝑔
gauge	𝑔	raged	𝜙	change	⌿

READING AND WRITING PRACTICE

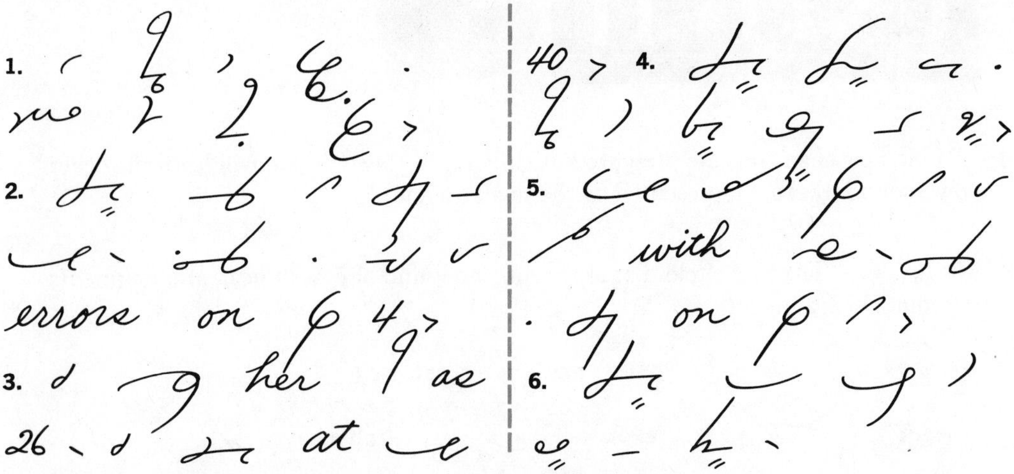
1.
2.
errors on 4
3. her as
26 at
40
4.
5.
with
on
6.

39. Long I. In Notehand, the sound of long ī, as in *my*, is represented by a broken circle.

I

my		sign		try	
might		file		time	
mine		light			

READING AND WRITING PRACTICE

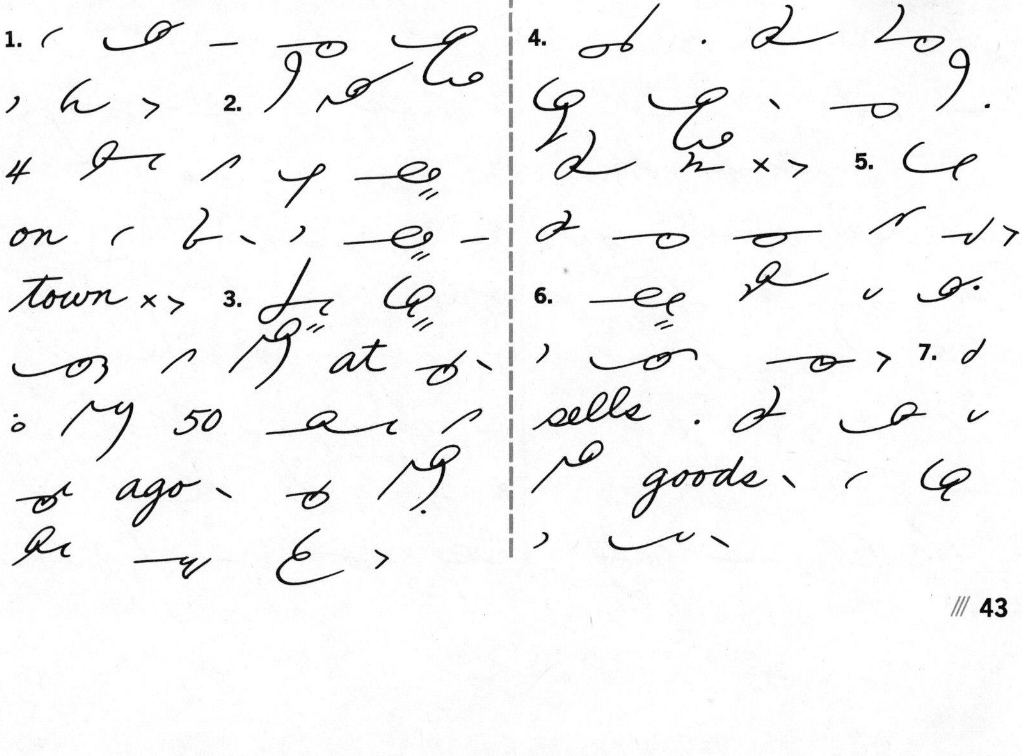
1.
2.
4
on
town
3.
at
50
ago
4.
5.
6.
7.
sells
goods

UNIT 11

No new characters are presented in Unit 11. In this unit you will learn the other vowel sounds that are represented by the small e circle.

40. **Ĕ.** The tiny circle that represents the sound of ē, as in *heat*, also represents the sound of ĕ, as in *get*.

Spell: **get,** *gay-e-t;* **set,** *s-e-t*

get		ever		check	
set		every		several	
telling		very		general	
letter		any		*next	

*In the word *next*, the x has the sound of *ks*; it is, therefore, represented by the Notehand characters *ks*.

READING AND WRITING PRACTICE

1.

2.

3.

4.

5.

6.

7.

8.

41. **Ĭ.** The small circle also represents the sound of ĭ, as in *him*.

Spell: **him,** *h-e-m;* **his,** *h-e-s*

him		give		bid	
his		little		business	
if		miss		mix	
bill		did		fix	

Did you notice that the *x* in *mix* and in *fix* is represented by *ks*?

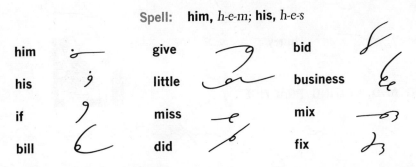

READING AND WRITING PRACTICE

1.　 $1,500

16 as

2.

5.

3.

6.

Fri.

4.

again

42. **Obscure Vowel.** The small circle also represents the obscure vowel sound heard in *her, firm, church*.

Spell: **her,** *h-e-r;* **church,** *chay-e-r-chay*

her		church		urged	
serving		nurse		major	

turn	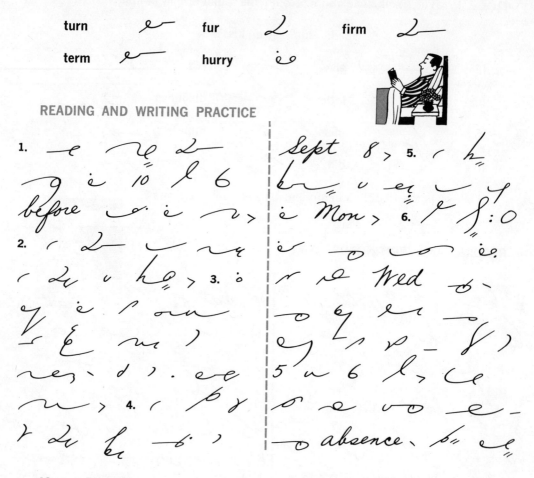	fur		firm	
term		hurry			

READING AND WRITING PRACTICE

43.   Past Tense.   As you no doubt have already noticed, in forming the past tense of a verb, we simply add the Notehand character for the sound that we hear in the past tense. In some words, the past tense has the sound of *t*, as in *baked* (b-a-k-t); in others, it has the sound of *d*, as in *saved* (s-a-v-d).

T

baked		missed		mixed	
reached		priced		faced	

D

saved		changed		urged	
tried		showed		stayed	

46

READING AND WRITING PRACTICE

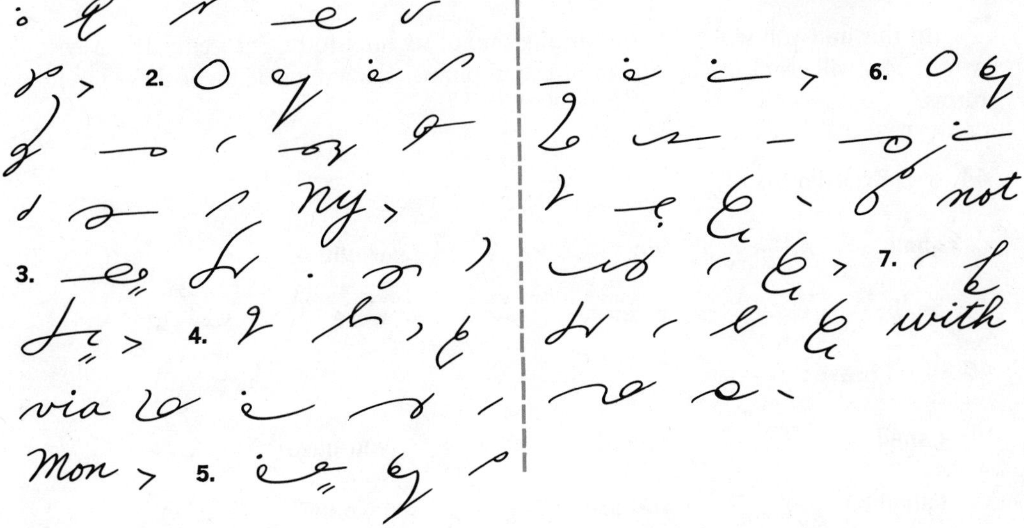

UNIT 12

In this unit you will study the third group of six brief forms for frequently used words. You will also learn a number of useful phrases that are made up of these brief forms.

44.   Brief Forms

shall	/	you	∩	would	/
be, by	(	when	⌐	were	℮

45.   Phrases

I shall	9	to you	⋔	you have	)
I shall be	9	you are	∿	I would	6
by the	(	you will	∿	he would be	6
for you	⟩	you may	∿	you would	∿

READING AND WRITING PRACTICE

Your Reading and Writing Practice for this unit consists of a number of personal letters. You will notice that these letters are written almost completely in Notehand, with only an occasional word in longhand—a sign of the rapid progress you are making.

As you work with each Reading and Writing Practice, are you making proper use of the key in the back of the book? Remember, the key is not to be used as a "last resort" after you have struggled unsuccessfully to decipher an outline. The key will serve you most effectively if you refer to it the moment you cannot read an outline after having spelled it. Your key is a timesaver!

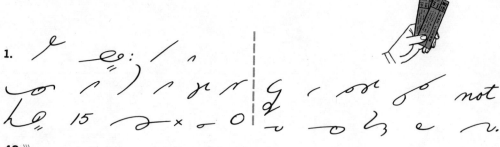

1.

2.

minutes

3.

My

Fri × with .

4. Dad :

a's and b's.

$10

$10 ×

but

Fri

12.

UNIT 13

In Unit 13 you will learn the other sounds that the a circle represents. You will also learn another alphabetic character.

46. **Ă.** In Unit 2 you learned that a large circle represents the sound of ā, as in may. This large circle also represents the sound of ă, as in *had*.

Spell: **had,** *h-a-d;* **has,** *h-a-s*

had		at		fast	
has		agree		arrive	
man		after		advice	
can		matter		appear	

READING AND WRITING PRACTICE

No Business Runs Itself

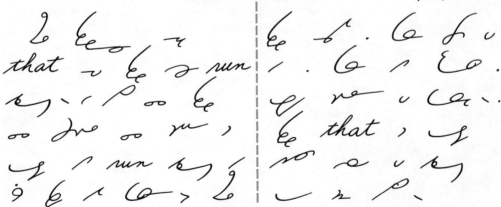

47. **Ä.** The large circle also represents the sound of ä, as in *mark*.

Spell: **mark** *m-a-r-k*

mark		car		start	

parked	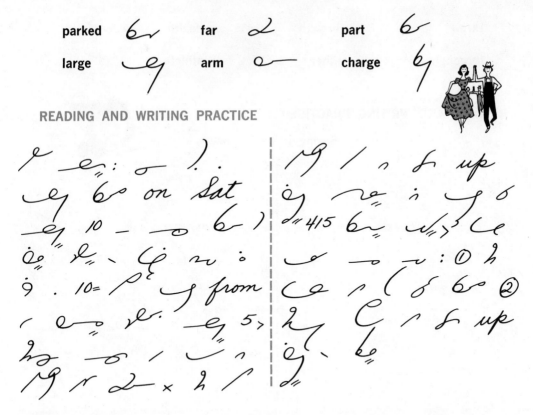	far		part	
large		arm		charge	

READING AND WRITING PRACTICE

48. **Th.** Two small upward curves represent the sound of *th*. (You are already familiar with one of them; it is the brief form for *the*.) Each of these strokes is called "ith." At this point you need not try to determine which *th* stroke to use in a given word; that will become clear to you as your study of Notehand progresses.

Over Th ⁀⁀   **Under Th**

Spell: **they,** *ith-a;* **though,** *ith-o*

Over Th

they		then		bath	
that		them		neither	
than		these		teeth	

Under Th

| though | | those | | rather | |

/// 51

throw	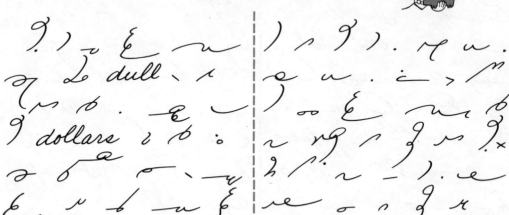	through		health	
thorough		either		athlete	

READING AND WRITING PRACTICE

Saving with a Purpose

UNIT 14

Unit 14 is a "breather"; it contains no new characters or principles for you to learn. By reading the recall chart that follows, you will review everything you have studied in Units 2-13. The material in the Reading and Writing Practice will help you expand your Notehand vocabulary further.

Before you begin your work on the recall chart and the Reading and Writing Practice, review quickly all the strokes you have studied so far.

Under Th	Over Th	I	J	Ch	Sh	K
‿	⌒	⟲	/	⁄	⁄	⌐

G	OO	Left S	B	P	H	L	R	O
⌢	⌒	⟋	⟍	⟍	·	‿	‿	∪

D	M	T	N	Comma S	V	F	E	A
/	—	⁄	—	⟩	⟩	⟩	∘	⟲

49.   Recall Chart.   This chart contains 108 words and phrases. Be sure to spell and say aloud each word as you practice it, but don't waste any time trying to decipher an outline that does not come to you immediately—refer to the key!

Time goal: 11 minutes.

Words

	1	2	3	4	5	6
1						
2						
3						
4						
5						
6						

7					
8					
9					
10					
11					
12					
13					
14					

Brief Forms

15					

Phrases

16					
17					
18					

50.   READING AND WRITING PRACTICE

Plans for Annual Sales Meeting

Time:

Place: ... from 9 ... 5 ... 20 ... on

on

Expenses: $15.

and it

and

Agenda:

Speakers: we

questions

Special Visits: On 12

how

How to Listen for Notemaking

Most of us take listening for granted. We do not rank it as equal in importance with reading, writing, and speaking. Yet it may surprise you to know that you spend more time listening than in any of the other three communication arts. In fact, of the total time spent communicating, about 45 per cent is spent in listening!

The ability to listen effectively should not be confused with the ability to hear. You may hear every word your Aunt Gracie said in that long telephone conversation and yet you may not actually have *listened* to any of it. You may sit on the front row during a speech by a political candidate, with your eyes and ears glued to the speaker, and still not be able to give even a hazy account of what he said.

CASUAL LISTENING AND ACTIVE LISTENING

Basically, there are two kinds of listening: casual listening and active listening. Casual listening usually results in absorbing just enough of the speaker's remarks to keep a conversation going. In a conversation with a friend, or a chat on the telephone, or a group discussion at the bridge table, you can get by with casual listening. It doesn't usually matter whether what you hear really "soaks in." Because we do so much of this kind of listening, we are inclined to forget that there is any other kind!

Active listening, on the other hand,

means concentrating on what you are hearing, trying to absorb and fix in your mind as much as you possibly can. It calls for actively participating mentally in what you hear, and thinking about the speaker's remarks as he makes them. Active listening is vitally important in many situations; for example, when a doctor listens to a patient describe an ailment; when a lawyer hears his client's account of an accident in which he was involved; when an employee receives instructions from his supervisor on how to do a job.

ACTIVE LISTENING VITAL FOR THE STUDENT

Much of the student's exposure to learning is through listening — to lectures, explanations and remarks of the instructor, and comments and discussions among the students. The typical college student attends some two thousand lectures during his four-year college career! For such an investment of time the student should be interested in improving his listening habits.

Classroom lectures call for the most difficult kind of listening. After all, the student goes to class for the purpose of learning. He cannot afford the ease of casual listening, but must strive to comprehend fully what he is listening to so that he can remember the essential ideas and information. Further, what he hears through lectures, explanations, and remarks of the instructor is perishable. If the student doesn't listen with understanding at the time of the lecture or discussion, he has lost the opportunity. What we read can usually be reread; what we hear can rarely be reheard.

GOOD NOTEMAKING AND ACTIVE LISTENING GO TOGETHER

Studies of listening show that, of what we hear, we forget most of what we are going to forget — about 50 per cent — immediately after we hear it. And we forget another 25 per cent about two months later. This factor of forgetting makes it imperative that the student make good notes while he is listening, because only through good notes can he retain in permanent form the important ideas he hears.

Good listening and good notemaking, therefore, go hand in hand. In fact, the process of making notes during a lecture encourages active participation in listening. At the same time, active listening is essential to good notemaking.

PARTICIPATE ACTIVELY IN LISTENING

Effective listening habits can be acquired. But, like any other art, active listening must be worked at if it is to be mastered. There is no magic formula for learning how to listen effectively. It is something you must do for yourself. First, *realize the importance* of good listening, then, *want* to listen effectively, and finally, *practice* listening effectively until it becomes an established habit.

For the student, participating actively in listening has six fundamental requirements:

1. A desire to listen
2. An open mind
3. Concentration
4. Alertness in grasping essential ideas

Hays from Monkmeyer

The typical college student attends some 2,000 lectures during his four-year college career. That's 2,000 opportunities to make notes!

5. Alertness in listening for related ideas
6. Notemaking

A Desire to Listen. Listening is a strictly voluntary activity, and the incentive has to come from you. Listening is important to your own goals. Since the basic purpose of a lecture or class discussion is learning, then you should "listen to learn."

An Open Mind. Bring an open mind to the listening situation. We often assess people and ideas in an introspective, personal manner, based on our pet likes and dislikes. For example, the speaker's appearance, his pronunciation, his voice, his mannerisms — perhaps even an occasional error in grammar — may annoy the listener so much that he cannot concentrate on what is being said. Or perhaps the listener has a special prejudice or strong feeling concerning the subject. These prejudices close the listener's mind and limit his ability to listen.

To be an effective listener try to overlook personal irritants, concentrate on what is "coming out" rather than on the person or on your prejudices.

Concentration. Do not allow the annoyances just mentioned to interfere with your receptivity to what is said. You are in a position to "tune in" or "tune out" the speaker as you wish. Your willingness to pay attention to what is being said is your "tuning device." And you may be tempted to "tune out," because many speakers speak much more slowly than many listeners can comprehend. In fact, the typical listener can comprehend at a rate approximately four times faster than some speakers talk. The listener should use this "spare" time for concentration — not for woolgathering.

The typical listener frequently indulges in daydreaming or detouring into unrelated thoughts. Once the listener is tuned out, he may get hopelessly lost when he tries to re-enter the discussion because he will have lost a part, perhaps a significant part, of what has been said. Concentration is practically a full-time job for the active listener — not something to "put on and take off" as the fancy pleases him. Concentration requires self-discipline and means paying attention and sustaining it throughout the lecture or discussion.

Alertness in Grasping Essential Ideas. Be on the alert to grasp the speaker's essential ideas. Try to think along with the speaker. You may even anticipate what he is going to say next — or at least the direction of his remarks. When an essential idea, fact, or piece of information is conveyed to you, *rephrase* it mentally in your own words. This process of *rephrasing* mentally to yourself what you hear will help you understand and remember what you hear. Note the example below.

Alertness in Grasping Related Ideas. Listen for related ideas and information, such as illustrations, anecdotes, and "asides" that elaborate, provide insight, and give support to the main ideas and information. For example, in the lecture on Venice just illustrated, the speaker may continue:

"Incidentally, this rivalry between Venice and Genoa had some interesting sidelights. Captains of Venetian ships were instructed to get there and back before the Genoese ships at all costs, regardless of who else was involved, and many unscheduled races were staged in the Mediterranean. To keep ahead of her rival, Venice even had an ambassador to England to smooth the way for her merchants there. The city fathers gave specific instructions, too, to the ambassador about putting up a good front. He was instructed to wear a fine scarlet gown and he was required to maintain four servants, two pages, a cook, and a secretary...."

You can see that these sidelights add both color and interest, even though not worth recording in your notes. If you are listening actively, however, your impressions of Venice as a leader in Mediterranean trade are much more vivid.

Notemaking. Make notes as you listen. Since what we hear is perishable, the main ideas (along with related and supporting ideas) must be captured and retained for reference, for reviewing, and for preparing for examinations. Making notes is no more

THE SPEAKER IS SAYING:	YOU MIGHT BE THINKING:
Many of the Mediterranean cities were already thriving veterans of trade. They had been toughened and enriched by the Crusades. In Italy, besides Venice, there were Genoa, Lucca, Pisa, Florence, Milan, and a good many others. In southern France, there were Narbonne, Montpellier, and Marseilles; and in Spain there was Barcelona. Through most of the thirteenth and fourteenth centuries, however, Venice was the undisputed mistress of Mediterranean trade. In the 1300's she won a feud with her strongest rival, Genoa, for leadership.	Several Mediterranean cities were old hands at trade. Crusades helped to build them. A number of cities were in Italy, France, and Spain. Venice, though, was undisputed leader through most of the thirteenth and fourteenth centuries. Surpassed her old enemy, Genoa, in 1300's.

than an extension of active participation in listening. It simply consists of putting on paper, in your own words, the essential ideas and information. And the very process of making notes contributes to concentration, learning, and remembering.

Gregg Notehand gives the listener more time to think about what is being said, and gives him time to record more complete notes. "More complete notes" does not mean verbatim notes. Even though Gregg Notehand gives the listener an efficient writing tool, he should not attempt to record lecture notes verbatim. Verbatim notes are seldom the most useful notes.

HOW TO MAKE NOTES AS YOU LISTEN

Following are practical suggestions to help you achieve active participation in listening and making good notes.

Prepare in Advance. The more you know about the subject that is being discussed the more fruitful your listening efforts will be. If possible, therefore, read in advance about the topic or subject on which you are to hear someone speak.

Choose a Good Location. Make sure you are seated where you can hear the speaker without strain. If the speaker uses the blackboard or other visual aids to outline important points or to illustrate complicated explanations, try to sit where you have a clear view of the visual device.

Come Equipped. Come equipped with proper and adequate supplies for making notes: plenty of note paper, a good pen, and an extra pencil or two.

Use a Good Writing Surface. Don't try to make notes on top of a pile of books or with your lap full of books. Give yourself as much uncluttered writing surface as you can manage.

Label Your Notes. Identify your notes — the name of the course ("History 202" or "Hist of Western Civ"), date, and, if there is a guest speaker or if instructors alternate, the name of the instructor.

Listen for Cues. If the speaker speaks from an outline, the framework of your listening and notemaking will be pretty well organized for you. The instructor may even have supplied you with a copy of the outline. If so, bring it to class with you each time for your notemaking "blueprint."

If there is no outline in either your or the instructor's hands, you will have to listen for cues from the speaker. The most important ideas and information will often be cued by such statements as "first," "second," "third," "another important consideration," and "finally." Or they may be cued by superlatives, such as "The most significant thing that happened during this period was," or "the best explanation is," or "the most successful method was." Watch for these cues; in many cases, they will provide important headings in your notes.

Contrasts and comparisons are often introduced by such cues as "on the other hand," "besides," "on the contrary," "moreover," "however," and "furthermore." In your notes these become subpoints or

Active listening and good notemaking are "musts" for the student.

Hays from Monkmeyer

parenthetical statements. Or, if you have followed the good practice of leaving a wide left margin on your notepaper, you may use this space to make notes of interesting contrasts and comparisons.

Questions posed by the speaker are helpful cues. For example, he may ask, "Why did Columbus return to Spain rather than to Italy after his discoveries?" or "What are some of the factors that influenced Lincoln's decision to retain Grant?" Since the lecturer is sure to proceed with the answers, the notemaker turns the questions into positive statements: "Columbus returned to Spain because . . ." and "Factors that influenced Lincoln's decision to retain Grant are. . . ."

Speakers will often cue in a listener with such signals as "in summary," or "note particularly that," or "now, let's turn our attention to." Pauses, intonations of voice, gestures, and other techniques used for emphasis are other helpful cues.

Flag Important Things in Your Notes. Flag your notes with signals of importance. These might be brackets, underscores, arrows, or indentions. Whatever the device, flagging notes will be helpful in using the notes later.

Listen for Special Instructions. Listen closely for, and note carefully, instructions and special directions—assignments, sources of other information, special preparation, examination dates and what they will cover, and so on.

Go Over Your Notes Promptly. After you have made your notes, go over them promptly. In this way you can review your notes, make additions and changes in them, plan further study, and so on. Using notes in reviewing is treated in detail in Unit 57.

PRACTICAL TIPS AND SUGGESTIONS FOR NOTEMAKING

SELECT A NOTEBOOK THAT BEST SUITS YOUR NEEDS

In some courses, instructors will specify the type of notebook to be used, but usually the selection of a notebook is left to the notemaker.

There are two types of notebooks that are commonly used by notemakers:

1. A *bound* composition notebook, 8 by 10, or a similar size. Some prefer a notebook with a stitched binding; others, one with a wire binding. While either type of bound notebook will serve the purpose, the wire-bound notebook is somewhat easier to use because it always lies flat when it is open. The wire-bound notebook is the more popular of the two types.

The bound notebook has an advantage in that the pages cannot come loose and be lost.

2. A *loose-leaf* ring binder that holds 8½ by 11 sheets. Many students prefer this type of notebook because removing and reinserting pages is easily done. It is also easy to add paper at any point.

The loose-leaf ring binder, however, has the disadvantage that the holes in the paper become worn and tear with use. Consequently, some pages may come loose and perhaps be lost or misplaced.

If you use a bound notebook, you will find it most convenient to have a separate notebook for each subject. If you use a loose-leaf ring binder, you will probably want to keep notes for all your subjects in one notebook; in that case, use an index tab to identify each subject.

Number the Pages. No matter what type of notebook you use, be sure to number the pages. Numbering the pages makes cross referencing more convenient and quicker.

If you use a bound notebook, the best plan is to number the pages consecutively throughout the book. If you use a loose-leaf ring binder in which you keep notes for several subjects, number the pages within each subject. Thus, if you find it necessary to add paper for a particular subject, you will not have to disturb the entire numbering plan.

PRESERVE DIFFICULT LONGHAND SPELLINGS

When you are listening to a lecture, the lecturer will sometimes write an unusual word on the board. By all means preserve the word in longhand in your notes.

When you are making notes or copying from a book, you can preserve the correct spelling of unusual or troublesome words.

It may be a common "spelling demon" like *embarrass* or a very unusual word like *syzygy*. Either word would be easy to write in Gregg Notehand; but if either word pre-

Notebooks for making notes.

sents a spelling problem to you, and if you have the correct spelling available when making your notes, by all means use longhand to keep that spelling conveniently available in your notes. If the word is repeated in the course of the same set of notes, write it in Gregg Notehand because of the saving of time.

MOST-USED GREGG NOTEHAND FORMS

If in all your written work you have made a real effort to use the Gregg Notehand forms for the ten common words, as given in Unit 8, you are now ready for another ten.

to	you	your	that	he

as	at	if	very	not

Research shows that the ten words given here, plus the ten in Unit 8, make up almost one-third of all the writing you will ever do. Be sure to use them constantly. Try to read them from your card a few times each day. Read them as rapidly as you can, sometimes forward, sometimes backward. The faster you can read them, the faster you will be able to write them.

PUTTING GREGG NOTEHAND INTO PRACTICE

Read and make a copy of the lecture notes on page 62. Notice that some of the words are written in longhand, but the common words are always written in Gregg Notehand.

The key to these lecture notes appears on page 285.

Making a Speech

Appearance

⌐◡ ◡ ◡ with ◡. (
sure ◡ look "◌." ◡ 2.
�⌐ ◡ well ◡ ◡◡
◡ confidence.

Posture

(◡ ◡ weight evenly on
◡ ◡ and ◡ forward.
◡ ◡ ◡ ◡ ◡ ◡ hang
loosely from ◡ shoulders.
◡. "◡ ◡ ◌" occasionally
(◡ ◡ hands — ◡ ◡ ◡
put ① hand — ◡ pocket.

Platform Manners

◡ wait ◡ ◡ ◡ ◡ ◡ ◡
attention ◡ ◡ ◡ ◡ ◡ ◡
(not exceed ◡ ◡ ◡ ◡ ◡ allotted
◡. ◡ end ◡ ◡ ◡ thank ◡ audience.

Delivery

Adopt ◡ ◡ ◡ ◡ use ◡ ◡ ◡
friends. (sure ◡ everyone ◡
◡ ◡. Look ◡ ◡ audience. (
not look ◡ ◡. ◡ on ◡ ◡◡.

UNIT 16

In Unit 16 you will learn two additional sounds that are represented by the Notehand o. You will also learn a shortcut for a very common word ending.

51. **ŏ.** The small hook that represents the sound of ō, as in *low*, also represents the sound of ŏ, as in *hot*.

Spell: **hot,** *h-o-t*

hot		sorry		often	
not		copy		operate	
got		stopped		on	
spot		office		from	

READING AND WRITING PRACTICE

The Tonic of Praise

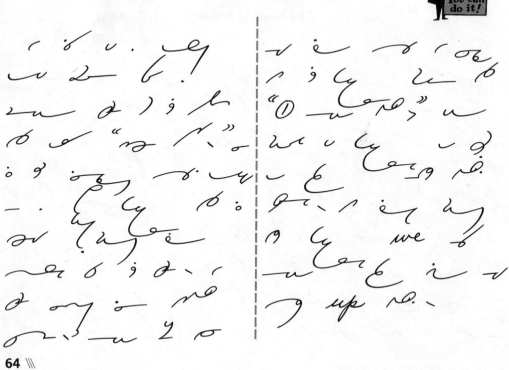

52. **Aw.** The o hook also represents the sound of aw, as in *law*.

Spell: law, *l-o*; **cause,** *k-o-s*

law		ought		all	
cause		taught		also	
fall		brought		call	
bought		broad		small	

READING AND WRITING PRACTICE

You Can Do It

53.   Word Ending -ly.   The word ending *-ly* occurs in hundreds of English words. In Notehand, *-ly* is represented by the *e* circle.

Spell: badly, b-a-d-lee

badly		finally		readily	
only		sincerely		easily	
early		specially		daily	

Did you notice, in the words in the third column, the joining of the *-ly* circle to words ending in a vowel, as in *readily* and *daily*.

READING AND WRITING PRACTICE

Four Ways to Be a Happier Person

(shorthand outlines)

① ... things ...

② ...

③ ... and ...

④ ... — good ...

In this unit you will study another set of six brief forms for commonly used words. After Unit 17, you will have only three more groups of brief forms to learn.

In addition, you will study a number of useful phrases made up of these brief forms.

54.   Brief Forms

with		their, there		this	
what		was		about	

55.   Phrases

with the		what is		in this	
with our		what are		on this	
with this		what will		for this	
there was		about the		there is	
I was		about this		there are	

READING AND WRITING PRACTICE

Your reading and writing practice consists of two humorous stories. You will enjoy them!

Tom

heard ⌐ ⌐ — ⌐ ⌐ ⌐ ⌐ ⌐ ⌐ ⌐.:

"⌐ ⌐ ⌐ ⌐ ⌐ ⌐

mumble ⌐ ⌐ ⌐ ⌐ ⌐."

Proof

⌐ ⌐ ⌐ ⌐ ⌐ ⌐

⌐ ⌐ (30 ⌐ ⌐)

⌐ ⌐ ⌐ ⌐ ⌐)

$500 ⌐ . ⌐ ⌐

⌐ ⌐ ⌐ (⌐ ⌐.

⌐ ⌐) ⌐ ⌐ ⌐ .

⌐ ⌐ ⌐ ⌐ ⌐ —

⌐ ⌐ ⌐ ⌐) ⌐

⌐ ⌐ ⌐ ⌐ ⌐)

⌐ ⌐ $500 — ⌐ ⌐ ⌐

"⌐ . ⌐ ⌐ ⌐"

⌐ ⌐ ⌐ ⌐ ⌐ ⌐

⌐ ⌐ ⌐ ⌐ ⌐

"⌐ ⌐ ⌐" ⌐ ⌐ ⌐ ⌐.

"⌐ ⌐ ⌐ ⌐ ⌐ ⌐.

⌐ ⌐ ⌐ ⌐ ⌐

$1,000 ⌐ ⌐ ⌐ " "⌐ ⌐ ⌐

$500 " ⌐ ⌐ ⌐ " "⌐

⌐ ⌐ ⌐ ⌐ $500.

⌐ ⌐ ⌐ ⌐ ⌐ ⌐

$1,000 ⌐ ⌐ ⌐ ⌐ ⌐ ⌐

⌐ ⌐ ⌐ ⌐ ⌐ $500.

⌐ ⌐ ⌐ ⌐ — ⌐.!"

UNIT 18

In Unit 18 you will learn the Notehand sign for *oi* and two word endings that occur in many useful words in the English language.

56. **Oi.** The sound of *oi*, as in *boy*, is represented by ↄ.

Spell: **toy,** *t-oi*

toy	ↄ	oil	ↄ	annoy	ↄ
boy	ↄ	soil	ↄ	noise	ↄ
join	ↄ	toil	ↄ	voice	ↄ
enjoy	ↄ	boil	ↄ	choice	ↄ

READING AND WRITING PRACTICE

The Apple Eater

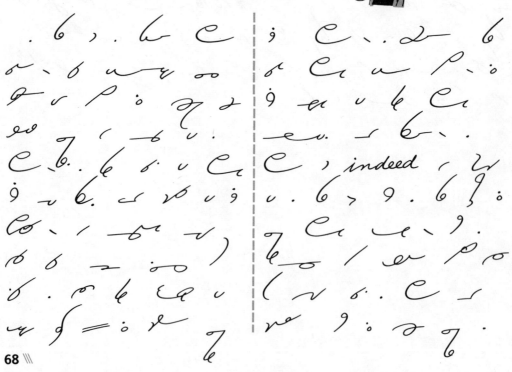

68 \\\

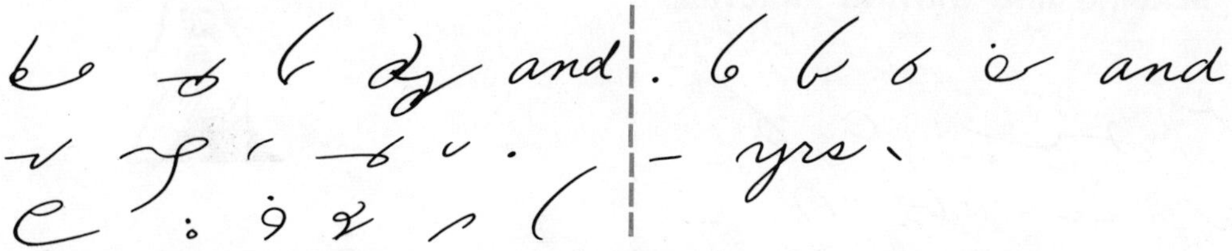

57. Word Ending -ure. The word ending *-ure*, as in *secure*, is represented by the Notehand r.

Spell: secure, *s-e-k-r*

secure	procure	picture
failure	figure	lecture
nature	feature	furniture

READING AND WRITING PRACTICE

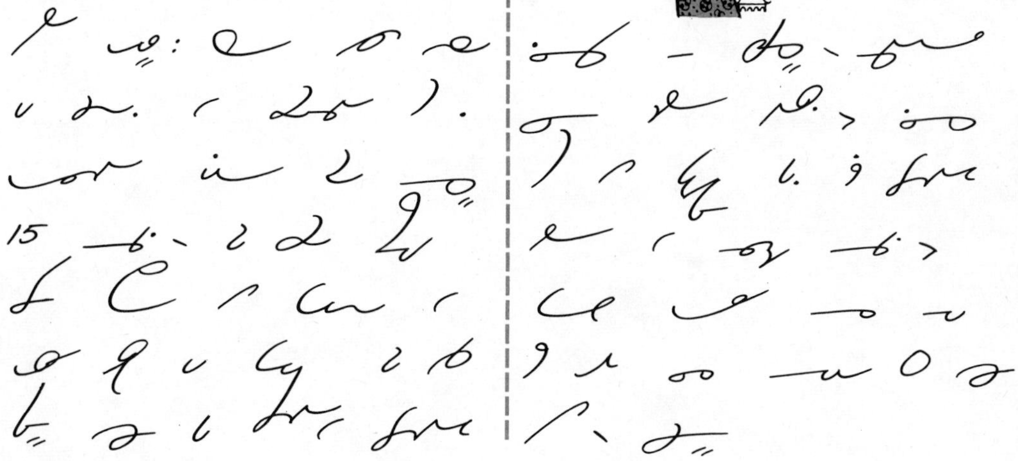

58. Word Ending -ual. The word ending *-ual*, as in *actual*, is represented by the Notehand *l*. (Sometimes this ending is spelled *uel*, as in *Samuel*, or *ule*, as in *schedule*.)

Spell: actual, *a-k-t-l*

actual	gradual	equal
factual	annual	schedule

UNIT 19

Unit 19 introduces another useful word ending and two additional sounds represented by the oo hook.

Reminder: If you practice the words in this unit as suggested in Paragraph 5 (Why not take a few minutes to review the suggestions in Paragraph 5?), each Reading and Writing Practice will be a "snap" for you.

59.   Word Ending -tion.   The word ending *-tion* (sometimes spelled *-sion*, *-cean*, or *-shion*) is represented by the Notehand *sh*.

Spell: **nation,** *n-a-shun*

nation		selection		ocean	
action		vacation		fashion	
section		provision		occasion	

READING AND WRITING PRACTICE

Vacation

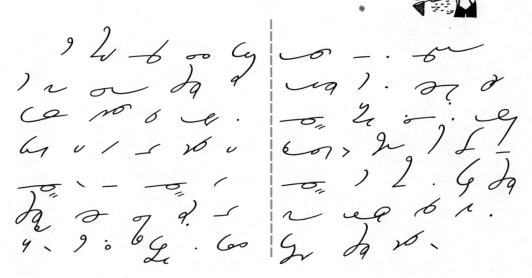

60. **Ŭ.** The hook that represents ōō, as in *to*, also represents the sound of ŭ heard in *but*.

Spell: **but,** *b-oo-t*; **up,** *oo-p*

but		product		touch	
up		succeed		brush	
does		us		must	
other		just		number	

Did you notice that:
   a. In *us*, the oo hook and the *s* join without an angle?
   b. In *must* and *number*, the oo hook is on its side?

READING AND WRITING PRACTICE

Five Principles of Selling

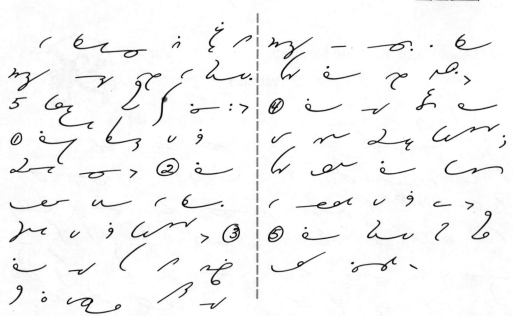

61. **ŎŎ.** The oo hook represents a third sound—the sound of ŏŏ heard in *book*.

Spell: **book,** *b-oo-k*

book	⟋	looked	⟋	pushed	⟋
foot	⟋	good	⟋	full	⟋
cooked	⟋	took	⟋	pulling	⟋

READING AND WRITING PRACTICE

Spare-Time Learners

[Shorthand outlines]

Burchell

UNIT 20

In Unit 20 you will learn how to express *w* in Notehand. You will also learn how to express the sound of *ū*.

62. W. W at the beginning of words is expressed by the oo hook.

Spell: we, oo-e; way, oo-a

we	*∂*	week	*ɔ*	watch	*ɣ*
way	*∂*	well	*ɔ*	won, one	*n*
wait	*ɣ*	war	*u*	wall	*u*

Sw at the beginning of words is expressed by *s-oo.*

Spell: swell, s-oo-e-l

swell	*ɔ*	swim	*ɔ*	sweet	*ɣ*

Wh, as in *while*, is pronounced *hw*. As the *h* is pronounced first, it is written first.

Spell: while, h-oo-ī-l

while	*ɔ*	wheat	*ɣ*	why	*∂*
wheel	*ɔ*	whether	*ɣ*	white	*∂*

READING AND WRITING PRACTICE

Be Calm

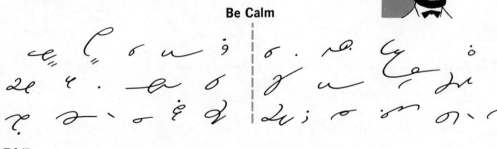

(Shorthand outlines)

(Concluded in Paragraph 63)

63. **W in the Body of a Word.** When the sound of w occurs in the body of a word, as in *always*, it is represented by a short dash underneath the vowel following the w sound. The dash is inserted after the rest of the outline has been written.

Spell: **always,** o-l-oo-a-s; **quite,** k-oo-ī-t

always	*(outline)*	**quite**	*(outline)*	**twin**	*(outline)*
railway	*(outline)*	**quick**	*(outline)*	**twice**	*(outline)*
roadway	*(outline)*	**quote**	*(outline)*	**liquid**	*(outline)*

READING AND WRITING PRACTICE

Be Calm (Concluded)

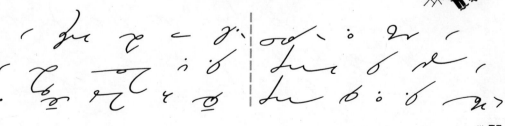

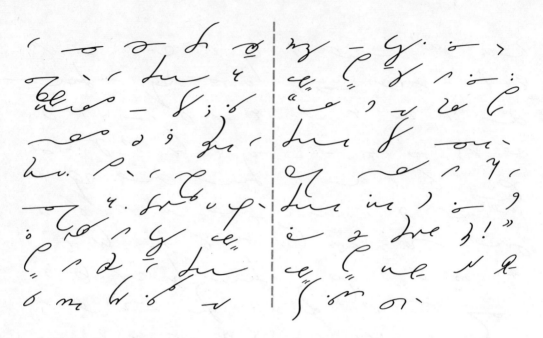

64. **Ū.** The sound of ū, as in use, is written ⟋ .

Spell: **use, ū-s; few, f-ū**

use	⟋	few	⟋	beauty	⟋
unit	⟋	view	⟋	tube	⟋
unite	⟋	fuel	⟋	value	⟋
utilize	⟋	pure	⟋	usual	⟋

READING AND WRITING PRACTICE

Memory

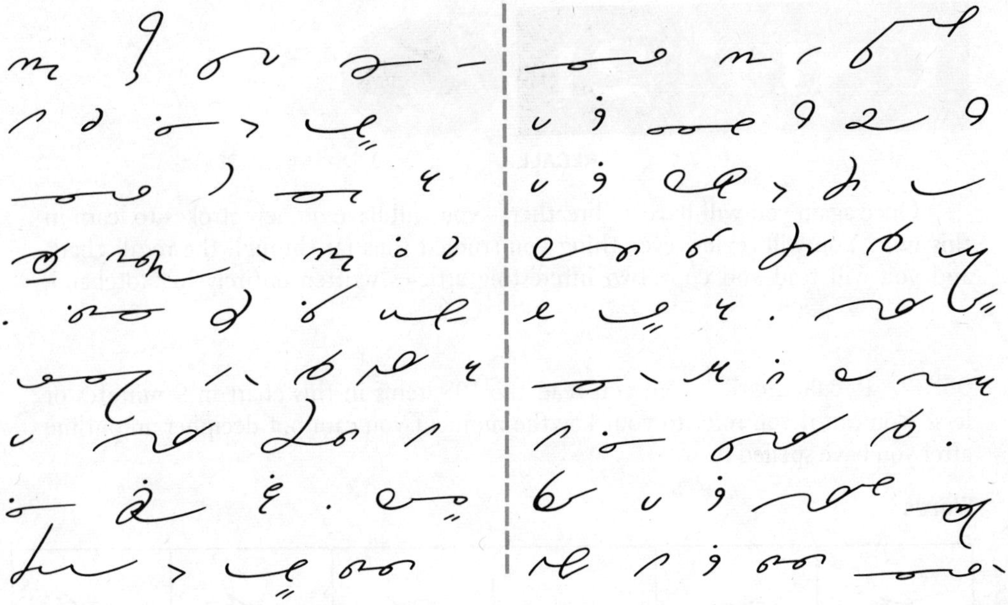

RECALL

Once again you will have a "breather"—you will have no new strokes to learn in this unit. You will review everything you studied thus far through the recall chart, and you will read and copy two interesting articles written entirely in Notehand.

65. **Recall Chart.** Can you read the 108 items in this chart in 9 minutes or less? You can if you refer to your key the moment you cannnot decipher an outline after you have spelled it.

Words

1					
2					
3					
4					
5					
6					
7					
8					
9					
10					
11					
12					
13					
14					

Brief Forms

15					

Phrases

16					
17					
18					

66. READING AND WRITING PRACTICE

Follow the Leader

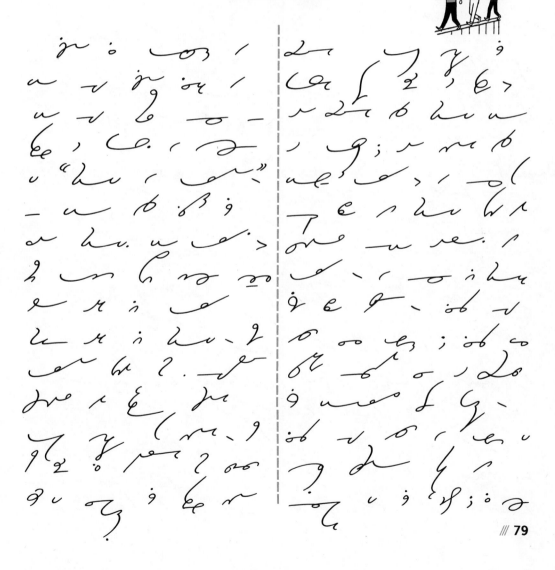

The Miser

How to Read for Notemaking

For many people, reading is the principal source of notes. To make good notes from your reading, you need to know how to read effectively.

ACTIVE PARTICIPATION IN READING

You are more likely to understand and remember what you read if you actively participate in what you read. The degree to which you participate depends in part on your purpose in reading. Some kinds of material — such as the morning paper, a sports or fashion magazine, or a novel — you read primarily for general information, for enjoyment, or in the pursuit of some special interest. Such reading does not ordinarily require a high degree of participation and effort. But this is not the case when you read for educational purposes in school or for personal improvement. Such reading requires a high degree of active participation by the reader if he is to understand and remember what he reads.

Active participation in reading means, essentially, reciting to yourself mentally and in your own words the gist of what you read. Let's suppose you read the following two paragraphs:

Spring used to be an unhappy season. Along with the swallow's chirp, wails of anguish were heard throughout the land as people wrestled with their income tax blanks. They used to have to pay taxes for the previous year's income—which often had already been spent.

Now things are better. All through the year our employers automatically withhold from each pay check most of what we shall have to pay the government. This puts us all on a pay-as-you-go basis, so that by the end of the year we are more or less all paid up even if our pay checks have all been spent.

After reading these paragraphs, stop and recite to yourself *mentally* and in your own words the gist of what you have read. The gist of the two paragraphs might be as follows:

People used to be unhappy in the spring because at that time they had to pay taxes on their previous year's income, which they often had already spent. Things are better today because employers automatically withhold a portion of the tax from each pay check. Consequently, by the end of the year most of our taxes are paid up even though we have spent all that we earned.

SOME RULES FOR UNDERSTANDING AND REMEMBERING WHAT YOU READ

At first, you may find it difficult and awkward to recite to yourself mentally and in your own words what you read. But after you get accustomed to the process, you will find that you can do it more naturally. Even so, it will require some effort.

If you will observe the following rules conscientiously, you will be able to participate actively in what you are reading.

Survey What You Are Going to Read. Glance over the material before actually reading it. Read only the main headings and the subheadings to get an idea of what the material is about. Look at the illustrations—photographs, charts, tables, diagrams, and the like. Read summaries and review questions. This survey will give you a perspective of the material and help you determine the important points to understand and remember.

Read Actively. After you have read a paragraph — usually an author develops a single idea in a paragraph — recite to yourself mentally and in your own words the gist of what you have read. As you do this, emphasize particularly the main idea and the significant details. These are what you want to remember; by concentrating on them you will fix them in your mind.

Reread If Necessary. Sometimes the material is hard to understand. If you don't understand something at the first reading, put it aside for a little while. Then come back to it later and read it again. If after several rereadings you still don't understand it, the chances are that you need some background improvement in order to grasp the ideas presented. For example, the author's vocabulary may be difficult or technical. In that case, skim through the pages you don't understand and make a list of all the words that are strange or unfamiliar. Then look them up in a dictionary, trying to establish their specific meaning in the context of the material you are reading.

Study Examples and Illustrations Carefully. Examples and illustrations are prepared to help you understand and remember what you read.

An author often states or explains a principle and then follows with a specific example that applies the principle. For emphasis, this example is often printed in a style or size of type different from that used in the explanation. Do not pass over such examples; they will help you get a clearer picture of what the author is trying to say. In addition, study carefully all charts, draw-

A. Devaney

As you read, recite to yourself mentally and in your own words the gist of what you have read.

ings, graphs, tables, and other visual illustrations.

Review Your Reading. Even though you have read the material with a full and clear understanding, you will need to review from time to time. A quick skimming of the material may be adequate.

Reviewing should be done shortly after the material is first read. Otherwise, you may have to start "from scratch" again because you have forgotten so much of what you read.

How often you review will depend on the difficulty of the material, its importance, and on such other considerations as preparing for examinations.

SELECTING THE ESSENTIALS FOR NOTEMAKING

Finding the Central Idea. The first essential to select in making notes from reading is the *central idea* in what you read. Finding the central idea involves recognizing the main or controlling idea. Most people who are good at selecting the central idea probably couldn't tell you how they do it. However, there are some general guides that will help you find the central idea.

There Is Usually Only One Idea Per Paragraph. You will remember this rule about only one central idea in each paragraph from your study of English grammar. This is particularly true if the paragraphs are short. For example:

> Great literature is not limited to one country. Shakespeare (England), Goethe (Germany), Corneille and Racine (France), Dostoevski and Tolstoi (Russia), Ibsen (Scandinavia), Dante (Italy), and Cervantes (Spain) rank among the great immortals. In any compilation of the 100 great books there are authors from all parts of the earth.

Of course you know the central idea in this paragraph is that great literature comes from all parts of the world, not just from one country.

Look for Key Phrase or Sentence. In finding the central idea, look for the phrase or sentence in the paragraph upon which everything else depends. It is the one thing in the paragraph that can stand alone; everything else is related to it and depends upon it. Let's take a look at this example:

> The report that is most inviting in appearance has the best chance of being read. To make it inviting, the writer types it neatly on good white paper. He makes sure that erasures, if any, are undetectable. He keeps the right-hand margins as even as possible. He is careful to see that the type is clean. If the report is to be bound, he selects a cover that is eye-appealing.

Notice in the example how everything in the paragraph relates to the central idea: the report that is most inviting in appearance has the best chance of being read. This statement stands alone, and the rest of the paragraph merely gives further explanations and examples. These explanations and examples are important, of course, in giving the reader an accurate picture of what the author is writing about and should not be ignored in notemaking.

First Sentence Often Conveys Central Idea. Usually the first sentence in the paragraph gives you the key to what the paragraph is about. More often than not, it *is* the central idea, as in the following example:

> George Washington was by everyone's choice the chairman of the Constitutional Convention. There simply could be no other; he was foremost in everyone's mind. There was no one less the politician and more the disinterested leader. He was a Virginian, to be sure, but was not identified with sectional interests. Even Ben Franklin, the Federation's elder statesman, lacked Washington's stature. Washington was the most eminent American of his day as well as the one most responsible for the formation of his country.

The key sentence in this paragraph is clearly the first one. The rest of the paragraph is given over to reasons why Washington was chosen as chairman.

Last Sentence May Convey Central Idea. Occasionally the author deliberately buries the most important idea somewhere in the middle or at the end of the paragraph. This may be because the key idea has already been given in the heading; more often it is because the author feels he can make his central point better by first providing some dramatic background material. Can you find the central idea in the following paragraph?

> The question of fall versus spring plowing is frequently debated. Such a question cannot be correctly answered without knowing what crop is to be grown. Plowing for spring-grain crops, which give their best yields when sown early, requires fall plowing to get maximum returns. If plowing is done in the spring, seeding of the crop is delayed and reduced yields result. In states where winter grains are grown, best yields have been obtained from

plowing in the middle of July. Time of plowing is determined by the crop to be grown.

The theme of this paragraph is obviously centered around the statement, "Time of plowing is determined by the crop to be grown." The central idea is the last sentence; everything else in the paragraph supports it.

Watch for Two Central Ideas in a Paragraph. Some paragraphs contain two or more central ideas, and the notemaker must find them. Notice the two central ideas in the following paragraph:

Credit is, from the point of view of the seller, simply confidence that a buyer will be willing and able to pay his bills when they become due. The seller gives evidence of his confidence by lending merchandise to the buyer. From the point of view of the buyer, credit is the power to obtain goods or services by giving a promise to pay money on demand or at a specified date in the future.

We won't argue the fact that this might have been better stated if it had been broken into two paragraphs — the first, a definition of credit from the viewpoint of the seller

Look for the central ideas as you read; they will provide the framework for your notes.

H. Armstrong Roberts

and the second, from the viewpoint of the buyer. But this is an actual paragraph from a textbook, and the fact remains that there are two central ideas. The notemaker must be on the alert for them and give them equal prominence in his notes.

Sometimes the Central Idea Is Elusive. In some paragraphs it is not easy to extract the central idea or a single statement that gives the key to the meaning of the paragraph. What is the central idea in the following?

The development of the radio placed a new burden upon presidential candidates. No longer could they escape the limelight by a "front-porch" campaign. The public wanted to hear them and if possible also to see them. Smith yielded to the new technique and toured the country extensively, speaking at various points before nationwide hook-ups. With radio broadcasting still in its infancy, he failed to make a good impression. He spoke from notes rather than from manuscript. While he was fascinating enough to the audience before him, he was often inaudible or inarticulate to the listeners. Moreover, his unusual accent and his occasional mispronunciations caused much unfavorable comment. Hoover, on the other hand, although a far less effective public speaker, poured what he had to say directly into the microphone; and it came out better than it went in. His pronunciation was no better than Smith's, but it was the kind that most Americans were themselves accustomed to use and so gave little offense.

This paragraph has to be read carefully two or three times in order to grasp the central idea. Did you find it? The author is telling you the general effect of radio on presidential elections. But in addition to telling you that the radio had a great impact on presidential elections, he is also revealing one of the factors that caused the defeat of presidential candidate Alfred E. Smith. In fact, this is the central idea.

In making good notes from reading, you must be interested in more than the central idea in what you read. You are interested also in facts, information, examples, and other ideas that explain, develop, and support the central idea. These essentials must not be overlooked, for they can be an important part of good notes.

To illustrate, let's take another look at the example on page 83. For notemaking purposes your analysis of this paragraph might be as follows:

Central idea: Report with inviting appearance has best chance of being read.

Related ideas: Typed neatly on good paper
Erasures, if any, undetectable
Right-hand margins even
Clean type
Attractive cover, if bound

Selecting the central idea and selecting related ideas, facts, information, examples, and so on, for notemaking requires recognition and judgment as to what is important and what is relatively unimportant. Whatever is pertinent should be included in your notes. Good notes are sufficiently complete but not too complete. They are just complete enough to serve your purposes effectively as tools for learning and performance.

PUTTING THE PRINCIPLES INTO PRACTICE

1. Read the following paragraphs. As you complete each paragraph, recite the gist of it to yourself in your own words.

a. The connection between word knowledge and business success has been proved by scientific study. We have all wondered why one man with very little education has been able to advance to a high executive position while another man with, perhaps, a college degree has not been able to reach the top level of management. One of the answers is that the first man continued to educate himself by reading a great deal and by listening attentively to people from whom he could learn. In order to read and listen intelligently, this man had to understand the meaning of words.

b. In order of authority, our existing law may be classified as the Constitution of the United States; laws of Congress; constitutions of the individual states; laws of the state legislature; and the common law. No law is valid if it violates the Constitution of the United States.

c. In early colonial times, the British, Dutch, and French all made settlements on the coast of South America; but the British claimed the largest area. When the Dutch surrendered New York to the British, the latter gave them a large area of Guiana in exchange. It was a poor bargain for the Dutch. Only in fairly recent years have these hot countries begun to produce much of value.

d. Right up until the middle 1930's, there was bitter opposition to unions. But finally the pendulum of government swung in support of collective bargaining; and since the Wagner Act (1935), most manufacturing industries have become unionized. The result has been less violence but still vigorous collective bargaining between the opposing groups. By 1947 Congress felt that the Wagner Act was one-sided in favor of labor and passed the Taft-Hartley Act to define illegal collective bargaining practices of unions.

e. Plowing has been called a major operation on the land. It results in rapid loss of organic matter and promotes availability of plant-food materials. These are desirable in the production of high-yielding crops, but with some crops it is not so essential. Whenever crops can be started and grown successfully without plowing, do so. Some lands should not be plowed.

2. Read the following paragraphs and find the central idea in each.

a. What the listener should strive for, then, is a more *active* kind of listening. Whether you listen to Mozart or Duke Ellington, you can deepen your understanding of music only by being a more conscious and aware listener — not someone who is just listening, but someone who is listening *for* something.

b. One of the reasons why Shakespeare gave such a fresh interpretation to the English language is that he was not hampered by formal English grammar. Little boys in Elizabethan England did not have to learn formal English. All the rules and ritual and reverence were focused on Latin, with the result that Shakespeare and the other writers of his day leapt into English lighthearted and free. There was no English dictionary to hamper them. They could pick up words where they found them, put them into any combinations, or make up new words.

PRACTICAL TIPS AND SUGGESTIONS FOR NOTEMAKING

USE LONGHAND INITIALS FOR NAMES

When an expression recurs frequently in a lecture or in the reading on which you are making notes, devise a special abbreviation for it, using small longhand initials. You will often know beforehand that some expression will recur frequently, and you can then put at the top of your notes a key to your use of such initials.

If the subject of the material on which you are preparing notes is *de Gaulle*, for example, you can write at the top of your sheet *dg=de Gaulle*. Even though you did not know beforehand that you would use such an abbreviation, you would find that after the name had occurred once or twice in the lecture and had been written out, you could use *dg* thereafter with perfect clarity.

Don't try to remember such abbreviations from month to month. Use them the day you devise them or as long as that subject continues to be part of your work. Somewhere at the beginning or end of the notes make a record of them. Then forget about them. Perhaps the next day, perhaps even the same day, you may use the same abbreviation to represent a totally different expression. In the morning you may make notes from a lecture on the rise of the Dutch Republic, and you use the small joined longhand initials *da* to represent the Duke of Alva. In the afternoon you may be making notes for a talk on law enforcement in your community, and *da* will represent *district attorney*.

ABBREVIATION TECHNIQUES MAY VARY

Sometimes it seems better to write the full name in Gregg Notehand because the full name will be used so frequently. In any study of the Civil War, for instance, the names of Grant and Lee will recur frequently. Since they may be written so easily in full in Gregg Notehand, it would be a waste of time to use longhand except in a rare instance when you might want to write the name in full in longhand as a heading.

In Civil War material you will also find the name McClellan occurring often. For such a name, it is better to write the small longhand initial *m* or perhaps the initials *mc* after having written the name at least once in longhand in the notes for positive identification.

In studying the Civil War, the name of Lincoln will also occur with great frequency. Neither the Gregg Notehand character for Lincoln nor the small longhand initial would stand out sufficiently on a page of notes. In such a case you may write a large block capital *L*. This can be written as rapidly as the Gregg Notehand form or the small letter *l*. It has the additional advantage of being easy to spot in a page of notes.

These three suggested methods of representing names are given here to illustrate the flexibility and adaptability of these note-making devices. As you learn to use your ingenuity, you will find many rapidly written, yet legible, devices in the happy combination of Gregg Notehand and longhand.

LONGHAND HEADINGS

In all notes, it is best to write the major headings in longhand to make them stand out so that you can spot them readily when you review your notes. The longhand headings in your notes are as helpful as the use of large, bold type on a printed page. Notice how the longhand headings stand out on the actual page of notes on page 88.

MOST-USED GREGG NOTEHAND FORMS

By this time you should have learned to use easily the twenty common words that were presented in Units 8 and 15. Here are ten more of the most frequently used words in the English language. Add these to the forms already on your card. Remember to keep the card near you whenever you are writing and refer to it as often as necessary. The ten additional words are:

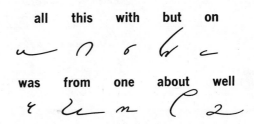

all	this	with	but	on
was	from	one	about	well

PUTTING GREGG NOTEHAND INTO PRACTICE

Read and make a copy of the outline summary of a discussion of the life of Woodrow Wilson. Notice the timesaving use of longhand initials for names.

The key to this material appears on page 288.

Woodrow Wilson

Education
1. ~ edu. ~ south.
2. Entered Princeton U. – 1875.
3. ~ debater ~ ~ ~
   ~ .
4. ~ 9 prof. and ~ 9 pres. ~ pu.

Politics
1. Dems. elected W Gov. ~
   N. J. – 1910.
2. Dems. elected W Pres. – 1912.
   ~ ~ ~ ~ possible (~
   – Rep. 6~.

Domestic ~
1. Dem. ~ called) ~
   ~. W ~ ~ and Cong.
   ~ Underwood ~ ~.
2. W ~ and Cong. ~ ~
   Reserve ~ ~.

Foreign ~
1. W ~) neutrality ~ ~
   ~ ~ – 1914.
2. W's ~ ~ (~ ~ elected ~
) second ~ – 1916 (~ ~.

In this unit you will study another group of six brief forms for frequently used words. You will also practice phrases that these brief forms enable us to build.

67.   Brief Forms

*under	⌒	which	/	should	✓
*over	⌣	opportunity	ℰ	could	⌐

*The words *under* and *over* are written above the following Notehand character. They may also be used as prefix forms as in the following words:

underneath		underpaid		oversight	
undertake		overcame		overlook	

68.   Phrases

under the		I should		which the	
under that		he should		I could	

READING AND WRITING PRACTICE

Easy Profit

"$125" $35 and

"$90"

$35

$125

$35,

$50

$50

$15

$75!

In Unit 24 you will take up three new alphabetic strokes. You have only a few more to go. You will also take up another principle for the omission of vowels.

69.   Ow.   The sound of *ow*, as in *how*, is written ⟋ . In writing ow, be sure to make the a circle large and the oo hook deep and narrow.

Spell: **how,** *h-ow*

how	⟋	**doubt**	⟋	**proud**	⟋
out	⟋	**town**	⟋	**now**	⟋
house	⟋	**down**	⟋	**mouse**	⟋
ounce	⟋	**brown**	⟋	**mouth**	⟋

READING AND WRITING PRACTICE

Temper

(shorthand practice text)

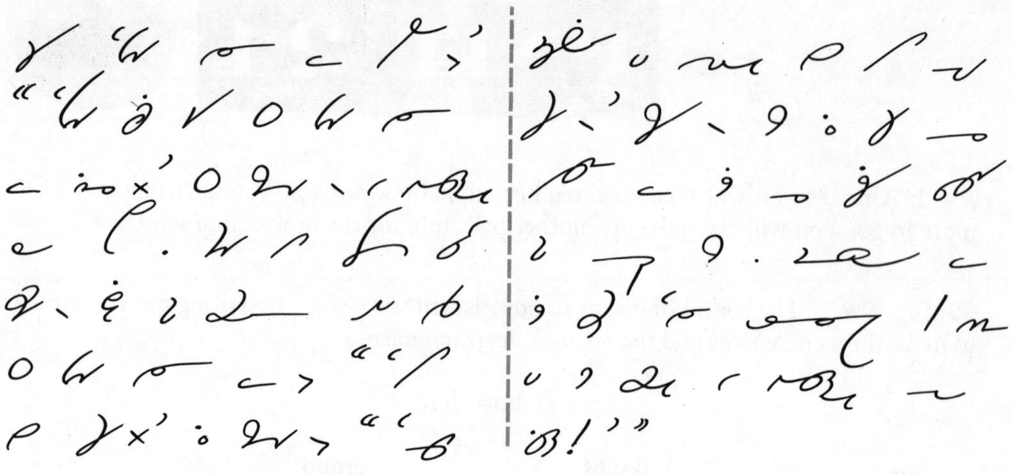

70. Ng. The sound of *ng*, as in *sing*, is written

Compare: **seen** **sing**

Spell: **ring,** *r-e-ing;* **long,** *l-o-ing;* **young,** *e-oo-ing*

ring	bring	single
rang	thing	young
wrong	sing	length
long	sang	strong

READING AND WRITING PRACTICE

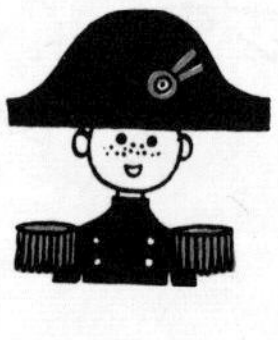

A Boy

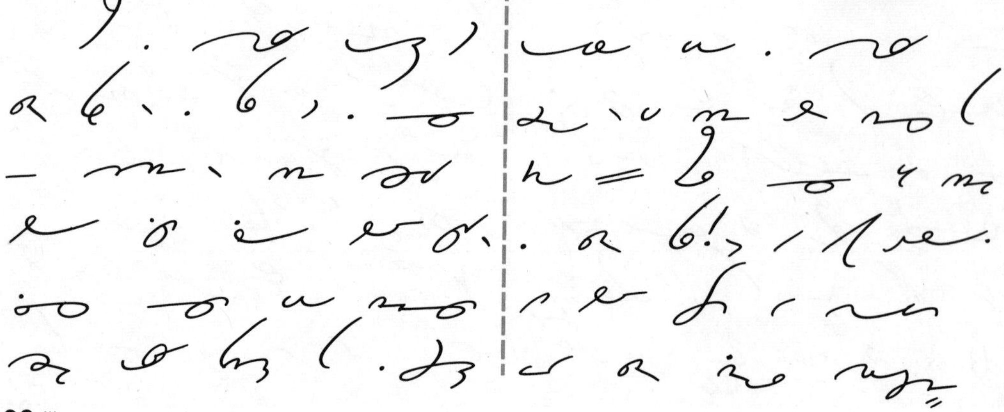

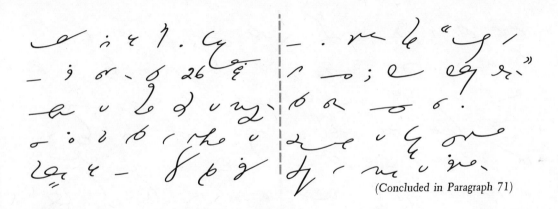

(Concluded in Paragraph 71)

71. **Ngk.** The sound of *ngk* (usually spelled *nk* in longhand), as in *sink*, is written ⌒ .

Compare: **seen** ⌒ **sing** ⌒

seem ⌒ **sink** ⌒

Spell: **link,** *l-e-ink;* **thank,** *ith-a-ink*

link	⌒	crank	⌒	think	⌒
thank	⌒	blank	⌒	rank	⌒
sank	⌒	blanket	⌒	drink	⌒
bank	⌒	ink	⌒	frank	⌒

READING AND WRITING PRACTICE

A Boy (Concluded)

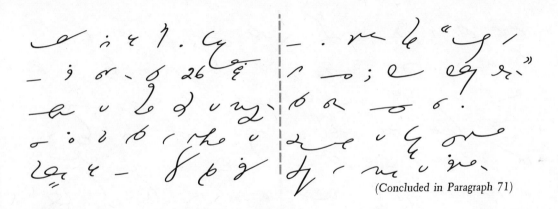

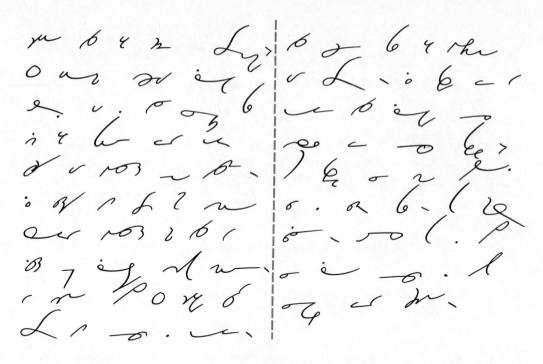

72. **Omission of Short U.** In the body of a word, the hook representing the sound of short *u*, as in *run*, is omitted before *n* or *m*.

Before N

run	⌒	gun	⌒⌒	ton	⌐
sun	⌒	fun	⌒	lunch	⌒⌐

Before M

come	⌒	summer	⌒⌒	column	⌒⌒
some	⌒	lumber	⌒⌐	welcome	⌒⌒

READING AND WRITING PRACTICE

Dither

Watterson

H.W.

In this unit you will take up two new alphabetic strokes, which you will find very easy because they are simply combinations of strokes you already know.

73. **Nd.** The Notehand strokes for *n* and *d* are joined without an angle to represent the sound of *nd*, as in *lined*.

Nd

Compare: **line**   **lined**

Spell: **lined,** *l-ī-end;* **land,** *l-a-end*

land		signed		end	
trained		kind		spend	
joined		mind		friend	
band		bind		wonder	

READING AND WRITING PRACTICE

The Lark and Her Young Ones

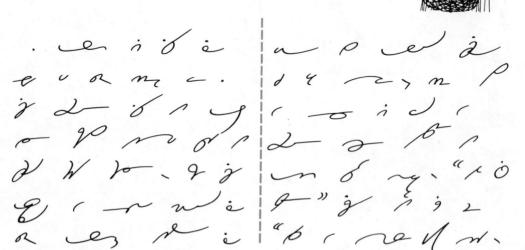

(shorthand outlines)

(Concluded in Paragraph 74)

74. **Nt.** The stroke for *nd* also represents the sound of *nt*, as in *rent*.

Spell: **rent,** *r-e-ent*; **paint,** *p-a-ent*; **enter,** *e-ent-r*

rent	*(outline)*	center	*(outline)*	spent	*(outline)*
went	*(outline)*	paint	*(outline)*	gentle	*(outline)*
prevent	*(outline)*	want	*(outline)*	enter	*(outline)*
sent	*(outline)*	plenty	*(outline)*	interest	*(outline)*

READING AND WRITING PRACTICE

The Lark and Her Young Ones (Concluded)

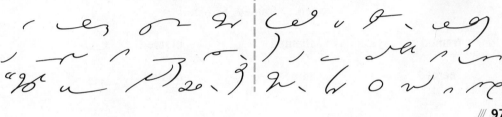

(shorthand outlines)

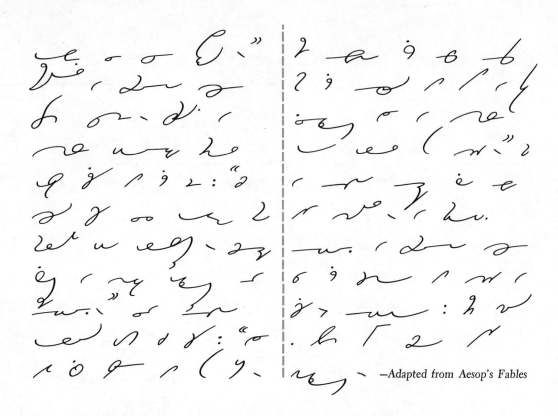

—Adapted from Aesop's Fables

75.   Md, Mt. The Notehand strokes for *m* and *d* are joined without an angle to represent the sound of *md*, as in *framed*. The same stroke also represents the sound of *mt*, as in *prompt*.

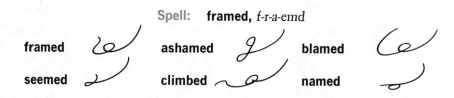

Did you notice that the *md*, *mt* stroke is considerably longer than the *nd* stroke —at least twice as long?

Md

Spell: **framed**, *f-r-a-emd*

framed   ashamed   blamed

seemed   climbed   named

Mt

Spell: **prompt**, *p-r-o-emt*

prompt ⌒ promptly ⌒ empty ⌒

READING AND WRITING PRACTICE

Study

[Shorthand outlines]

UNIT 26

In this unit you will learn one more group of six brief forms. After that, only one more group to go!

76.   Brief Forms

and	/	short	✓	important, importance	⌐
suggest	⌒	work	⌣	where	ℓ

77.   Brief-Form Derivatives

suggestion	⌒	shortly	ℓ	worked	⌣
suggested	⌒	shorter	ℓ	working	⌣

READING AND WRITING PRACTICE

Fast Shrinkage

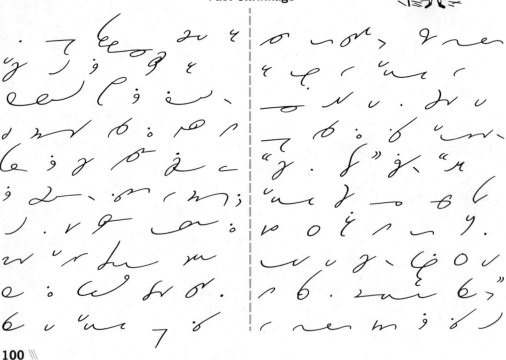

The Measure of a Man

—W. C. Brann

78. **Brief Forms as Word Beginnings.** It is often possible to use the brief forms *in*, *be*, and *for* as prefixes in longer words.

In

Spell: **income,** *in-k-m*

income   inside   invite

Be

Spell: **beneath,** *b-n-e-ith*

beneath   believe   belong

For

Spell: **forget,** *for-gay-e-t*

forget   form   force

READING AND WRITING PRACTICE

Surprise

UNIT 27

In Unit 27 you will study two new strokes, which are really combinations of strokes you already know. You will find these timesaving strokes easy to learn.

79.   Ted.   The combination *ted*, as in *heated*, is formed by joining *t* and *d* together as one long stroke.

Ted

Compare: **heat**   **heed**   **heated**

Did you notice that the stroke for *ted* is about twice as long as the stroke for *d*?

Spell: **acted,** *a-k-ted;* **instead,** *in-s-ted*

acted	**visited**	**located**
waited	**quoted**	**instead**
adjusted	**noted**	**steady**

READING AND WRITING PRACTICE

Loyalty

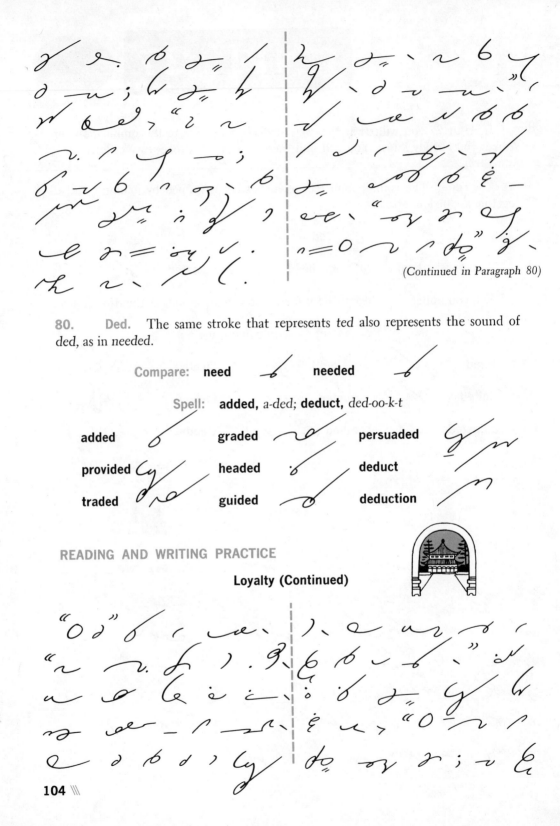

(Continued in Paragraph 80)

80. **Ded.** The same stroke that represents *ted* also represents the sound of *ded*, as in *needed*.

Compare: **need** ⟋ **needed** ⟋

Spell: **added,** a-ded; **deduct,** ded-oo-k-t

added		graded		persuaded	
provided		headed		deduct	
traded		guided		deduction	

READING AND WRITING PRACTICE

Loyalty (Continued)

(Continued in Paragraph 81)

81.   **Men.**   The combination *men*, as in *mend*, is written by joining *m* and *n* together in one long stroke, which is about twice as long as the stroke for *m*.

Men _____→

Compare: **in** ___   **am** _____   **men** _____

Spell: **meant,** *men-t;* **women,** *oo-e-men*

men _____	mend _____/	mention _____7
meant _____/	mended _____/	immense _____
mental _____	many _____	women _____

READING AND WRITING PRACTICE

Loyalty (Continued)

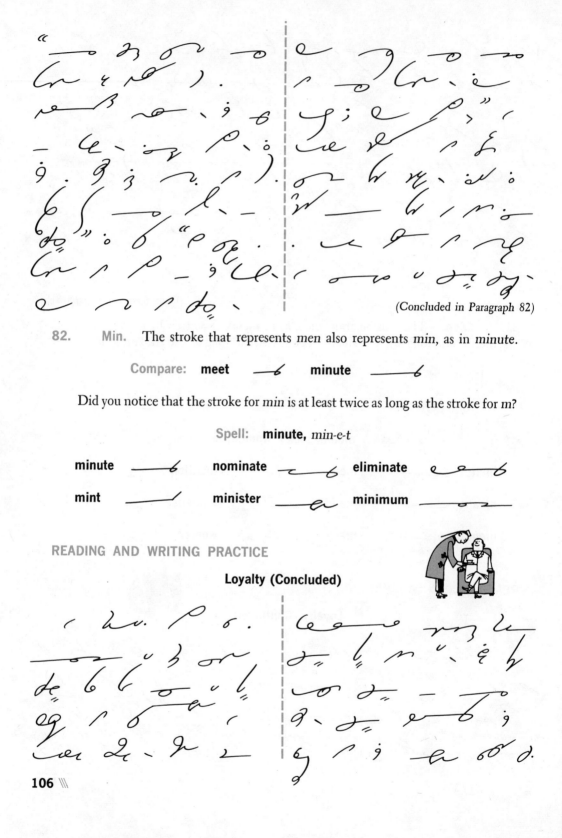

(Concluded in Paragraph 82)

82. **Min.** The stroke that represents *men* also represents *min*, as in *minute*.

Compare: **meet** ⟋ **minute** ⟋

Did you notice that the stroke for *min* is at least twice as long as the stroke for *m*?

Spell: **minute,** min-e-t

| **minute** ⟋ | **nominate** ⟋ | **eliminate** ⟋ |
| **mint** ⟋ | **minister** ⟋ | **minimum** ⟋ |

READING AND WRITING PRACTICE

Loyalty (Concluded)

—Adapted from Elbert Hubbard's Notebook

RECALL

In Unit 28 there are no new Notehand devices for you to learn; you will have a little time to digest the material you studied thus far. You will get a hearty chuckle out of the story in the Reading and Writing Practice entitled "Green Dye."

83.   Recall Chart.   Can you read the 96 words and phrases in this chart in 9 minutes or less? After you have read the chart from left to right, read down each column. If you can also read the entire chart in this way in 9 minutes, you are to be congratulated; you are making fine progress!

Words

1					
2					
3					
4					
5					
6					
7					
8					
9					

Brief Forms

10					
11					

Brief-Form Derivatives

12					
13					

Phrases

14						
15						
16						

84.   READING AND WRITING PRACTICE

Green Dye

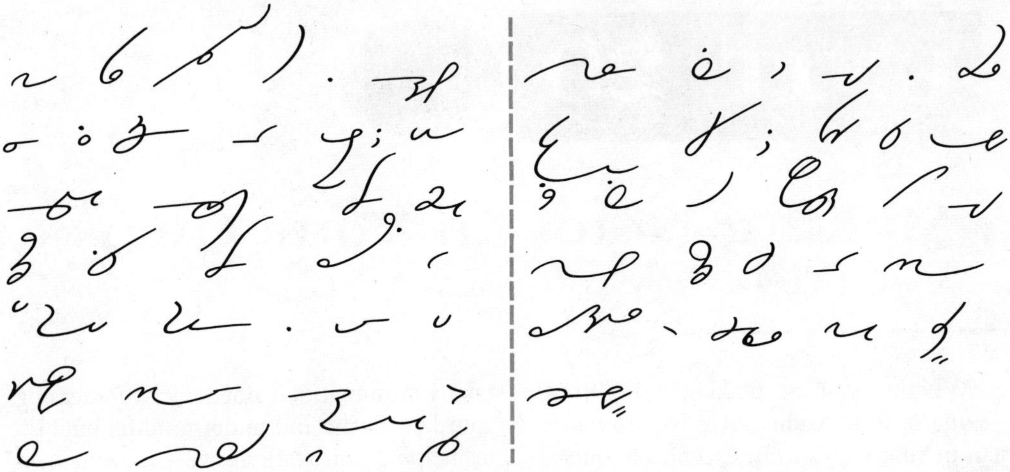

Making Notes in Your Own Words

Whether you are making notes from listening or from reading, it is best to make them in your own words, except, of course, for statements you wish to recall exactly or to quote. Fortunately, making notes in your own words is but another application of effective listening or effective reading. In either case, you recite to yourself mentally and in your own words the gist of what is said or read.

HOW MAKING NOTES IN YOUR OWN WORDS WILL HELP YOU

Making notes in your own words will help you in five significant ways:

1. It will help you prepare more useful notes — notes that convey in your *own vocabulary* only the essentials of what you have heard or read.

2. It will help you think for yourself. Making notes in your own words requires you to analyze, interpret, relate, and summarize what you hear and read.

3. It will help you learn because it requires you to participate actively in what you hear and what you read.

4. It will help you review. Notes made in your own words are a helpful source of material for reviewing. Ideas, facts, information, and examples that are put into your own words may help you recall the entire reasoning process that you followed in making the notes initially.

5. It will aid you in preparing for and taking examinations, not only by increasing your knowledge and understanding but also by helping you state answers in your own words. It will help you to relate ideas, facts, information, and examples. It will help you to approach examinations with confidence and to think creatively.

AN EXAMPLE

Read the following paragraph for the purpose of putting into your own words the essential ideas that it contains.

Gluck himself had written a great many operas in the conventional Italian style of his day before he assumed the role of reformer, so that he knew whereof he spoke when he said that opera was in need of purification. Gluck tried above all to rationalize opera — to have it make more sense. In the older opera, the singer was supreme, and the music served the singer; Gluck made the dramatic idea supreme and wrote music that served the purposes of the text. Each act was to be an entity in itself, not a nondescript collection of more or less effective arias. It was to be balanced and contrasted, with a flow and continuity that would give it coherence as an art form. The ballet, for example, was not to be a mere divertissement introduced for its own sake but an integral part of the dramatic idea of the work.

The central idea in the foregoing paragraph is that Gluck assumed the role of a reformer in opera after having written many operas in conventional Italian style. The paragraph also contains several ideas related to the central idea. Put into your own words, the essential ideas of the paragraph might be as follows:

Gluck had written many operas in conventional Italian style. He thought opera should make sense; the drama was more important than the singer. Each act should be complete in itself and coherent. Ballet should be a real part of the story, not just something thrown in.

As you will observe, the ideas have been selected, interpreted, and described briefly in words that in several instances are different from those in the original paragraph.

BREVITY IN MAKING NOTES IN YOUR OWN WORDS

In making notes in your own words, strive to put down *just enough* — not too much or too little. The note that you make of each idea, fact, piece of information, or example should be brief and to the point, eliminating unnecessary words.

Nearly everything we read except telegrams has more words than are really necessary for comprehension. "Why, then," you may ask, "don't writers cut out the extra words?" Well, the extra words make the material easier to read and understand. Books and other types of literature would be very hard to read if they were written like telegrams. Also, extra words make it possible for an author to say things in more interesting and striking ways.

When you make notes, however, you should eliminate most of the extra words. Every unnecessary word you include requires time for the writing and later requires additional time for reading in using your notes. You must get down to the bare essentials. For example, read the following paragraph:

In all the pages of history, from the be-ginning of time, there is no blacker example of infamous treachery and inhuman cruelty than the campaign in which the Spaniards under Pizarro ravaged Peru and traitorously executed the Inca after extorting a vast treasure of gold as his ransom.

Notice how much more interesting and colorful this paragraph is because of the use of such words and phrases as *from the beginning of time, in all the pages of history, blacker example, infamous treachery,* and *traitorously.* Yet these words are not necessary in notes. As a matter of fact, your notes might simply read:

Spaniards under Pizarro were treacherous and cruel when they executed Inca after collecting ransom.

Thus, the 14-word note tells all that is necessary about the 48-word paragraph. The brevity of the note has saved about two-thirds of the time that would have been required to write the paragraph in full.

Include Useful Little Words. Brevity does not mean that you should write notes in telegraphic style from which useful little words like *and, to,* and *from* are omitted.

It is best to make notes in your own words; but when you must copy verbatim, do it accurately.

Because of the ease with which these little words may be written in Gregg Notehand, they can be used without any appreciable loss of time. Furthermore, notice in the preceding illustration how much the inclusion of the word *and* helps the sense of the notes.

Words like *to* and *from* can be important in interpreting your notes long after they were written. This is not always the case, but it is important not to leave them out just because they are short words.

Don't Be Too Brief. The effort to keep your notes brief must not be carried too far. Sometimes it may be quicker to write a slightly longer note than to take the time to decide how best to abbreviate it. In addition, notes must not be so brief that they are inadequate and difficult to use after they are made. Read the following paragraph:

Although medieval culture abounded in local, regional, and eventually national differences, the feudal upper classes throughout the West shared the way of life we call *chivalry*. This term comes from *chevalier*, the French word for *knight*. This chivalric code began as the simple creed of fighting men, and like most things medieval it came into full maturity about the thirteenth century.

The central idea of the paragraph might be reworded in your own notes as follows:

Feudal upper classes shared way of life called chivalry.

For good notemaking purposes, however, this description of the central idea of the paragraph is too brief. It would be more useful if it were worded as follows:

Chivalry was a way of life for feudal upper classes in West. Originally a simple creed for fighting men (term comes from French word for *knight*), it came into full maturity about the thirteenth century.

Notice, again, in this illustration the usefulness in notemaking, and especially in reading notes, of such little words as *a*, *of*, *for*, *in*, and *from*.

VERBATIM NOTES

Sometimes you need to make notes of what you hear or read exactly as it is said or written. Examples of such occasions are as follows:

1. You wish to make a direct quotation from what you hear or read.

2. You wish to memorize a statement, such as a famous quotation, a poem, or a rule of law.

3. The material on which you are making notes contains many technical or commonly used terms for which there are no satisfactory substitutes.

When material is difficult to paraphrase in your own words, you have no choice but to use the original words. For example:

Conjunctions join sentence elements with each other. They may join words, phrases, and clauses (both dependent and independent). There are two principle kinds of conjunctions: co-ordinating and subordinating. When used in pairs, they are called correlative conjunctions.

In your study of English grammar you know that specific nomenclature must be used. Thus, in making notes on this subject, you cannot use your own words; you must adhere to the established terms. Your notes on the foregoing paragraph might be as follows:

Conjunctions join sentence elements with each other. May join words, phrases, and clauses. Two kinds of conjunctions — co-ordinating and subordinating. When used in pairs, they are called correlative conjunctions.

Although these notes are not absolutely verbatim, you can see that the original paragraph is almost impossible to condense. Almost every word is necessary.

PUTTING THE PRINCIPLES
INTO PRACTICE

In each of the following paragraphs (a) find the central idea or ideas and (b) condense the material in your own words for notemaking purposes. Be brief, but not too brief.

1. Fortunately, duress does not enter into many business contracts. Businessmen do not ordinarily carry guns to threaten their customers, nor lock them up until they agree to sign contracts! Although you should be able to recognize the elements of duress should they occur in some future business relationship, it is very unlikely that you will be involved in a case of duress. (Hint: Your notes on this paragraph should be contained in one brief sentence of five to ten words.)

2. Strictly speaking, the civil service includes all elected or appointed public officials of the federal, state, county, city, and town governments. In actual practice, however, the term is used to designate those public employees who have obtained appointments to their jobs by competitive examinations or by merit.

3. The army reached France far more slowly than Pershing had hoped. By August, he had only 45,000 men; by January, less than 200,000; and by March, well under 300,000, of whom about half were "technical troops," the builders and operators of the American military plant in France. But from then on, the Atlantic ferry began to achieve results. In April alone, 120,000 men were transported overseas, and 311,359 in July, an average of over 10,000 a day. On a single trip, the *Leviathan*, once the German *Vaterland*, carried 11,500 Americans to France; and while it was engaged in transport service, it took over a total of approximately 100,000 men. By the end of the war, Admiral Gleaves had records to show that the American contribution in manpower had reached a grand total of 2,079,880. Out of this number, Pershing netted forty-two divisions of fighting men.

PRACTICAL TIPS AND SUGGESTIONS
FOR NOTEMAKING

LEAVE WIDE MARGINS

A good set of notes should have wide margins all around the page, for the following very important reasons:

1. Wide margins make the notes more readable. A page crowded with notes from edge to edge and from top to bottom always appears considerably more difficult to read.

2. Wide margins leave room for corrections and for the insertion of afterthoughts. Otherwise such additions must be squeezed illegibly into some cranny of an already crowded page.

3. Wide margins permit the notemaker to add key words that make finding and reviewing easier and faster.

COPY WITHOUT WATCHING WHAT YOU WRITE

The simplest and quickest way to copy long extracts verbatim from printed or typewritten material is to copy without watching what you write, using as much Gregg Notehand as possible. You can learn to do this with a little practice.

To copy in this way, write on every other line, with just an occasional glance at the writing to be sure that you are not overlapping.

Copying without watching is no special advantage if you must write everything in longhand, because most English words require so much writing time that you have plenty of time to glance back and forth from the textbook to the notebook.

But copying without watching is not difficult for the Gregg Notehand writer. The Gregg Notehand outlines for most words, particularly for the frequently used words of the language, are so short that constant glancing back and forth considerably slows down the speed of copying. Because the Gregg Notehand outlines are so short, they need less watching than the more cumbersome longhand words.

MOST-USED GREGG NOTEHAND FORMS

If you have made a real effort in your everyday writing to use the Gregg Notehand outlines for the most-used words presented in Units 8, 15, and 22, those outlines should be old friends by this time.

Here is another group of ten common words in the English language. Add them to your card.

and   **which**   **some**   **out**   **now**

The student copies an extract without watching what he writes.

find   **sent**   **over**   **how**   **work**

PUTTING GREGG NOTEHAND INTO PRACTICE

1. In your stenographic notebook, copy the two paragraphs under the preceding heading, "Most-Used Gregg Notehand Forms" without watching what you write. Use longhand whenever the Gregg Notehand outline for a word does not come to you immediately.

2. Read and make a copy of an extract from a book on practical psychology that appears on page 117. You will find the key on page 293.

[illegible] – Personality Development

1. [illegible] Dependence. [illegible] completely dependent [illegible] weaned [illegible]

2. [illegible] Comfort [illegible] Eating. [illegible] child's [illegible] yrs [illegible] comfort [illegible]

3. Show-Off [illegible] child [illegible] attention [illegible] uses [illegible]

4. [illegible] Low-Boiling Point. [illegible] into [illegible]

5. Gang [illegible] Toward [illegible]

UNIT 30

In this unit you will study your last set of brief forms for frequently used words. First, however, you will review all the brief forms you have studied up to this point.

85.   Brief-Form Review.   The following chart contains the 36 brief forms you have studied thus far. Can you read the entire chart in half a minute or less? Can you then make a copy of the brief forms in your notebook in one minute or less?

1						
2						
3						
4						
5						
6						

86.   Brief Forms.   This is the last set of brief forms that you will have to learn.

question	send	difficult
yesterday	probable	into

87.   Phrases

to question	send them	into this
send the	into the	into that

READING AND WRITING PRACTICE

Ten Signs of a Mature Man

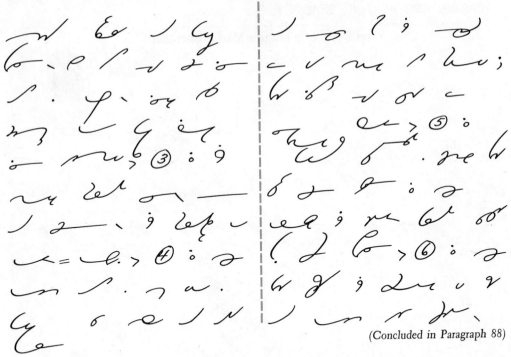

(Concluded in Paragraph 88)

88.   Ses.   The sound of *ses*, as in *senses*, is represented by joining the two forms of *s*.

Compare: **sense**   **senses**

face   **faces**

Spell: **addresses**, a-d-r-e-ses

addresses		**chances**		**closes**	
glasses		**sizes**		**realizes**	
leases		**cases**		**necessary**	

This stroke also represents the similar sounds heard in *sis*, as in *sister*; and in *sus*, as in *versus*.

Spell: **sister**, ses-t-r;   **versus**, v-e-r-ses

sister		**basis**		**census**	
system		**analysis**		**versus**	

Ten Signs of a Mature Man (Concluded)

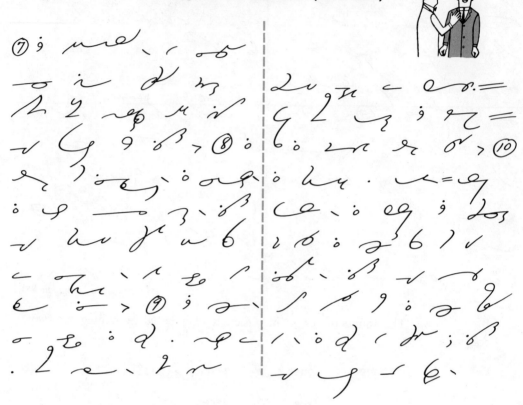

UNIT 31

In this unit you will study three new alphabetic strokes.

89.   Ten.   The combination *ten*, as in *written*, is represented by an upward curve about three times as large as the curve for the over *th*.

Ten

Compare: **Th**   **Ten**

Spell: **written,** *r-e-ten;* **stand,** *s-ten-d;* **bulletin,** *b-oo-l-e-ten*

written		intend		tonight	
threaten		tender		stand	
attend		gotten		bulletin	

This blend also represents *tain.*

Spell: **captain,** *k-a-p-ten*

| captain | | maintain | | retain | |
| certain | | obtain | | attain | |

READING AND WRITING PRACTICE

Strictly the Truth

/// 121

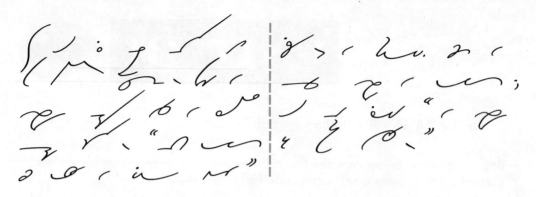

90. **Den.** This stroke also represents the sound of *den*, as in *sudden*.

Spell: **sudden,** *s-oo-den;* **dinner,** *den-r;* **guidance,** *gay-ī-den-s*

sudden		deny		evident	
hidden		dentist		guidance	
broaden		dinner		incident	

READING AND WRITING PRACTICE

Time to Forget

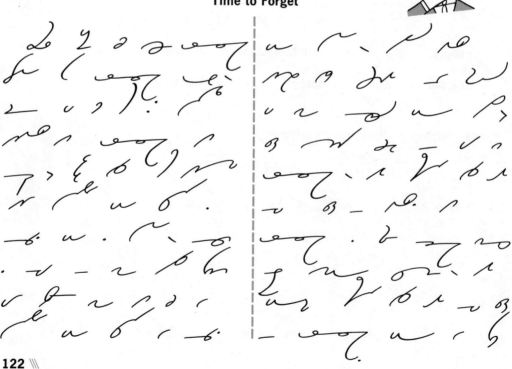

[Shorthand outlines]

91. **Word Ending -ment.** The word ending -ment, as in *agreement*, occurs in a great many English words. The ending is expressed by the Notehand *m*.

Spell: **agreement,** *a-gay-r-e-ment*; **elementary,** *e-l-e-ment-r-e*

agreement *[outline]*	payment *[outline]*	moment *[outline]*
arrangement *[outline]*	judgment *[outline]*	elementary *[outline]*
measurement *[outline]*	appointment *[outline]*	fundamental *[outline]*

READING AND WRITING PRACTICE

Big Business and Small Business

[Shorthand outlines]

—Abraham Lincoln

UNIT 32

In Unit 32 you will take up two new strokes and a common word ending.

92.   Rd.   The combination *rd*, as in *heard*, is represented by giving the *r* an upward turn at the end.

Compare: **hear** ⌒   **heard** ⌒

Spell: **hired,** *h-ī-ard*; **garden,** *gay-a-ard-n*

hired	⌒	**hard**	⌒	**card**	⌒
tired	⌒	**word**	⌒	**garden**	⌒

READING AND WRITING PRACTICE

Hard Work

(shorthand outlines)

(Concluded in Paragraph 93)

93. **Ld.** The combination *ld*, as in *told*, is expressed by writing the *l* with an upward turn at the end.

Compare: **roll**  **rolled**

Spell: **field,** *f-e-eld;* **seldom,** *s-e-eld-m*

field		settled		sold	
cold		drilled		gold	
spoiled		hold		seldom	

READING AND WRITING PRACTICE

Hard Work (Concluded)

94. **Word Ending -ble.** Another frequent word ending in the English language is *-ble*, as in *available*. It is represented by the Notehand *b*.

Spell: **available,** *a-v-a-l-bul*

available	**obtainable**	**agreeable**
capable	**payable**	**possible**

READING AND WRITING PRACTICE

Boiling Water

(shorthand outlines)

UNIT 33

In Unit 33 you will take up one word ending and three word beginnings.

95. **Word Ending -ful.** The word ending *-ful*, as in *careful*, is expressed by *f*.

Spell: **careful,** *k-a-r-ful*

careful	*(shorthand)*	beautiful	*(shorthand)*	thoughtful	*(shorthand)*
grateful	*(shorthand)*	tactful	*(shorthand)*	useful	*(shorthand)*
doubtful	*(shorthand)*	faithful	*(shorthand)*	helpful	*(shorthand)*

READING AND WRITING PRACTICE

Wasted Time

(shorthand practice material)

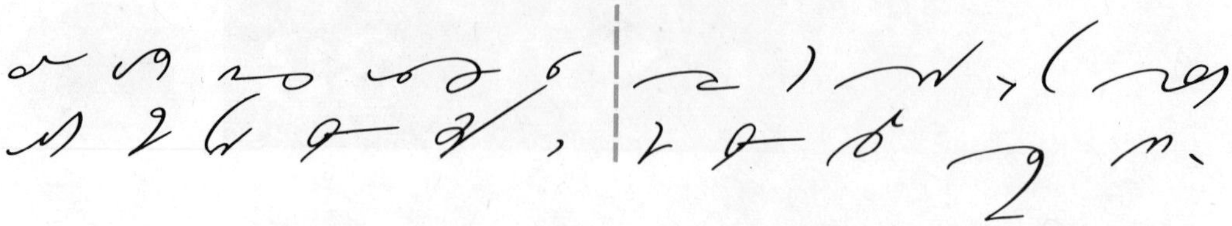

96. Word Beginning Con-. The word beginning *con*, as in *concern*, is expressed by the Notehand *k*.

Spell: concern, *con-s-e-r-n*

concern	contest	conclude
conduct	contract	constant
consider	contain	conscious

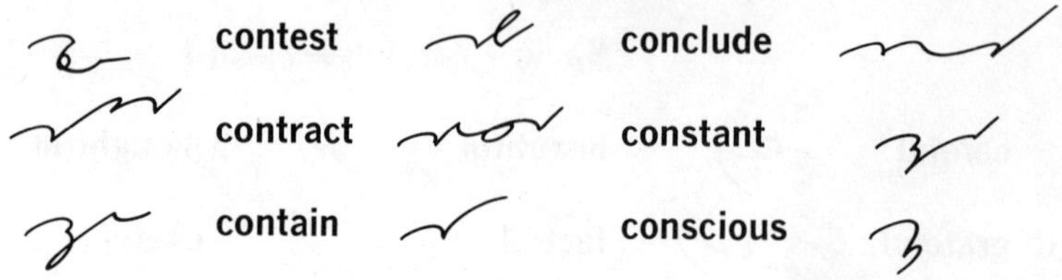

READING AND WRITING PRACTICE

On the Alert

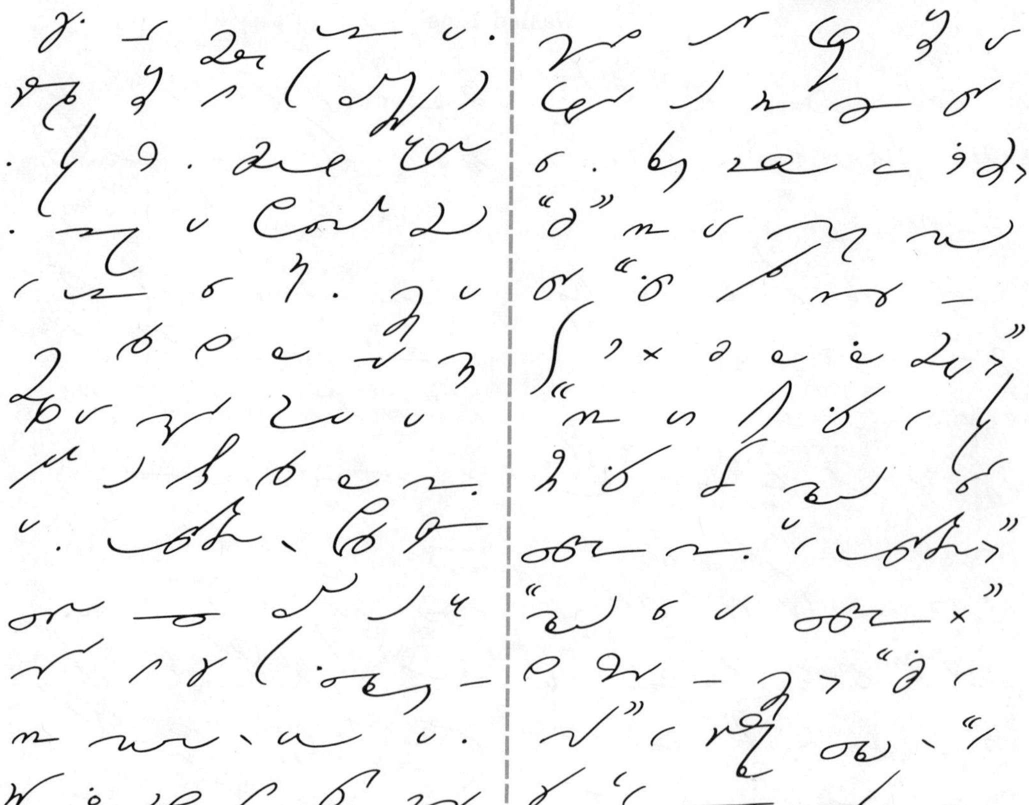

(shorthand outlines)

97. Word Beginning Com-.

The Notehand *k* represents the word beginning com-, as in *comply*, as well as the word beginning con-, as in *consider*.

Spell: comply, com-p-l-ī

comply	compliment	combine
competent	complain	comparative
compare	complete	comfortable

READING AND WRITING PRACTICE

Hearing Aid

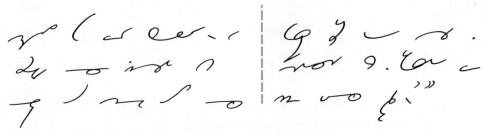

(shorthand practice outlines)

[shorthand outlines]

98. Word Beginning Trans-.

The word beginning *trans-*, as in *transmit*, is expressed by a disjoined *t* placed above the following character.

Spell: **transact,** *trans-a-k-t*

transact	*[outline]*	**translation**	*[outline]*	**transfer**	*[outline]*
transmit	*[outline]*	**transformed**	*[outline]*	**transcript**	*[outline]*
transport	*[outline]*	**transcribe**	*[outline]*	**transparent**	*[outline]*

READING AND WRITING PRACTICE

A Little Late

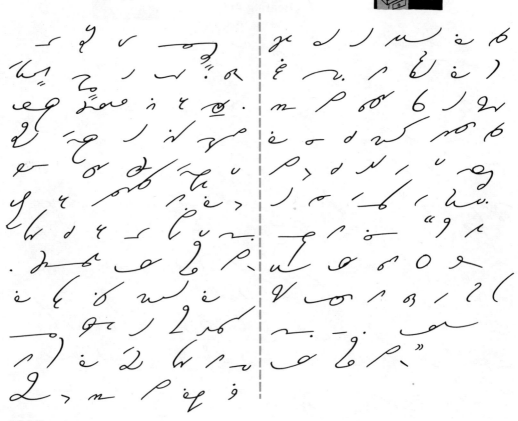

[shorthand practice text]

In this unit you will take up four easy word beginnings, all of which are frequently used in the English language.

99.   Word Beginning Ex-.   The word beginning ex-, as in express, is represented by the Notehand characters for es.

Spell: express, ex-p-r-e-s

express	*Ɛ*	explain	*Ɛℓ*	extent	
excellent		experiment		extra	
except		expense		extreme	
export		exclude		excessive	

A Tooth for a Tooth

[Shorthand notation symbols appear at the top of the page]

100. **Word Beginnings De-, Di-.** The word beginnings de-, as in delay, and di-, as in divide, are expressed by the Notehand character for d.

Spell: **delay,** d-l-a; **direct,** d-r-e-k-t

delay		desire		direct	
deliver		debate		different	
definite		develop		divide	
decide		devised		division	

READING AND WRITING PRACTICE

Shock

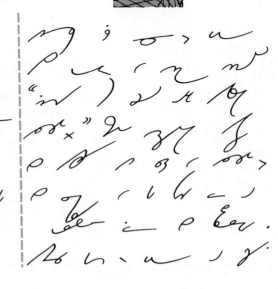

[Shorthand notation symbols fill the lower portion of the page]

(shorthand outlines)

101. Word Beginning Re-.

The word beginning re-, as in *repeat*, is expressed by the Notehand character for r.

Spell: **repeat,** re-p-e-t

repeat	*(outline)*	**replace**	*(outline)*	**refuse**	*(outline)*
report	*(outline)*	**revise**	*(outline)*	**reform**	*(outline)*
reveal	*(outline)*	**reply**	*(outline)*	**recent**	*(outline)*
residence	*(outline)*	**reverse**	*(outline)*	**react**	*(outline)*

READING AND WRITING PRACTICE

No Smoking!

(shorthand outlines)

$127.50

12

45

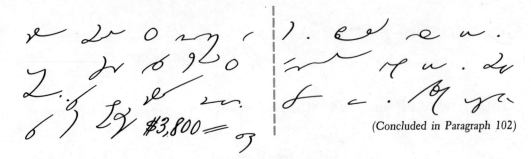

$3,800 =

(Concluded in Paragraph 102)

102. Word Beginnings Dis-, Des-.

The word beginnings *dis-*, as in *display*, and *des-*, as in *describe*, are expressed by the Notehand characters ds.

Spell: **display,** *dis-p-l-a*; **describe,** *dis-k-r-ī-b*

display		dissolve		describe	
discover		distance		description	
dispose		dismissed		despite	
dispute		district		destroy	

READING AND WRITING PRACTICE

No Smoking! (Concluded)

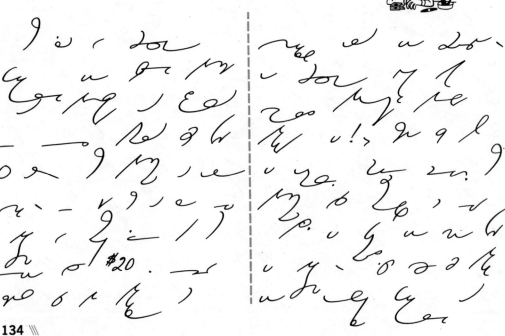

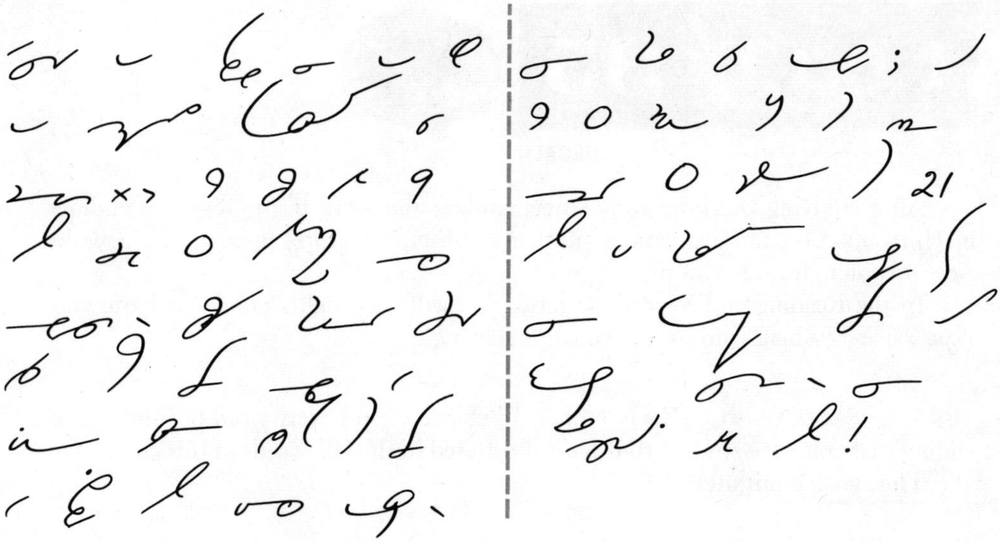

After studying the brief forms, new strokes, and word beginnings and endings in Units 30–34, you have earned another breather; therefore, there are no new devices for you to learn in this unit.

In the Reading and Writing Practice you will thoroughly enjoy the harrowing experiences of a man who cut his ear while shaving.

103. **Recall Chart.** Every Notehand character and every word beginning and ending that you have studied thus far is illustrated in the 102 words in this chart.

Time goal: 8 minutes!

Words

1						
2						
3						
4						
5						
6						
7						
8						
9						
10						
11						
12						
13						
14						

Brief Forms

15					

Brief-Form Derivatives

16					
17					

104. READING AND WRITING PRACTICE

Medicine Cabinet

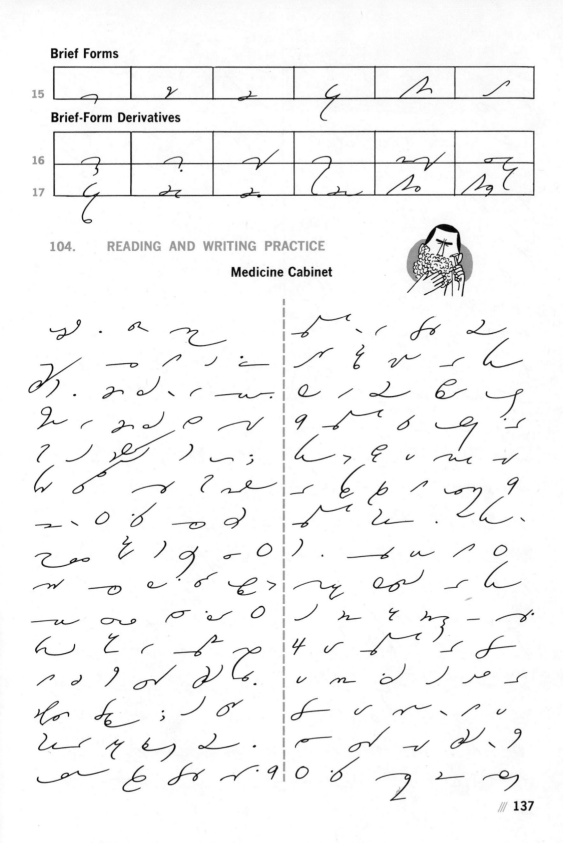

35

—James Thurber

UNIT 36

Organizing Your Notes as You Make Them

Notes may be organized in two basic forms: as narrative summaries of the essential ideas you have grasped from listening or reading; or in outline form.

Organizing your notes as you make them will help you get more out of your listening and reading. Moreover, it will result in notes that are much more useful to you after they are made.

ORGANIZING NOTES IN NARRATIVE SUMMARIES

Narrative summaries are restatements in your own words of the essential ideas in what you are reading or listening to. The following is an example of a narrative summary.

Packaging

Packaging is a primary function of marketing. Industry growth has been phenomenal. Retail packages are not just containers but often works of art. Packaging increases cost of distribution, but most retailers and consumers don't object. Smart packages are "silent salesmen" for the retailer; consumer appreciates beautiful things and will pay more for them.

Narrative summaries are especially useful in organizing notes:

1. In discussions and conferences
2. When listening to a speaker whose remarks range over a number of topics and do not treat any one topic in depth
3. In reading one or more reference sources for general information on a topic or a variety of topics

Headings in Narrative Summaries. Headings in narrative summaries will be helpful when you use the notes later. Headings should be surrounded by plenty of white space so they can be spotted readily.

An Example of Making Notes in Narrative Summaries. Study the following example of notes organized into narrative statements. Notice the use of headings.

JOHANN SEBASTIAN BACH

THE MAN

More than an intellectual musician. He was a lovable, warm-hearted man. Probably never danced, but enjoyed dance music. Had a cheerful heart, wrote cheerful music, such as his Gavotte in E Major and Minuet.

Bach had a deep and sincere piety. Loved the service of the church, for which he wrote great music.

140

COUNTERPOINT

    Brought old church counterpoint to life.
    Called his counterpoint tunes <u>fugues</u>.
    In a fugue the melodies seem to chase each other. Musician's eye
as well as his ear tells him the first tune begins with the left hand
and proceeds for four measures. While left hand goes on with new
theme, the right hand repeats first pattern. At measure 9, the right
hand plays a new pattern, which the left hand immediately begins to
imitate at measure 11, etc.

CANTATAS

    Wrote over 200 cantatas. His Christmas oratorio is really a
collection of six cantatas.

ORATORIOS

    Bach was organist many years for German Protestant Church of
St. Thomas. Here he wrote magnificent oratorios (church singing plays).
    Called his oratorios "Passions."
    In his Passions, Bach used the language of the gospels of John,
Mark, and Matthew.

B MINOR MASS

    Among Bach's greatest works is the "Mass in B Minor."

In the foregoing notes the headings are placed at the left, with plenty of white space around them so that the eye can readily spot them.

ORGANIZING NOTES IN OUTLINE FORM

Organizing notes in outline form involves the use of main headings and subheadings. Main headings are used for items of primary importance, with subheadings for items of secondary importance. The degree of importance of the items and the relationship between them are shown by levels or ranks of headings. Thus, essential ideas are main headings or subheadings, depending upon the level of their importance and their relationship.

Outline form is generally regarded as the most efficient form in which to organize notes. This is especially true in making notes *in depth*; that is, making notes that involve several levels of headings and subheadings and that run to considerable length.

Make your notes in outline form if you can; it will not only help you organize your thinking but also make your notes more useful for study and reference.

H. Armstrong Roberts

Organizing notes in outline form offers these advantages:

1. It will help you to think through carefully what you hear or read. It will help you select the essential ideas, facts, and information and to understand their relative importance and relationship.

2. It will help you to make useful notes — notes that can be used readily for studying, for review, and for reference.

3. It will help you save time both in making notes and in using them.

Informal and Formal Outlines. The two basic kinds of outlines are the informal and the formal. In the informal outline, simple indentions are used to indicate the relationship and relative importance of headings and subheadings. For some of your notemaking, the informal outline will do very well.

A more elaborate, and often more efficient, form for organizing notes is the formal outline. This uses a system of numbers and letters to indicate the importance and the relationship of headings and subheadings. The most commonly used system is as follows:

SUBJECT OR TOPIC (Not part of numbering system)

I. . . . .
  A. . . . .
    1. . . . .
      a. . . . .
        (1) . . . .
        (a) . . . .

Note that each succeeding level is indicated by a wider indention.

The following outline illustrates the number-letter system.

TRANSFER OF HEAT

I. Importance of transfer of heat

    A. Life on earth dependent on radiation from the sun
        1. Plants receive radiation from the sun
        2. Energy from coal, oil, etc., largely from fossil plants
    B. All man's sources of energy ultimately derived from radiation except atomic energy

II. Methods of transfer of heat

    A. Conduction
        1. Definition: Transfer of heat between materials in contact
        2. Method: Molecules in motion on surface of "hot" object striking molecules on surface of "cool" object and imparting kinetic energy
            a. Molecules do not pass from "hot" to "cool" object
            b. Kinetic energy the "heat" that flows from one object to another
    B. Convection
        1. Definition: Movement of molecules of gas
        2. Method: Kinetic energy of molecules increased
            a. Causes gas to become less dense
            b. Gas pushed upward by buoyant force of colder air
            c. Hence the gas circulates
        3. Convection responsible for movement of winds, ocean currents, as well as heating from a "steam radiator"

C. Radiation
    1. Definition: Energy emitted by a body whose molecules
       are in state of kinetic energy
        a. Radiation not transmitted by moving molecules
        b. May be transmitted across a vacuum
    2. Types of radiation
        a. Heat
        b. Light
        c. Electric waves
        d. "X-radiation," etc.
    3. Factors that determine radiation
        a. Energy radiated and absorbed by all bodies
        b. Radiation determined by temperature (kinetic energy)
        c. Type of material
           (1) Some substances radiate more than others
              (platinum more than silver)
           (2) Rough surface radiates more than smooth
              (because there is _more_ surface when it is
              rough)

Once you adopt a system of outlining for organizing a set of notes, use it consistently. Select your headings carefully. Indent subheadings consistently to show degrees of importance and relationship. That is, keep headings of equal importance at the same level. Watch the sequence of main headings and subheadings carefully so that each level develops and supports the next higher level.

Topic or Sentence Headings? In outlining, headings may be in the form of topics (that is, brief phrases or single words) or complete sentences. Or a combination of the two forms may be used. That is, main headings may be in the form of topics, and subheadings may be in the form of sentences.

There is no hard-and-fast rule for deciding when to use topics and when to use sentences. Topic headings are more concise and quicker to write. Sentence headings require more time and effort to construct. Sentence headings force the notemaker to think through more carefully what he reads or hears in order to make complete statements. The use that is to be made of the notes is also a consideration. For example, in outlining notes from the usual reading and listening, topics are more commonly used. In outlining notes for a research paper, sentence headings are probably preferable.

OUTLINING NOTES FROM READING

The first step in outlining notes from reading is to find the subject or topic for your notes. This may be a chapter title, a section heading, or a title that you make up yourself. The subject or topic is easy to find; but when you begin to fill out the outline with main headings and subheadings, it gets more difficult. Of course, if the author of the book you are studying has been generous with paragraph headings, your problem is greatly simplified. Often you can use these headings as your principal outline structure.

The technique you use in finding the main headings and subheadings is not so important. What is important is the preliminary survey, for you can't begin a good outline without some notion of the nature of the material.

OUTLINING NOTES FROM LISTENING

Outlining notes from listening is usually more difficult than outlining notes from reading. In listening, you must rely primarily on the organization used by the speaker or lecturer and on your alertness as a listener. A speaker may announce the organization of his remarks in advance or as he proceeds. This assistance will be helpful to you in organizing your notes.

A speaker may also provide cues that will help you in outlining your notes. He may cue you in with such a statement as, "There are five functions of distribution — transportation, packaging, processing, stor-

age, and advertising. First, let's take up transportation. . . ." Your subject or topic is, of course, DISTRIBUTION. Under this, you will note five main headings: Transportation, Packaging, Processing, Storage, and Advertising.

Be on the alert for cues that will help you in outlining your notes. These cues will also help you to think through carefully what you hear and to make notes that will be of better quality and therefore of greater usefulness to you for reference.

PUTTING THE PRINCIPLES INTO PRACTICE

Read a section from a textbook on history, government, or another subject of your choice. Make notes of this material in outline form.

PRACTICAL TIPS AND SUGGESTIONS FOR NOTEMAKING

Indicate Important Dates Distinctively. A frequent reason for referring to notes is the necessity for finding some date. It is easy for a date to get lost in surrounding masses of notes unless some special measures are taken to make it conspicuous.

The simplest method of doing this is to leave plenty of space before and after each date. When the date is written or when

it appears later that it is more than usually significant, it may be further emphasized by enclosing it within a rough rectangle.

In the example below the date of the discovery of America is of more historical importance than the date of the death of Columbus. Therefore, 1492 is surrounded by the rectangle, while 1506 has merely the emphasis of space on each side.

Key: Columbus discovered America in 1492 and did not die until 1506, but it is possible that he died without realizing that he had discovered a new continent.

MOST-USED GREGG NOTEHAND FORMS

By this time you have probably completely mastered many of the most-used
Gregg Notehand forms that you wrote on
your special card in the early part of your
study of Gregg Notehand. Perhaps some of
the more recent words added to the card
may not yet be thoroughly familiar. Read
through the forty Gregg Notehand forms
you now have on the card as rapidly as you
can. Put a circle around any forms on which
you had to hesitate ever so slightly. Then
transfer those words to a new card. Thus,
instead of the forty words, you will now
have fifteen or twenty that you need to keep
for constant reference as you make notes in
Gregg Notehand. Then add the ten new
words given below. You could already have
written any of these new Gregg Notehand

forms, but they are given here for special
practice and attention.

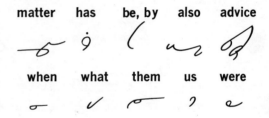

matter	has	be, by	also	advice
when	what	them	us	were

PUTTING GREGG NOTEHAND INTO PRACTICE

Read and make a copy of the outline
on page 146. Notice how the wide margins
and plenty of white space make the notes
easy to review.

The key to this outline is given on page
298.

Essentials ⌐ . Good Savings Program

I.). *⌐o plan*
 A. . ⌐e ⌐ ⌐ ⌐ ⌐ ⌐ ⌐
   ⌐, , ⌐.
 B. ⌐ . ⌐e ⌐ ⌐ ⌐⌐
   ⌐,) ⌐⌐

II. ⌐ ⌐ ⌐ , *safe*
 A. ⌐ ⌐ ⌐ ⌐ — . ⌐ ⌐
   ⌐.
 B. ⌐ ⌐ ⌐ ⌐:
   1. Savings ⌐
      a. ⌐ ⌐ ⌐ ⌐ ⌐.
   c. savings b. ⌐ ⌐ ⌐ ⌐ ⌐
   ⌐   ⌐ ⌐ ⌐ ⌐ ⌐.
   ⌐   2. ⌐ savings ⌐ ⌐ E

III. ⌐ ⌐ savings ⌐ ⌐ ⌐ *earn interest*
 A. — . ⌐. ⌐) convenience —
   ⌐. ⌐ ⌐ ⌐ ⌐ ⌐.
 B. ⌐ ⌐ ⌐ ⌐ ⌐:
   1. ⌐
   2. ⌐
      a. — ⌐ ⌐ ⌐ ⌐ ⌐.
      b. ⌐ , ⌐ ⌐ ⌐
        ⌐.

In this unit you will take up (1) the principle of abbreviation of long words and (2) two additional word endings.

105.   Abbreviation.   As you make notes in Notehand, you should always feel free to use any longhand abbreviations that are familiar to you. You may also abbreviate long words in Notehand simply writing enough so that your outline suggests the word to you; for example, *s-a-t-e-s* for *satisfactory*. However, before you abbreviate a word in Notehand, be sure that it occurs frequently in your work. A word that does not occur frequently is better written in full.

Here are some examples of the abbreviating principle:

Mr.	**anniversary**	**privilege**
Mrs.	**convenient, convenience**	**mathematics**
satisfy, satisfactory	**consequent, consequence**	**memorandum**
particular	**arithmetic**	**reluctant, reluctance**

READING AND WRITING PRACTICE

Table Conversation

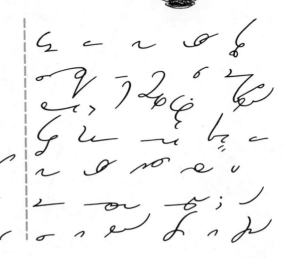

(shorthand outlines) × (Continued in Paragraph 106)

106. **Word Ending -ingly.** The word ending -ingly, as in accordingly, is represented by a disjoined e circle.

Spell: **accordingly,** a-k-o-ard-ingly

accordingly *(shorthand)* **knowingly** *(shorthand)* **seemingly** *(shorthand)*

increasingly *(shorthand)* **willingly** *(shorthand)* **convincingly** *(shorthand)*

READING AND WRITING PRACTICE

Table Conversation (Continued)

(shorthand outlines)

(Shorthand outlines)

(Concluded in Paragraph 107)

107. **Word Ending -ings.** The word ending -ings, as in *feelings*, is represented by a disjoined left *s*.

Spell: **feelings,** *f-e-l-ings*

feelings	*(outline)*	**earnings**	*(outline)*	**drawings**	*(outline)*
savings	*(outline)*	**awnings**	*(outline)*		

READING AND WRITING PRACTICE

Table Conversation (Concluded)

(Shorthand outlines)

—Robert Benchley

/// **149**

UNIT 38

In this unit you will learn the last of the signs of Notehand. At this point, you could, if you had to, construct an outline for any word in the English language. All that remains for you to learn in the remaining units is a number of timesaving abbreviating devices.

108. *Ĭa, Ēa.* The sound of *ĭa* or *ēa*, heard in *piano* and *create*, is represented by placing a dot within the *a* circle.

Compare: **crate** ⟿ **create** ⟿

Spell: **create,** *k-r-ĭa-t*

piano	appropriate	mania
area	initiate	recreation
appreciate	brilliant	created

READING AND WRITING PRACTICE

The Value of Reading

[shorthand outlines]

Fishbein

150 \\\

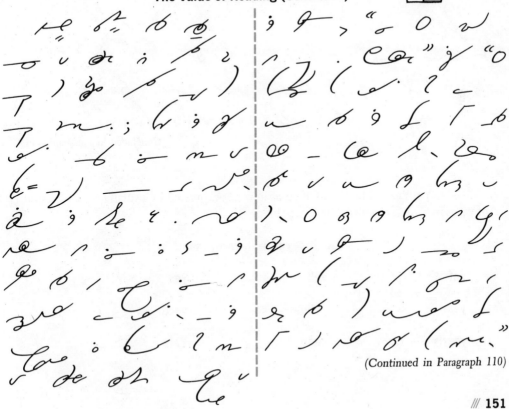

(Continued in Paragraph 109)

109. **Long I and a Following Vowel.** The sound of long ī followed by any other vowel, as in *diary, diet,* is expressed by a double circle.

Compare: **signs** ⟨shorthand⟩ **science** ⟨shorthand⟩

Spell: **science,** *s-ī-a-n-s*

diary ⟨shorthand⟩	**quiet** ⟨shorthand⟩	**diagnosis** ⟨shorthand⟩
diet ⟨shorthand⟩	**dial** ⟨shorthand⟩	**appliance** ⟨shorthand⟩
prior ⟨shorthand⟩	**trial** ⟨shorthand⟩	**reliance** ⟨shorthand⟩

READING AND WRITING PRACTICE

The Value of Reading (Continued)

(Continued in Paragraph 110)

110. **Aw, Ah.** When *aw* or *ah*, as in *away* and *ahead*, occur before a vowel, the initial a is expressed by a dot.

Spell: **away,** a-oo-a; **ahead,** a-h-e-d

away	∂	award	.ᴜ	await	.ɣ
awake	.ʒ	aware	.ɔ	ahead	.ϐ

READING AND WRITING PRACTICE

The Value of Reading (Continued)

(shorthand text)

(Concluded in Paragraph 111)

111. **Ye, Ya.** The sound of ye, as in yet, is expressed by a small loop; the sound of ya, as in yard, is expressed by a large loop.

Spell: **yet,** ye-t; **yard,** ya-ard

yet	/	yell	⌣	yes	9
year	⌣	yellow	⌣ᴜ	yard	⌣
yearly	⌣ᴗ	yield	⌣	Yale	⌣

The Value of Reading (Concluded)

[Shorthand content]

UNIT 39

In Unit 39 you will study a timesaving principle of vowel omission, another word beginning, and two word endings.

112.   **Omission of Vowel Preceding -tion.**   When *t, d, n,* or *m* is followed by *-ition, -ation,* the circle is omitted.

Spell: station, s-t-shun

station		transmission	foundation
quotation		permission	explanation
combination		termination	reputation
examination		hesitation	addition

READING AND WRITING PRACTICE

The Traits of Successful People

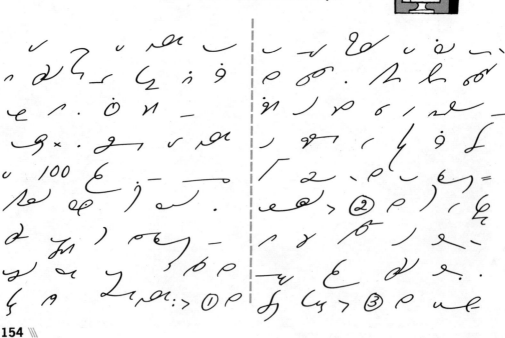

154

(shorthand notation)

113. Word Beginning Sub-.
The word beginning *sub-*, as in *submit*, is expressed by either form of the Notehand *s*.

Spell: **submit,** *sub-m-e-t*

submit	*(shorthand)*	substantial	*(shorthand)*	suburb	*(shorthand)*
subscribe	*(shorthand)*	subway	*(shorthand)*	sublease	*(shorthand)*
subject	*(shorthand)*	subdivide	*(shorthand)*	sublet	*(shorthand)*

READING AND WRITING PRACTICE

The Art of Saying "No"

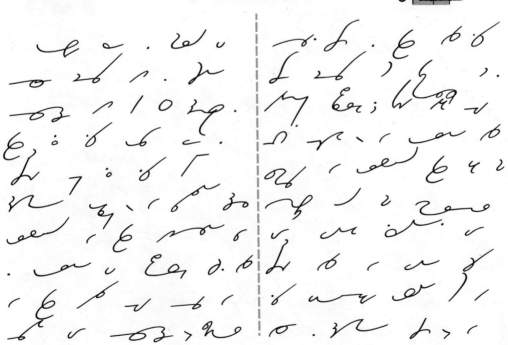

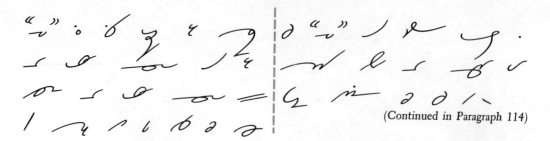

(Continued in Paragraph 114)

114. **Word Endings -cal, -cle.** The word endings -cal and -cle, as in *chemical* and *article*, are expressed by a disjoined *k*.

Spell: **chemical,** *k-e-m-ical;* **article,** *a-r-t-ical*

chemical		typical		bicycled	
surgical		medical		mechanically	
logical		clerical		articles	

READING AND WRITING PRACTICE

The Art of Saying "No" (Continued)

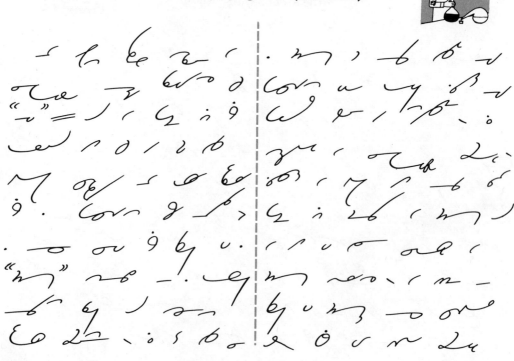

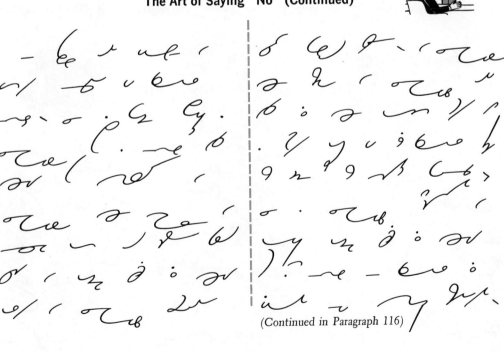

(shorthand outlines)

(Continued in Paragraph 115)

115.   Word Ending -ward. The word ending -ward, as in backward, is expressed by a disjoined d.

Spell: backward, b-a-k-ward

backward	*(outline)*	upward	*(outline)*	afterwards	*(outline)*
forward	*(outline)*	downward	*(outline)*	inwardly	*(outline)*
onward	*(outline)*	awkward	*(outline)*	rewarded	*(outline)*

READING AND WRITING PRACTICE

The Art of Saying "No" (Continued)

(shorthand outlines)

(Continued in Paragraph 116)

In this unit you will study two more word endings—the last—and two more principles of vowel omission.

116. **Word Endings -lity, -lty.** The word ending -lity, as in *locality*, is expressed by a disjoined *l*.

Spell: **locality,** *l-o-k-ality*

locality		reality		reliability	
utility		ability		personality	
mentality		possibility		quality	

The word ending -lty, as in *faculty*, is also expressed by a disjoined *l*.

Spell: **faculty,** *f-a-k-ulty*

faculty		loyalty		penalty	

READING AND WRITING PRACTICE

The Art of Saying "No" (Continued)

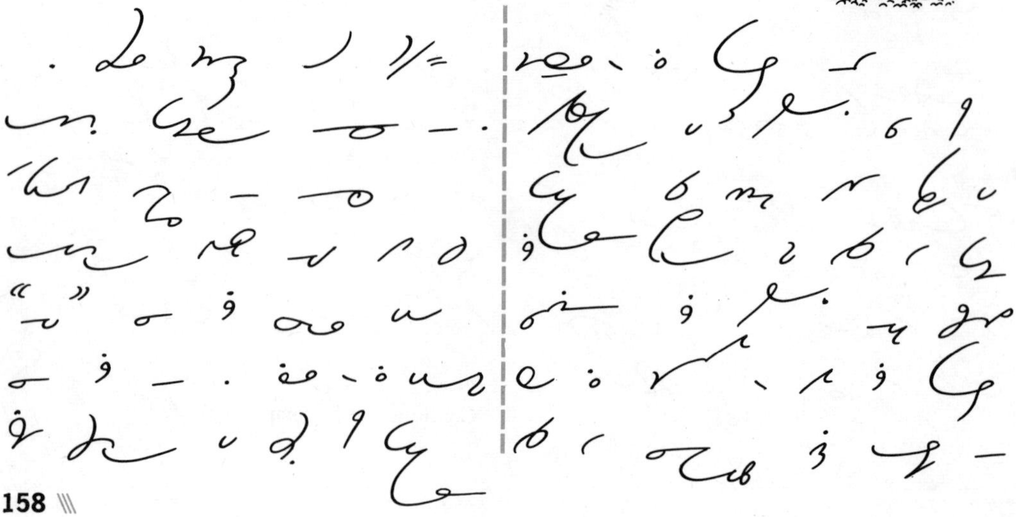

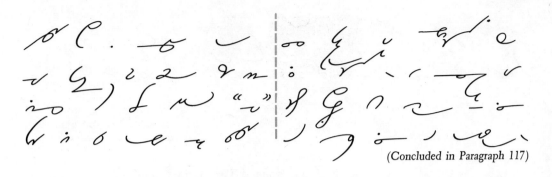

(Concluded in Paragraph 117)

117.   Word Ending -rity.   The word ending -rity, as in majority, is expressed by a disjoined r.

Spell: majority, m-a-j-rity

majority	**authority**	**charity**
sincerity	**prosperity**	**clarity**
regularity	**securities**	**minority**
integrity	**maturity**	**popularity**

READING AND WRITING PRACTICE

The Art of Saying "No" (Concluded)

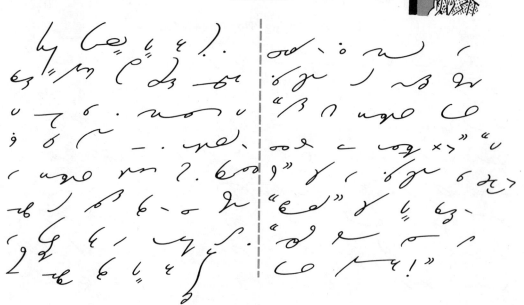

118. Omission of Vowel in -ious, -eous.

The endings *-ious* and *-eous*, as in *various* and *courteous*, are expressed by *oo-s*.

Spell: serious, *s-e-r-oo-s*

serious	*(outline)*	tedious	*(outline)*	envious	*(outline)*
curious	*(outline)*	obvious	*(outline)*	erroneous	*(outline)*
previous	*(outline)*	industrious	*(outline)*	courteously	*(outline)*

READING AND WRITING PRACTICE

Dominoes

119. **Omission of E in U.** The small e circle may often be omitted from the diphthong ū, as in new.

Spell: new, n-oo

new	⟋	reduce	⟍	issue	⟍
numerous	⟋	produce	⟍	avenue	⟍
tune	⟋	induce	⟍	duty	⟍
renew	⟍	music	⟍	suit	⟍

READING AND WRITING PRACTICE

Press the Button

[shorthand outlines]

UNIT 41

In this unit you will learn the last group of Notehand devices. You will learn to express the days of the week, the months of the year that are not written in full, and the helpful intersecting principle.

120. Months and Days

Months

January		May		September	
February		June		October	
March		July		November	
April		August		December	

Days

Sunday		Wednesday		Friday	
Monday		Thursday		Saturday	
Tuesday					

READING AND WRITING PRACTICE

Revenge

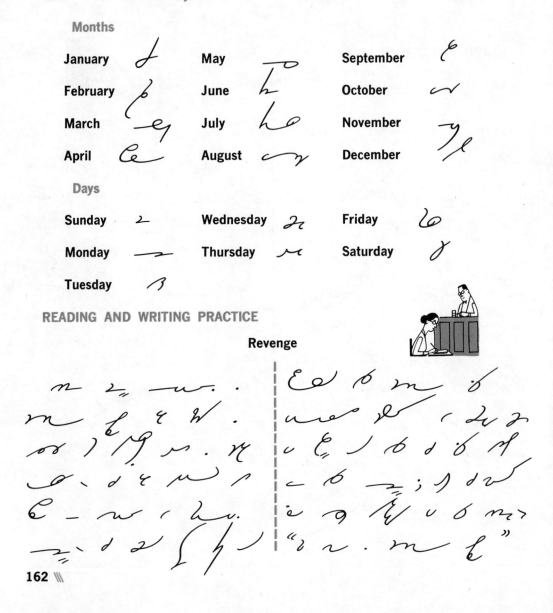

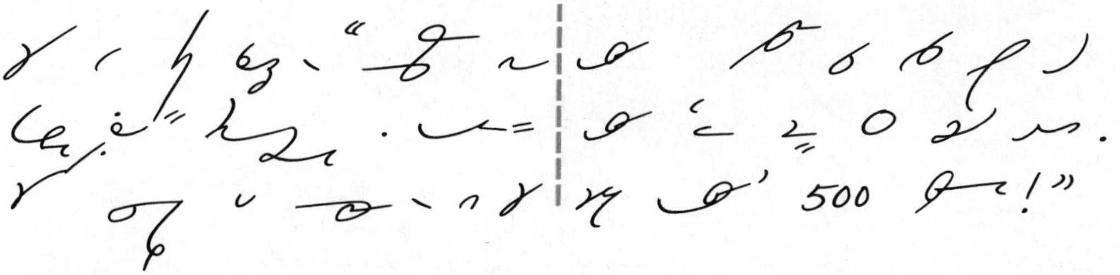

121. Compounds. It is often possible to join the two parts of a compound word. Sometimes, however, it is more convenient to write the two parts of the word separately but close together.

-body

everybody **anybody** **somebody**

-thing

everything **anything** **something**

-ever

however **whenever** **whatever**

-where

everywhere **anywhere** **somewhere**

With-

within **withstand** **without**

READING AND WRITING PRACTICE

He Liked Everybody

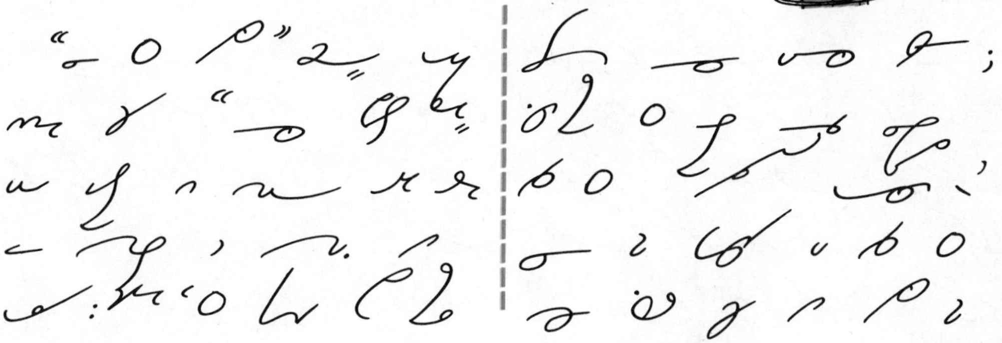

[Shorthand writing — top section]

122. Intersection.

Intersection, or the writing of one character through another, is sometimes useful for special phrases. Before you apply this principle, however, be sure that the expression to which you apply it occurs frequently in the writing you do.

a.m.	*[shorthand]*	**chamber of commerce**	*[shorthand]*
p.m.	*[shorthand]*	**school board**	*[shorthand]*
vice versa	*[shorthand]*	**Associated Press**	*[shorthand]*

READING AND WRITING PRACTICE

[Shorthand writing — practice section]

Through the chart and Reading and Writing Practice in this unit, you will review every character and abbreviating device (except brief forms) in Notehand.

123.   **Recall Chart.**   Can you read the 108 items in this chart in 7 minutes or less?

Words

1					
2					
3					
4					
5					
6					
7					
8					
9					
10					
11					
12					
13					
14					
15					
16					

17						
18						

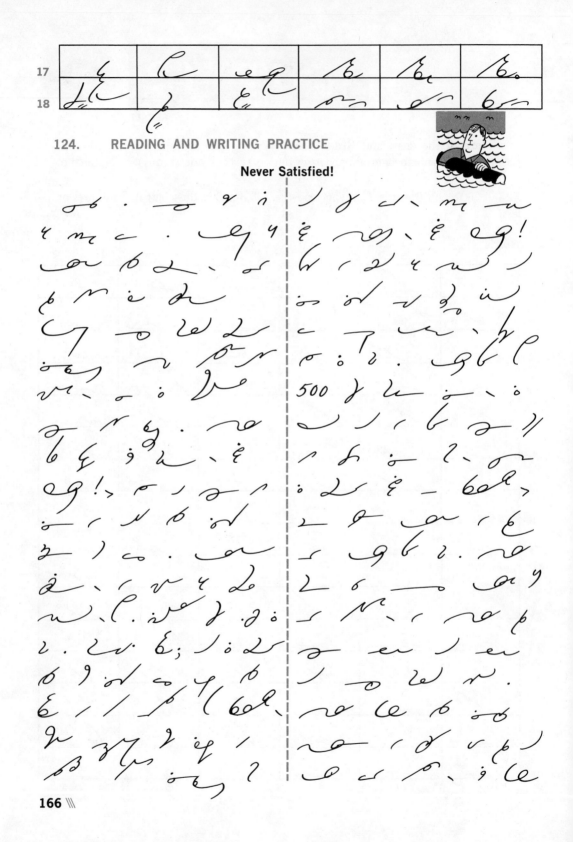

124.   READING AND WRITING PRACTICE

Never Satisfied!

PART TWO

Applications of Gregg Notehand and Notemaking — Extended Practice

What's Ahead

In Part I you studied the entire alphabet and all the word-building principles of Gregg Notehand. You now have at your disposal the tools with which to construct an outline for any word in the English language. If you practiced each unit in Part I faithfully, you no doubt have already developed considerable fluency in writing Gregg Notehand for notemaking.

OBJECTIVES

In Part II your objectives are as follows:

1. To review systematically the alphabet and the word-building principles of Gregg Notehand so that they will be firmly fixed in your mind.

2. To develop further your ability to construct without hestitation a readable Gregg Notehand outline for any word you see or hear, whether it is familiar or unfamiliar to you.

3. To learn additional ways in which to use your Gregg Notehand to best advantage in your personal notemaking.

The following types of exercises in Part II will help you achieve these objectives:

Word Drills. Each unit in Part II contains a word drill that has a specific review objective.

Of special value to you will be the word-family lists that enable you to take advantage of the principle of analogy in developing your Gregg Notehand vocabulary.

Many of the words in these drills occur in the Reading and Writing Practice exercises of the unit.

You are to practice these word drills in the same way that you practiced the word lists in Part I; that is,

1. Cover up the type key while you read the words.

2. Spell any word that you cannot read immediately.

3. Refer to the key if the spelling does not give you the meaning immediately.

4. Make a Gregg Notehand copy in your notebook of the entire list. Make a second copy of the list if time permits.

Reading and Writing Practice. You will enjoy your work with the articles and letters in Gregg Notehand in each unit. These articles and letters were chosen not only for the contribution they will make in developing your Gregg Notehand vocabulary, but for their informational, inspirational, and entertainment value as well.

Follow the same procedure with each Reading and Writing Practice that you followed in Part I; that is,

1. Read from the Gregg Notehand article or letter until you come to a word that you cannot read.

2. Spell the word; if the spelling does not give you the meaning immediately, refer to the key. (Remember, detailed suggestions on how to use the key are given in Paragraph 16.)

3. Make a Gregg Notehand copy of the Reading and Writing Practice. If time permits, make a second copy.

Notemaking. In Part II you will find four additional units containing helpful suggestions designed to make you a more efficient notemaker.

UNIT 43

How to Use Gregg Notehand in Original Writing

Hardly a day goes by that you as a student are not called upon to do some original writing; for example, summarizing a chapter from a history book, writing a theme or an essay for an English class, describing an experiment for a chemistry class, or preparing a research paper. Original writing plays an important part in your formal education; in fact, the success you ultimately achieve scholastically depends in large measure on the quality of your original writing.

Your ability in original writing may also play a significant part in your success in later life. It may, for example, help you get that first job through a well-written letter of application and personal data sheet.

Should you enter the field of business, you will have letters, memorandums, reports, and talks to prepare. If your choice lies in the professions, you will have articles for professional journals and papers, even books, to write. Your ability to prepare written material will stand you in good stead even though you do not enter the field of business or professions. The modern housewife finds time for the Cub Scouts or the PTA or the Red Cross or the community chest; and all these activities require some writing in the form of social letters, announcements of meetings, committee reports, and even the preparation of informal talks.

In short, ability in original writing is a valuable asset for just about everyone.

GREGG NOTEHAND IS AN AID TO ORIGINAL WRITING

Three forms in which you can do original writing are (1) in longhand, (2) on the typewriter, (3) in Gregg Notehand.

In Longhand. Longhand is least efficient because of the time required to write down your thoughts. Longhand is slow and cumbersome. Each time you make a false start or change a word or a phrase all the time and effort expended in the original writing is wasted. In addition, you may lose your train of thought simply because your longhand writing cannot keep up with your thinking.

On the Typewriter. Typewriting is more efficient than longhand, assuming that you have a fair degree of typing skill. Much time can be lost, however, when you make additions or corrections or deletions in the process of x-ing out and moving the carriage back and forth. Then, too, a typewriter may not be available to you when you wish to compose — while you are working in the library, for example.

In Gregg Notehand. Gregg Notehand is a very efficient medium for original writing. Why?

1. You can record your thoughts rapidly as they come to you.

2. You are not likely to lose an idea or interrupt your train of thought because your thinking outruns your writing speed.

The condition of the State was thus - viz. The Rump after being disturbed, by my Lord Lambert, was lately returned to sit again. The Officers of the Army, all forced to yield — Lawson, lies still in the River, & Monk is with his Army in Scotland.

An extract from the diary of Samuel Pepys written about 1700.

Sir G. Kneller, Pinxt.   J. W. Steel, Sculpt.

3. When you make changes or corrections and must scratch out, you waste only a fraction of the time it would take if you had written in longhand or on the typewriter. Insertions and additions can often be made in Gregg Notehand with a stroke or two of the pen.

4. Since corrections and additions are so easy to make with Gregg Notehand, you are likely to revise and correct more freely than you would in longhand or on the typewriter. As a result, you will produce a better composition.

5. With Gregg Notehand you can write anywhere — on the street car, bus, plane, in the study hall, in the library — places where it would be either impossible or impracticable to use a typewriter.

Many famous people have used some form of shorthand for original writing. Among them were Samuel Pepys, who wrote his diary in shorthand; Woodrow Wilson,

who drafted all his state papers in shorthand; and George Bernard Shaw, who wrote his plays in shorthand for his secretary to transcribe.

The briefest study of the following rough draft of a paragraph of a paper on "Differences of Opinion" written in longhand, on the typewriter, and in Gregg Notehand will convince you of the timesaving advantages of using Gregg Notehand for original writing.

Differences of Opinion

~~When you find yourself in dis-agreement~~ What usually ~~transpires~~ happens when you ~~do not agree~~ _disagree_ with another's opinion? ~~Does it~~ Do you ~~invariably~~ _always_ find it easy to ~~reconcile~~ settle your differences? Or ~~do you~~ does a ~~difference of opinion~~ _disagreement_ frequently lead to harsh words or strained feelings? _One of_ ^ The most important ~~principles~~ _things_ to remember is that ~~you~~ ~~cant always be right~~ your opinion cannot always prevail.

TYPEWRITTEN COMPOSITION

Differences of Opinion

~~When you find yourself in disagreement~~ What usually
disagree
~~transpires~~ happens when you ~~do not agree~~ with another's
always
opinion? ~~Does it~~ Do you ~~invariably~~ find it easy to

~~reconcile~~ settle your differences? Or ~~do you~~ does a
disagreement
~~differences of opinion~~ frequently lead to harsh words
One of   things
or strained feelings? The most important ~~principles~~

to remember is that ~~you cant always be right~~ your

opinion cannot always prevail.

[Gregg shorthand notes — "Differences of Opinion"]

ROUGH DRAFTS

An experienced writer would tell you not to attempt to make the final copy of an important paper on the *first* writing. It is the rare person indeed who can write a finished paper on his first effort. Most people — even the most talented writers — make many false starts. They scratch out. They insert. They transpose. They change a word here and there. Occasionally they tear up everything and start all over again. Their completed first draft often contains more corrections than it does original writing!

"Good writing comes about only through rewriting" is an axiom that applies to most writers, and it should guide you in your own work. You can improve your own writing only after you have put something down on paper.

PROCEDURES AND SUGGESTIONS FOR PREPARING ROUGH DRAFTS

Organize Your Materials. Before you begin your rough draft, organize your materials so that, once you sit down to write, you can complete the task without interruption. Assemble all the supplies* and reference books you will need within easy reach so that you will not have to leave your desk or table. By freeing yourself from all possible distractions, you will be able to concentrate uninterruptedly on recording your thoughts and you can complete your writing with the greatest economy of time.

Concentrate on Recording Your Thoughts. As you write your rough draft, concentrate

*A convenient place in which to do your rough drafting is the stenographic notebook that you use for your Gregg Notehand practice. However, almost any type of paper is satisfactory for the purpose.

on getting your *ideas* down on paper. In this creative stage don't worry about spelling, punctuation, grammar, etc. Your final paper must, of course, be correct in every grammatical detail; but the time to attend to grammar is when you reread your completed rough draft — after you have organized and recorded your ideas and thoughts.

Start Writing. Perhaps the hardest job for any writer is to get that first sentence down on paper. Get "a" first sentence down even though you are quite sure it will not be "the" first sentence you will ultimately use. Somehow, writing becomes easier and more fluent when that first sentence is on paper. As you continue writing, a more suitable first sentence may suggest itself to you.

Use Gregg Notehand. Write in Gregg Notehand all the words for which the outline comes to you readily. Write in longhand any words for which the Gregg Notehand outline does not immediately come to your mind. Do not take time to devise outlines for such words. As you progress with your study of Gregg Notehand and your skill develops, you will find yourself writing more and more Gregg Notehand and less and less longhand.

Make a special effort to write the commonest words in Gregg Notehand, especially those that you have recorded on your card.

Make Changes Freely. Do not hesitate to cross out and rewrite and make corrections and insertions; you can do it easily and quickly in Gregg Notehand.

If you discover that you are making a great many changes and additions in your notes, it is a good idea to write only on every second line in your notebook. And leave very generous right and left margins for changes and insertions.

Reread and Edit. After you have completed your rough draft, reread it before you begin to make your final copy. While you are rereading, you may want to revise that first sentence that you put down just to "get started." While you are rereading you should also take care of the following:

1. Insert all punctuation. Be sure each sentence ends with a period, each question with a question mark. Put in necessary commas.

2. Check the grammar. Does each sentence have a subject and a predicate? Does each noun agree with its verb? Do any participles dangle?

3. Indicate paragraphs.

4. Look up the spelling of words about which you are in doubt and write them in longhand—in the proper place in your draft. Don't take a chance on misspelling a word.

5. Make any other refinements in wording or construction that occur to you.

If you follow these steps in making your rough draft, your hardest work is done; all that remains is the preparation of your final copy.

The businessman often prepares a report while riding on the train.

Ewing Galloway

Gregg Notehand can be of great value to you not only in preparing papers, themes, and reports, but in many other writing situations.

In Taking Examinations. Many examinations consist of questions that require an essay-type answer of several paragraphs or even pages. If you read the question and immediately start writing down your thoughts, the result is usually a disorganized answer that doesn't do justice to your ability to answer the question. A thought may occur to you while you are writing the second paragraph that should be included in the first. When you reread your answer, you find many opportunities for improvement, some of which you can make; but others you cannot because they would mean rewriting the whole answer — and there just isn't time for that. As a result, you must turn in an answer that doesn't represent your best work.

The wise student will not start writing his final answer immediately but will take a little time to plan his answer in the form of a rough draft on a piece of scratch paper. This very act of drafting will suggest facts and information that will help him prepare a well-organized final answer, which he knows represents his best efforts.

But you may ask, "Won't this draft take up too much time so that I won't be able to complete the examination?" Not if you do your drafting in Gregg Notehand. With Gregg Notehand you can jot down your thoughts quickly, arrange them in logical order, and proceed with the writing of the final answer — which will be rapid and easy because you have already done your thinking while preparing your draft.

In Filling Out Forms. Perhaps you have already had some experience in filling out ap-

A. Devaney

After you have edited and polished your rough draft, you are ready to type your paper.

plication forms of various kinds — applications for jobs, for admission to college, for membership in a club. If you haven't, you soon will.

Many of the questions on these forms are routine and simple; for example, your name, your address, your age, etc. Some, however, call for an essay-type answer such as "Describe your duties on your last job," "Why did you choose Midwestern University?" Usually only a few lines are provided on the form for the answer.

Again, the average person will start writing the answers immediately on the final form only to find that he must make changes and insertions or that he has run out of space—with the result that the filled-out form does not present a pleasing picture to the person who must read it and perhaps act on it.

Doesn't it make good sense, therefore, to draft answers to such questions on a piece of scratch paper before you fill out your application form? It's easy and quick with Gregg Notehand.

PUTTING THE PRINCIPLES
INTO PRACTICE

Prepare a rough draft for a report of about 150 words on a topic that interests you or one that has been assigned in another class. Use as much Gregg Notehand as you can, but write in longhand any word for which the Gregg Notehand outline does not come to you immediately. Insert all punctuation and indicate the paragraphs. Be sure to check the spelling of any word about which you are in doubt.

PRACTICAL TIPS AND SUGGESTIONS
FOR NOTEMAKING

USE LONGHAND ABBREVIATIONS

In the English language there are many combinations that, because of their frequency of use, have acquired generally accepted longhand abbreviations. No doubt you are familiar with many such abbreviations. Because these longhand abbreviations are distinctive and can be written rapidly, you will find it best to use them in any notes you make rather than writing them in Gregg Notehand.

Here are three types of such longhand abbreviations.

Political

GOP   Grand Old Party (Republican)
NATO   North Atlantic Treaty Organization
TVA   Tennessee Valley Authority
DAR   Daughters of the American Revolution
UN   United Nations
VIP   very important person

In writing these longhand abbreviations when making notes, you will save even more time if you use the small, joined letters instead of capitals, thus:

Business

C.O.D.   cash on delivery
f.o.b.   free on board
c.i.f.   cost, insurance, and freight
CPA   Certified Public Accountant

Literary

c. or ca.   about (circa)
ibid.   in the same place (ibidem)
id.   same (idem)
i.e.   that is (id est)
loc. cit.   the place cited (loco citato)
n.b.   note well (nota bene)
n.d.   no date
q.v.   which see (quod vide)
t.p.   title page
viz.   namely (videlicet)

A combination of these literary abbreviations that you might find is:

This indicates that the book was copyrighted in 1887. There was no date on the title page to indicate when the book was printed or published, but it was probably about 1890.

Add the following ten to your card:

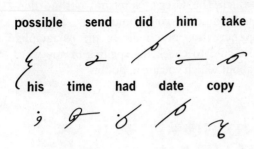

possible   send   did   him   take

his   time   had   date   copy

Read the rough draft on page 179. As you do so, notice how the principles of rough drafting presented in this unit are applied.

The key to this rough draft appears on page 302.

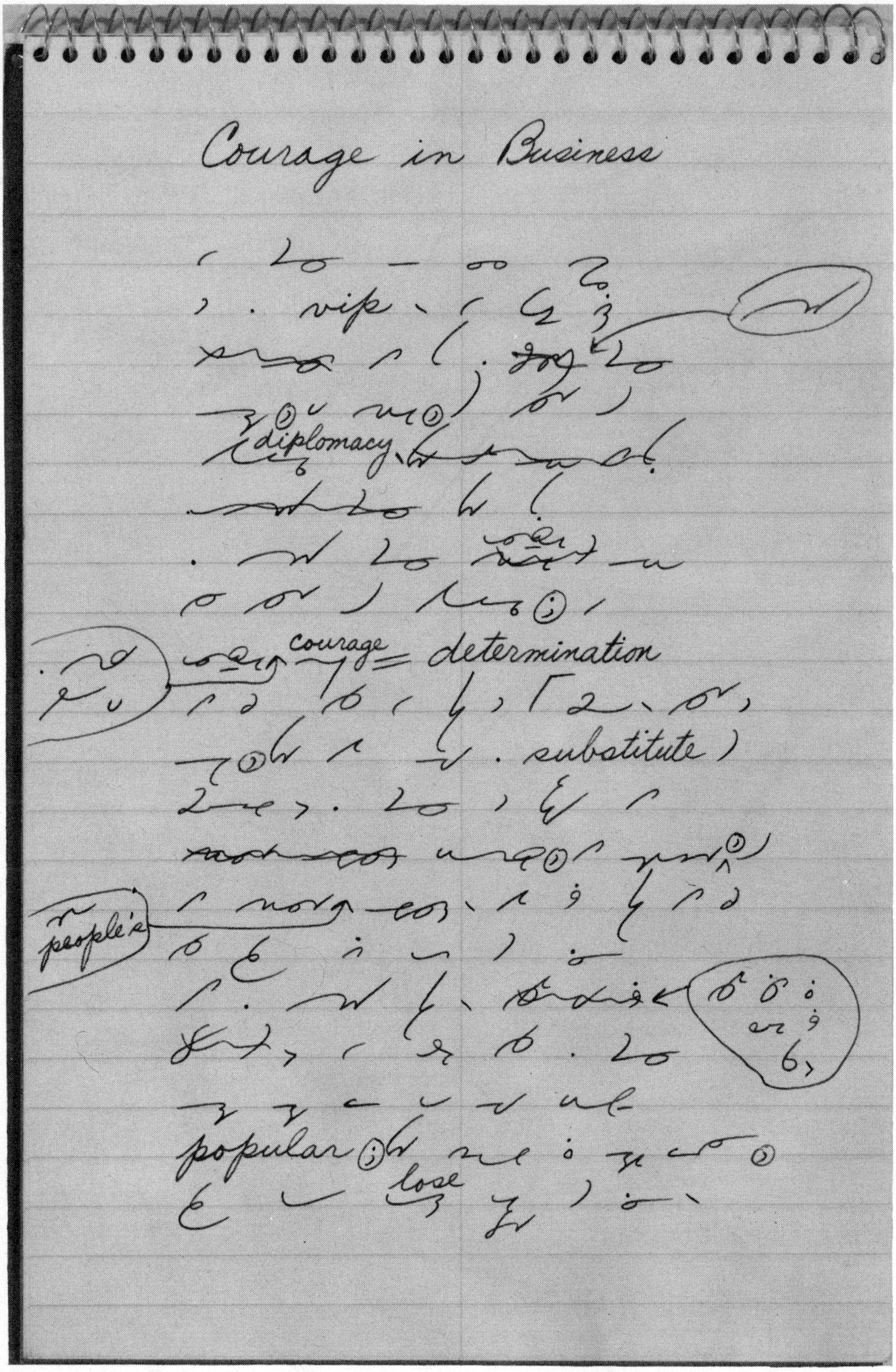

Courage in Business

(shorthand outline)

diplomacy

courage = determination

substitute)

people's

popular

lose

125.   Word Beginnings.   Can you read the 31 words in this drill in 20 seconds? make a Notehand copy of them in 1 minute?

Sub-

1 *[shorthand outlines]*

Re-

2 *[shorthand outlines]*

Con-

3 *[shorthand outlines]*

Dis-, Des-

4 *[shorthand outlines]*

De-

5 *[shorthand outlines]*

KEY

1. Substantial, substantially, submit, submission, subscribe, subtitle.
2. Replace, replacement, reported, resulted, reply.
3. Conceal, concern, consideration, contained, consist, conceivably, confer.
4. Discover, display, dispute, destination, describe, desolated.
5. Delightful, delay, departure, depend, desirable, depression, define.

126.   READING AND WRITING PRACTICE

If you received Letter No. 1 in this unit, would you write as pleasant and amusing an answer as Letter No. 2?

X 1.   *[shorthand outlines]*

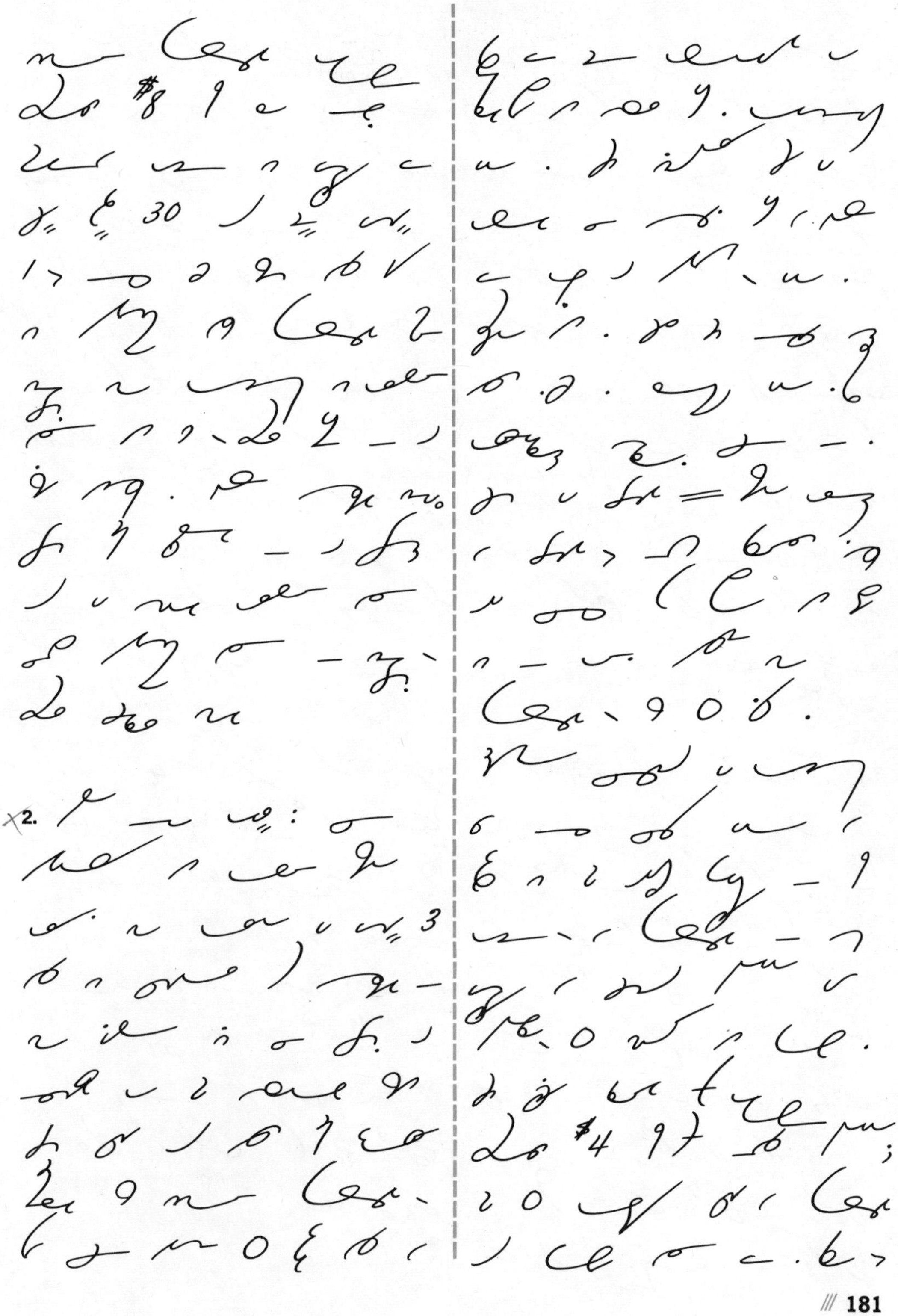

3.

$25,000

UNIT · 45

127. **Word Families.** There are 30 words in this drill. Because the endings in each family are alike, you should be able to read the entire list in 20 seconds and make a Notehand copy in 1 minute.

-ct

1 *[shorthand outlines]*

-ound

2 *[shorthand outlines]*

-or

3 *[shorthand outlines]*

-en

4 *[shorthand outlines]*

KEY
1. Act, fact, tact, exact, contact, contract, attract.
2. Found, sound, pound, ground, round, around, bound.
3. More, store, floor, door, nor, core, tore.
4. Often, even, oven, woven, driven, given, frozen, forgiven, uneven.

128. **READING AND WRITING PRACTICE**

Your Vocabulary

A large vocabulary is a great asset in both business and social life. You, too, can develop a large vocabulary if you will follow the five steps suggested in this article.

[shorthand outlines] 1. Read. *[shorthand outlines]*

/// **183**

3. Say the word.

4. Use the word.

5. Keep in touch

129. Blends. Goal: reading, 15 seconds; copying, 45 seconds.

Men, Min

1

Ted

2

Tain

3

Nd

4

Ses

5

KEY

1. Men, many, examine, minute, minimum.
2. Started, investigated, instructed, waited, treated, steady.
3. Certain, maintain, contain, retain, attain, detain, pertain, obtaining.
4. Returned, brand, beyond, around, found, kind, chandelier.
5. Success, expenses, dresses, causes, releases, pleases, passes, fences, uses.

130. READING AND WRITING PRACTICE

Mixer

You'll chuckle at the experiences of a young housewife in her efforts to get a mixer repaired.

It seems that

So she called

$15

① ②

③

#3 ; ④

#3

#15

The store

#3

We understand that

"..."

UNIT 47

131. **Vowels.** Goal: reading, 15 seconds; copying, 45 seconds.

Ow

1 *(shorthand outlines)*

Ū

2 *(shorthand outlines)*

Ĭa, Ēa

3 *(shorthand outlines)*

Oi

4 *(shorthand outlines)*

Ī

5 *(shorthand outlines)*

KEY

1. Round, down, town, cloud, outrun, proud, house.
2. Argue, tribute, few, human, unit, united, reviewed, refused.
3. Immediate, piano, enthusiasm, ideas, areas, appreciate, negotiate.
4. Voice, point, noisy, boil, toil, soil, annoy, annoyance.
5. Inclined, retire, find, wind, likely, appetite, timely.

132. **READING AND WRITING PRACTICE**

Miracle

In the following article, do you recognize yourself when you were a child?

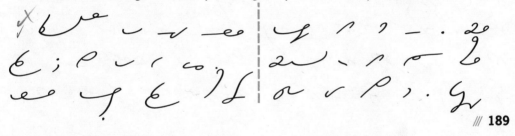

/// **189**

He may,

Only a teacher

It is amazing

Weariness

8:30

UNIT 48

✓ **133.** **Word Families.** Goal: reading, 10 seconds; copying, 30 seconds.

-lize

1 *(shorthand outlines)*

-er

2 *(shorthand outlines)*

-ory

3 *(shorthand outlines)*

-cated

4 *(shorthand outlines)*

-est

5 *(shorthand outlines)*

KEY

1. Capitalize, realize, analyze, centralize, generalize.
2. Ladder, batter, reader, matter, greater, leader.
3. History, factory, victory, memory, territory, inventory, advisory.
4. Located, educated, complicated, confiscated, dedicated.
5. Nearest, greatest, loudest, hardest, kindest, longest.

✓ **134.** **READING AND WRITING PRACTICE**

The Little Things

(shorthand outlines)

.250

$7,000.

.350

$30,000

10

7

10

Yesterday and Tomorrow

(shorthand)

An Educated Man

(shorthand)

— Henry Ford

UNIT 49

135. Word Families

-ther

1 *[shorthand outlines]*

-age

2 *[shorthand outlines]*

Al-

3 *[shorthand outlines]*

Out-

4 *[shorthand outlines]*

-self

5 *[shorthand outlines]*

KEY

1. Whether, other, brother, mother, another, together, either.
2. Cottage, baggage, luggage, storage, marriage, village, message.
3. All, almost, also, already, although, always.
4. Out, output, outside, outlay, outlast, outlet, outline.
5. Self, himself, yourself, myself, herself, itself.

136. READING AND WRITING PRACTICE

A Dissertation Upon Roast Pig

[shorthand outlines] 70,000 *[shorthand outlines]*

Ho-ti *[shorthand outlines]*

Some of the

The son raked out

196 \\\

x At length

x The judge,

— Charles Lamb

How to Make Notes for Research Papers

Many people — especially students and those in the professions — often need to make notes from reading for such purposes as writing an article, a report, a speech, a term paper, or any project that calls for research. Although the final product of each of these projects may vary in purpose and form, the procedures for each are quite similar. For our purposes, therefore, we shall consider the research paper.

THE RESEARCH PAPER

The research paper is sometimes called a term paper. Generally, however, a term paper is not so extensive as a research paper. A single reference may provide sufficient source material for a term paper although several sources are often required. The term paper ordinarily presents no recommendations or conclusions, but a summary statement at the end is usually desirable.

The research paper, on the other hand, is often much longer and more scholarly than a so-called term paper in that it requires the student to investigate some perplexing problem or controversial question. A topic for a research paper might be "The Defeat of Alfred E. Smith — Religion or Tammany?" For such a controversial topic, the researcher must read widely, seeking various points of view. A single source or two would not provide the depth he needs for a comprehensive treatment. For a research paper, the student must weigh the evidence collected and present conclusions and, in some cases, recommendations. These conclusions must, of course, be supported by the content of the paper.

CHOOSING A SUBJECT

The first step in getting ready to prepare a research paper is the selection of a subject. Avoid the pitfall of choosing a subject that is too broad. For example, unless you're writing a book you will stay away from such a broad subject as "Ulysses S.

Writing a research paper requires many sources. Whether you need as many as are shown here, it's better to have too many than too few references.

H. Armstrong Roberts

Grant" or "City Government." It is much wiser to limit your topic so that it is manageable. For example, instead of the two broad subjects just mentioned, you might select such manageable topics as "Ulysses S. Grant as President" and "An Appraisal of the Mayor-Council Plan of City Government."

You will do a better paper if you choose a subject in which you are personally interested. If, at the same time, it is one that will help you along toward your career goals, so much the better.

LOCATING YOUR SOURCES

In gathering material for a short paper you may have to consult only two or three sources. For more scholarly papers, however, you will probably have to consult many sources.

Most experts agree that the first step in locating your sources is to consult a good encyclopedia. There you will probably find an authoritative, albeit condensed, discussion of your topic or some important phase of it. At the end of the discussion may be a list of books that deal with the subject in detail. This list is a good starting point in locating sources. Write down the names of the authors and titles of these books, and then see whether these books are available in the library. The best way to find out is to use the card catalogue. Consulting the card catalogue will also help you locate additional sources to investigate. Make up a bibliography card for each of the books that you wish to consult. This bibliography card should contain all the following information:

1. The author's name (last name first)
2. The title (and edition if there is more than one)
3. The location and name of the publisher
4. The date of publication (latest copyright date)
5. The call number

For example:

Satin, Joseph

Ideas — Context. Boston:

Houghton Mifflin Company, 1958

808.88

Bibliography card for a book

Some of the books you come across will probably suggest other sources to you. Before long you'll doubtless find your problem to be one of selecting the most promising sources for your purpose. If you have no luck, however, ask the librarian to help you.

Don't overlook magazines and newspapers in your search. The best place to look for lists of magazine articles, according to subject, is the *Reader's Guide to Periodical Literature*; for newspaper articles, the *New York Times Index*. A bibliography card for each article should also be prepared. Here is one for a magazine article.

After you have collected the books and other materials you wish to consult for your paper, you are ready to begin to think seriously about your reading. Some researchers think it is a good idea, before reading a single book or article, to jot down on a piece of scratch paper any questions about the subject that you expect to have answered in your reading. For example, if you are writing a paper on "Ulysses S. Grant as President," you might ask such questions as: Why was he chosen to run for office? How

Perron, Alex J.

"Bacon's Interpretation o Nature," Classics Monthly

44:316-330 ⟨—⟩ 1933⟩

Bibliography card for a magazine

The number 44 at the bottom of the card indicates the volume number of the magazine; 316-330, the page numbers where the article may be found. For newspaper articles, you need the title of the article, the title and location of the newspaper, and the month, day, and year of publication.

Be sure to make up a bibliography card for every book or article that you use. These cards will come in handy later.

close was the race? What qualifications did he have? How did he fare during his first term? Second term? What was he like as a person? Whether you do this is up to you, but you should at least give a good deal of thought to your subject before you begin to dig into the materials you have gathered.

The next step in getting ready to make notes is to prepare a broad outline. Look at the table of contents of some of the books and perhaps read a chapter or two in a couple of them. This quick examination should give you a framework around which to build a tentative outline. You will need some directional signals, for you can't do a very intelligent job if you just start making notes without a purpose. You need a broad, general outline to start with. It might look something like this:

Grant 9 President
General Introduction
Civil War
Postwar Yrs
Nomination ✓ Election
First ℯ
Cabinet
Domestic Policy
Foreign Affairs
Associates
Second ℯ
Scandals
"Whiskey Ring"
Indian Service Graft
Panic ✓ 1873
Grant ∩ Man
Soldier
Father

MAKING NOTES

With your broad general outline before you, you are ready to make notes. Making notes is perhaps the most important activity in the research process. The ease with which you can organize your material and write the paper will depend largely on how well you have made notes from your reading.

Make More Notes Than You Need. Don't skimp on quantity; make more notes than you will probably use. A good news reporter, in conducting an interview with a famous person or in preparing a report on local crime, gathers three or four times as much material as he can actually use in his final article. It is through the process of sifting this mass of material that he arrives at his best story.

The same is true of making notes for use in a research paper. The more notes you make the more material you will have on which to draw as you write your paper. You can discover what is really important only when you have made a great many notes and begin to "shake them down" to write your paper. By gathering a great deal of material from several sources you also get many points of view, which help give balance to the finished paper.

Use Cards for Making Research Notes. You won't know until you are all through, how much of your notes you can actually use. You must, therefore, make these notes in such a way that (1) you can easily add new material and throw out useless material, and (2) you can reorganize in different ways the material you have collected. For these purposes cards are better than ordinary sheets of paper. Cards are sturdy and can be sorted and re-sorted without damage. And they are handy: you can spread a lot of them out in front of you as you work.

There are three common sizes of cards for this type of notemaking: 3 x 5 inches,

4 x 6 inches, and 6 x 9 inches. No one size is absolutely best, but of course you should use the same size throughout your project. The cards should be small enough to be convenient but large enough to enable you to write a fair amount on each card. You can buy cards in a variety of sizes at nearly all stationery, school book, and other local stores. Most people prefer cards that are not ruled.

Identify Your Sources. As you make notes from reading, be careful to identify accurately the source of your material. Of course, your bibliography cards contain complete information about your sources. But you should also indicate the sources on your note cards. These do not have to be so complete as the bibliography cards, but there should be no question in your mind about the source. For example, your note card on Satin, Joseph, *Ideas in Context* (see bibliography card illustrated on page 199) might be merely: Satin, *Ideas*, p. 46.

Write Summary Statements. For most notemaking for research papers, your notes will appear in the form of summary statements. Since there is little continuity when you read several different authors with several different approaches to a subject, you will find it almost impossible to outline as you make notes. Study carefully the examples of note cards shown below and on page 203.

Note in the illustrations that each card carries a brief identification of the source, including the page number. If more than one card is used from one source, number the cards and group them together.

Here are two important rules for making notes on cards:

1. Write on one side of the card only.
2. Limit each card to one subject.

When you rearrange your cards later, you will be glad you followed these rules.

Did you notice in the illustrations of note cards the liberal use of Gregg Note-

(Key appears on page 307.)

Grant = second term

... "Whiskey Ring") ... (persecuted) ... investigators ... investigations ... corruption ... admin ... propaganda.

Faulkner, Am Pol + Soc Hist p 421

(Key appears on page 307.)

hand? Gregg Notehand not only enables you to write the material down more rapidly than you could in longhand, but it also makes it possible for you to get more material on a card.

Use a Slug Line. Notice in the last two illustrations, the "slug" lines or catch lines: GRANT—FIRST TERM and GRANT—SECOND TERM. These slug lines are picked up from the general outline that you made before you began to make notes. You can see now the value of making a tentative outline of your main topics—its major headings are your directional signals for notemaking to keep you on the right road. Later on, you will find these slug lines a help in putting related topics together. Some notemakers prefer to put the slug in a different color of ink, or at least in all capital letters.

Be Accurate in Quotations. When you take a statement verbatim from a book, be sure to enclose the statement in quotation marks. You would not want to take credit for someone else's writing (that's plagiarism); and unless you use quotation marks, you may forget that it isn't your statement. Another

caution: quote the author correctly; don't saddle him with something he didn't say! Always give the page number from which the quotation was taken.

Make Notes of Your Own Impressions. A third type of notes for research papers are notes to yourself. As you read and analyze the source from which you are gathering your material, make notes to yourself of your own interpretations of those data — your ideas, observations, impressions, and conclusions. Your finished paper will, after all, consist mainly of the impressions you have gained from your reading. Getting these impressions down while they are fresh in your mind will save you much time later. Prepare these cards in the usual manner, but flag them in some way so that you know the source. A large asterisk (*) in the upper left corner will do. Or just the word "Me" with a circle around it is sufficient identification. Keep these cards with the material to which they relate, numbering them in the same sequence. Note the following illustration.

Grant = the man

extrovert.

entertain

{30=

dynamically.

Me

(Key appears on page 307.)

MAKING AN OUTLINE OF YOUR PAPER

The final step before beginning to write your paper is the preparation of a complete outline from your notes. When you have assembled all your notes (and you should have a good-sized stack of cards), read them all carefully. Undoubtedly, you will find a few cards that contain information that is irrelevant or unimportant. Remove these from the cards you expect to use. Then arrange the remaining cards roughly in the order you are going to follow in writing the paper. Decide where each point can be most effectively presented. Don't be afraid to change your mind. The advantage of having notes on cards is that you can shuffle them as you wish until you find the organization that suits you best. If you have limited each card to one subject, you will not have the problem of overlapping.

When your cards are arranged correctly, the outline almost writes itself. By the way, don't try to get by without making a final outline. A good outline is like a candle in the dark — it will guide you on your way surely and safely.

WRITING THE PAPER

As suggested in Unit 43, no one expects to write a finished paper or an article on the first try. You should, therefore, prepare a rough draft, using a combination of Gregg Notehand and longhand (by this time, you'll probably write most of the material in Gregg Notehand). From this rough draft you can make a typewritten copy. You may find that even this is not exactly what you want as final copy. If so, edit and polish it carefully, and make another typewritten copy.

When you are finished, lay the paper aside for a few days (assuming you have given yourself a little time before the paper is due!) to allow your report to "age." Then read it again. You'll probably be glad you did—for it is only when you put your paper completely out of mind that you can approach it with a clear and fresh perspective.

You'll be surprised to find even at this late stage that your paper contains errors in punctuation, grammar, sentence structure, and perhaps even organization. Thus, a delayed final trip through the manuscript will often pay big dividends.

FORM OF THE PAPER

The final form of your paper will vary with the preferences of your instructor. Before you reach this stage you should, of course, have found out exactly the required form. Most instructors provide some kind of style sheet for guidance in preparing research papers. Some general suggestions can be given, however.

1. The typewritten paper should be double-spaced, with a minimum of one-inch margins all around. The only thing single-spaced in the body of the paper are verbatim quotations.

2. Provide a bibliography at the end; that is, a list of all the reference sources you have used. Include books, magazines, newspapers, pamphlets, and so on. If you have done a good job on your bibliography cards, you merely have to arrange them alphabetically and copy the information for your paper. If the bibliography is long, you may wish to group the cards by books, magazines, and pamphlets.

3. Be generous with white space. Leave plenty of space around major headings, tables, and other displayed material.

4. Use side headings liberally. The report will be much easier to read if you break up long paragraphs with apt, well-worded side headings. Be sure all headings of the same value within a section are parallel. Here is an example of nonparallelism and the same headings in parallel form:

Nonparallel:

> **Grant as a Soldier**
> **Grant Is Elected President**

Parallel:

> **Grant as a Soldier**
> **Grant as a President**

5. Prepare a title page. This usually includes the following:

a. The title of the paper (most prominent)

b. Your name

c. The course for which the paper is submitted

d. The name of the instructor

e. The date

6. A table of contents is usually in order. It need not be detailed — a listing of the major headings, with page numbers, is enough.

7. Bind the report in an art-paper cover, which can be purchased at almost any school bookstore. Paste a label on the outside, giving the title of the paper and your name.

In writing a research paper, the library will be your temporary home.

Frederic Lewis

PUTTING THE PRINCIPLES
INTO PRACTICE

Assume that you are gathering material for a paper on "The Development of Office Automation." One of your sources is a book; another a magazine. An extract from each of these sources follows.

Extract No. 1. This extract comes from page 54 of the book *Office Work and Automation*, written by Howard S. Levin for John Wiley and Sons, Inc., New York. The publication date is 1956.

The technology of our times provides much that can contribute to more effective information handling. There is promise that clerical costs can be reduced as more accurate, comprehensive, and timely information is made available.

But these are not the only, or even the most, important reasons for improving business information systems. The more significant advantages will result from new ways of using business information to form business decisions. These improved systems will place at our command new means for initially handling information, new methods for processing information, and new techniques for utilizing information in solving business problems.

Extract No. 2. This extract is taken from an article entitled "Automation in the Sixties," by Robert M. Smith. It begins on page 16 and ends on page 20 of the January, 1960, issue of *Office Management Magazine*, Volume 16.

Business had also fallen behind generally in assessing and planning for the psychological effects of automation, either on the production line or in the office. While most instances of clerical automation have included provisions for transfer of displaced workers to other parts of the company, and

some planned information program in advance of the change, all the ramifications of intelligent transfer have not by any means been fully worked out. For example, how many companies have really faced the problem of what to do with senior workers suddenly moved into a new area where, in spite of their years of service, they have less experience than their juniors? How many have considered the psychological problems involved in moving a worker with a responsible job into a less demanding one?

Here is what you are to do.

1. Prepare a bibliography card for each source.

2. Write a slug line for each note card.

3. Make appropriate notes from the extracts, identifying each note card according to the suggestions in this unit.

During the process of making notes it's a good idea to keep your note cards in a box.

PRACTICAL TIPS AND SUGGESTIONS
FOR NOTEMAKING

FOOTNOTES

In copying from books or composing a rough draft for a research paper, it is often necessary to provide for a footnote. The inexperienced notemaker usually puts the footnote at the bottom of the page of notes on which the reference appears, which seems reasonable. Actually, it is much better to follow the same practice in writing footnotes that is used in preparing manuscripts for the printer.

Instead of writing the footnote at the bottom of the page of notes, place it immediately below the line to which it applies. First, leave a blank line. Then draw a single line clear across the page, write the footnote, draw another line across the page and proceed with your notes or your draft. In your notes simply indicate the word to which the footnote belongs by placing an asterisk or a small cross after the word. Later, when you prepare your final copy, you can substitute raised numbers for the asterisks or crosses. See the example below.

Placing the footnote immediately following the reference is desirable for two reasons:

1. In your original draft it is sometimes difficult to know how much room to allow for footnotes; some footnotes are quite long.

2. As you prepare your final copy, you may find that the word on which the footnote hangs may be at the very bottom of the page, leaving no room for the footnote which was inconspicuously placed at the foot of the page. When the footnote follows on the line after the word on which it depends, it is considerably easier to plan for the placement of the footnote on the proper page.

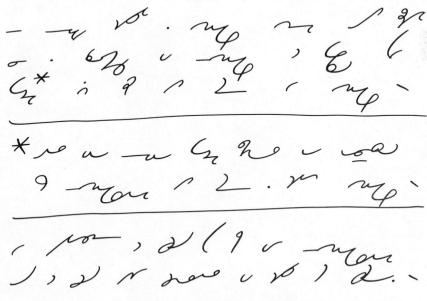

(Key appears on page 307.)

MOST-USED GREGG NOTEHAND FORMS

Here are ten more of the commonest words in the English language to be added to the card that you keep with you whenever you are making notes. Every day read over once or twice all the words that you now have left on the card. The more often you read them, the more rapidly you can write them.

same   **note**   **made**   **make**   **their, there**

just   **come**   **other**   **they**   **much**

PUTTING GREGG NOTEHAND INTO PRACTICE

Read the rough draft on page 209. Notice the following:

1. The heading in longhand
2. The indication of the footnote
3. The use of longhand for words that might present spelling difficulties in the preparation of the final copy

The key to this rough draft appears on page 307.

Stoppage — Transit

[shorthand]

[shorthand]

carrier *[shorthand]* occurs

[shorthand]

UNIT · 51

Disjoined Word Endings

-cal, -cle

1

-lity

2

-ings

3

-rity

4

-ward

5

KEY

1. Technical, medical, mechanical, vertical, particle, article.
2. Locality, facility, ability, quality, personality, possibility.
3. Proceedings, meetings, hearings, ratings, mornings, openings, feelings.
4. Sincerity, majority, minority, priority, clarity, authorities, security.
5. Outward, inward, onward, backward, upward, forward, reward, rewarded.

138.   READING AND WRITING PRACTICE

Just-a-Little-Late Club

I used

I was

— Bruce Barton

X139. Word Families

-nted

1 *[shorthand outlines]*

-kn

2 *[shorthand outlines]*

Moo, Noo

3 *[shorthand outlines]*

-ished

4 *[shorthand outlines]*

-fully

5 *[shorthand outlines]*

KEY

1. Planted, granted, rented, printed, wanted, hunted.
2. Chicken, weaken, shaken, waken, broken, spoken, darken, quicken.
3. Moon, moving, month, money, must, noon, number.
4. Astonished, finished, accomplished, furnished, abolished, punished, varnished.
5. Carefully, gratefully, forcefully, usefully, faithfully, skillfully, helpfully, cheerfully.

140. **READING AND WRITING PRACTICE**

Mr. Murphy's Chickens

[shorthand outlines]

Just as the

A few days later,

"Oh, I think

UNIT 53

141.   Word Families

-ier

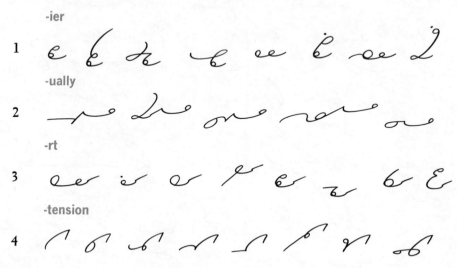

1

-ually

2

-rt

3

-tension

4

KEY

1. Easier, busier, fancier, lazier, earlier, happier, carrier, heavier.
2. Mutually, virtually, actually, gradually, annually.
3. Alert, hurt, art, dirt, exert, insert, part, expert.
4. Tension, attention, retention, contention, intention, detention, extension, inattention.

142.   READING AND WRITING PRACTICE

Open Door

Perhaps you have already made up your mind what field you would like to make your lifework. Perhaps it is advertising or television or publishing. This article will suggest to you an almost "sure-fire" way of getting your start in the field of your choice.

$200.

We did not

$275.

The critical shortage

— H. M. Overley

UNIT 54

143. Phrases

The

1 *[shorthand outlines]*

He

2 *[shorthand outlines]*

I

3 *[shorthand outlines]*

To

4 *[shorthand outlines]*

Should

5 *[shorthand outlines]*

KEY

1. Of the, in the, at the, on the, from the, with the, for the, is the, as the.
2. He is, he may, he was, he should, he did, he could, he might, he will.
3. I shall, I will, I have, I am, I said, I would, I know, I could.
4. To the, to it, to that, to talk, to go, to try, to take, to you.
5. He should, I should, you should, you should be, I should have, I should like, I should say, he should be.

144. READING AND WRITING PRACTICE

Profit

[shorthand outlines]

Our primitive

Then one day 100

990

16

99

50

The enterpriser, 16

100

99

$\frac{1}{10}$

99

(Concluded in Paragraph 146)

UNIT 55

145. Word Families

-tive

1 

-ser, -cer

2 

-vent

3 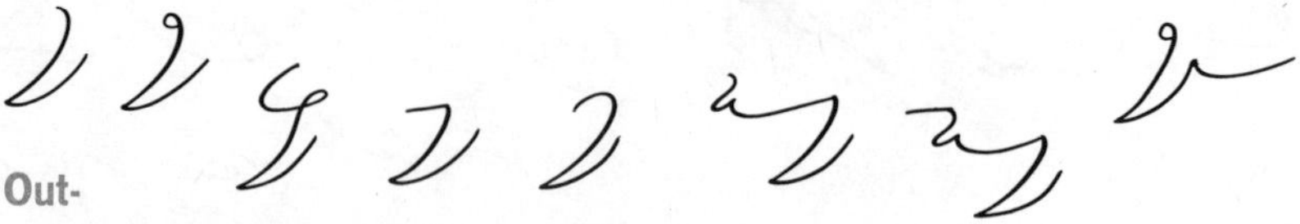

Out-

4 

Al-

5 

KEY

1. Relative, primitive, active, positive, incentive, creative, effective.
2. Enterpriser, miser, tracer, eraser, closer, grocer, dancer.
3. Vent, event, prevent, invent, convent, solvent, insolvent, eventual.
4. Outlay, outline, output, outside, outward, outright, without.
5. Also, almost, already, although, alteration.

146. READING AND WRITING PRACTICE

Profit (Concluded)

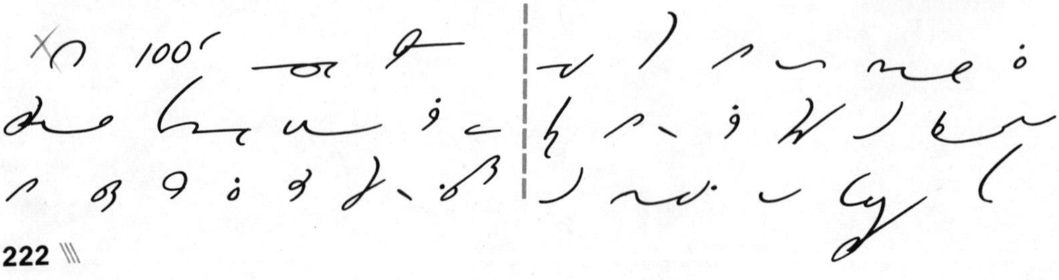

The other 98

You can see

UNIT 56

147. Word Families

-ally

1 

-man

2 

-eral

3 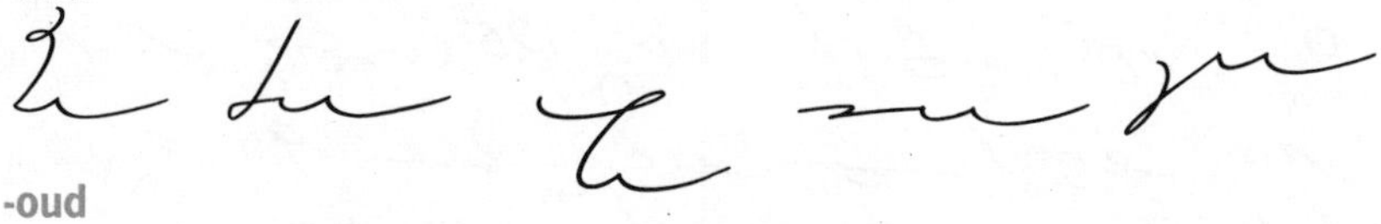

-oud

4 

-plied

5 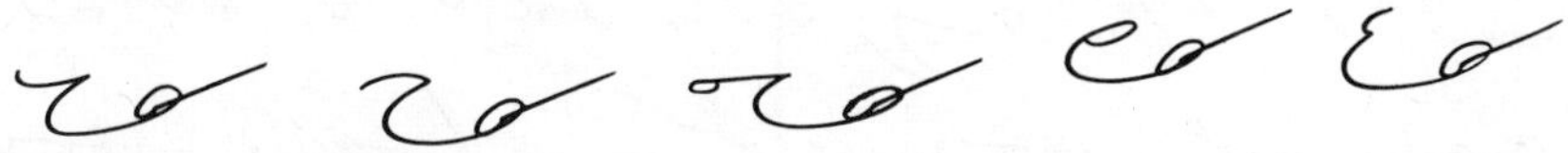

KEY

1. Finally, vitally, totally, normally, partially.
2. Human, woman, foreman, workman, salesman.
3. Several, general, liberal, numeral, federal.
4. Loud, cloud, plowed, aloud, crowd, proud.
5. Replied, complied, implied, applied, supplied.

148. READING AND WRITING PRACTICE

Silly Advice

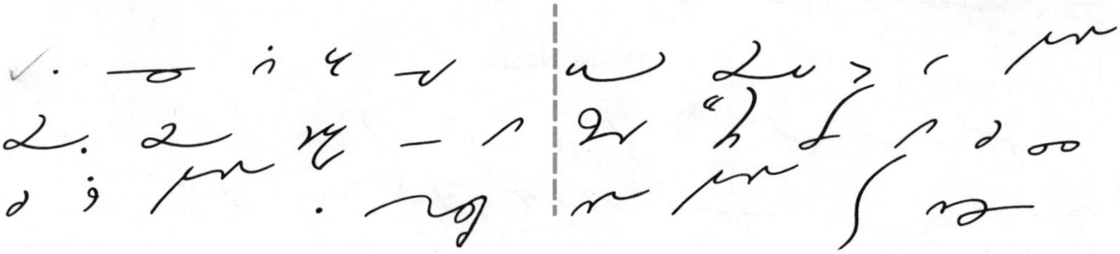

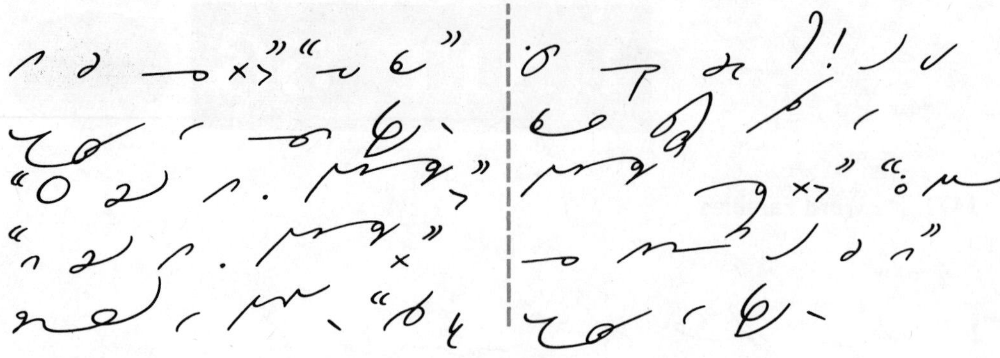

Long Life

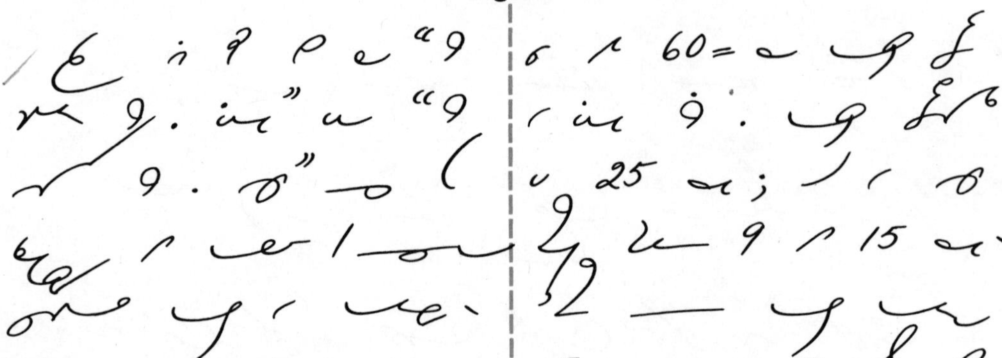

— Charles Adams

Office Hours

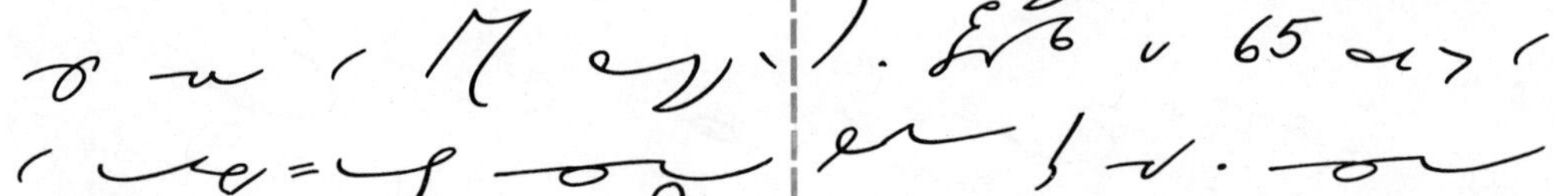

Solution

Darkness

UNIT 57

How to Use Notes in Reviewing and Preparing for Examinations

Notes are virtually indispensable in reviewing and preparing for examinations. An even more permanent value of notes is that they serve as a "memory storehouse" for you. They are always available to refresh your thinking, your recall, your memory.

USING YOUR NOTES IN REVIEWING

Reviewing is an essential process in learning. We tend to forget what we learn, and reviewing is an effective means of relearning. In addition, through reviewing we often learn things that were not learned — or only partially learned — the first time.

Notes are an invaluable source of material for reviewing, whether they were made from reading a book, from a discussion, or from listening to a lecture.

Review Your Notes Promptly. By reviewing notes promptly, you need less time to relearn and to fix previous learning. Also, notes can be "filled in," if need be, with pertinent bits of information, comments, facts, or ideas that were omitted when the notes were first made. Reviewing promptly also gives you an opportunity to change the content or organization of your notes while they are still fresh in mind. For example, a point made in the latter part of a lecture may have significant bearing on a point made in the early part of the lecture.

Reviewing promptly also helps you plan further reading and studying. A review of your notes may reveal a point on which you need additional information or a theory or a problem that you do not fully understand. You can then do something about it while there is still time.

Review Your Notes More Than Once. How often you review notes depends on the subject, how difficult it is for you, and how well you are learning it. How often you review your notes also depends on the lecturer or instructor: how well he teaches for your purposes, whether he gives unannounced quizzes, and so on. Incidentally, if unannounced quizzes are usual, you will need to review your notes more frequently.

Review your notes as frequently as you need to in order to *learn well* and *do well* in a particular learning situation. At any rate, review more than once — the first time promptly following the making of the notes and again before taking an examination related to the notes. It is far better to review too often than not often enough.

Review for Examinations. To be effective, reviewing for examinations should be done well in advance of the examination. All too often, reviewing is put off until the last minute. Delaying review until the eleventh hour tempts you to "cram"—and cramming is never so productive as *deliberate reviewing.* Last-minute reviewing leads to fears and anxieties, which impair mental and physical efficiency. It interferes with the adequate sleep and rest one should have before an examination. It makes difficult, if not impossible, checking information, obtaining additional facts, and other preparations for the examination.

Recite to Yourself As You Review. Notes may be reviewed *passively* or *actively*. In passive review, you simply "spin your wheels" and waste time. If you review notes actively, your time and effort will be productive. To review actively means to *think* as you review and to *recite to yourself* the essential information, ideas, events, facts, and formulas. For example, review a relatively short segment at a time — a section, a paragraph, or even a statement in your notes — striving to grasp the essentials, and then recite it back to yourself for fixation and mastery.

If you are reviewing your notes for the first time — which means promptly after making them — read them verbatim. It is also good to read verbatim if you are relatively unfamiliar with them, perhaps because considerable time has elapsed since you last reviewed them.

Notes should also be reviewed by skimming — running through them quickly just to pick up cues, and using the cues to recite to yourself the facts and other information related to the cues. This process will help you to organize the essentials in your own mind and relate them in the notes reviewed. It facilitates fixation and mastery of the material and the recall of what has been learned. Progressing from reviewing through verbatim reading to reviewing through cues is particularly effective in preparing for examinations.

How you review will depend on such things as your purpose, familiarity with the notes, and amount of relearning required. But all review must involve *effective reciting back* to produce anything in the way of learning results.

MAKING DERIVED NOTES

Making "derived" notes is a helpful technique in reviewing notes and in relearning. *Derived notes* are simply revised notes made from original notes. They are, in effect, condensations and summaries of notes; in some cases, they may be a reorganization of notes as well. Derived notes may bring together notes from several sources, such as notes from lectures, from textbook reading, from discussions, and from supplementary reading — all on the same topic.

The purpose of derived notes is to make original notes more useful. For example, suppose you have made a set of notes in biology and you wish to use your original notes to prepare a table comparing all the major divisions of the animal kingdom (the phyla). Your derived notes might resemble the example shown on page 230.

Good notes are helpful in relearning.

Harold M. Lambert

Or suppose you are taking a course in American history, and your instructor does not discuss the events of a particular episode or period in chronological order. You might make derived notes from your original notes by preparing a table or a list of the events in chronological order.

Derived notes can be helpful in reviewing as well as in preparing new notes. Preparing derived notes is in effect a reviewing process. In addition, derived notes themselves provide a source of material for reviewing. They are condensations and summaries of cues or reorganizations of cues.

Derived notes may be used effectively in recalling and reciting to yourself the more detailed essentials that appear in the original notes. If you cannot readily recall the details, however, be sure to review the original notes.

The quality of derived notes depends almost entirely on the quality of the original notes. If the original notes were carefully recorded, many good derived notes can be made.

SPECIAL NOTES FOR REVIEWING

Some subjects lend themselves to special kinds or forms of notes for review and recall. An example of such special notes are vocabulary cards for a foreign language. To prepare a vocabulary card, simply write the foreign word or phrase on one side and the translation in English on the other. You can then use these cards easily and in different sequence for review and recall. Look at the word on one side of the card and try to remember the translation of the word. Check yourself for accuracy by reversing the card if necessary.

This special form of notes can be applied to chemical formulas, structures, names, dates, laws, and so on.

Major Divisions v Animal Kingdom

Phylum (kind v animal)	Germ Layers	Digestive System	Other Characteristics
Protozoa	Doesn't CC (single cell)	Within cell	Single celled organisms
Porifera	2 layers	Special cells (within cell)	Canal &
Coelenterata	2 layers	Cavity	Radial symmetry
Ctenophora	3 layers	Cavity	Biradial symmetry

DISPOSITION OF YOUR NOTES

Whether you should keep or discard your notes after they have served their immediate purpose, such as completing a course, depends upon what the notes cover, how complete they are, how important they are, how likely it is that you may want them in the future, how difficult it would be to replace them, and so on. It is a good policy to keep notes for a reasonable period of time. You may wish to refer to them soon after they have served your immediate purposes. They may contain information that would be helpful to you — information that would otherwise be difficult to obtain.

In doing advanced work, you will find it helpful to be able to refer to previous notes for information and explanations. Courses in science and mathematics are examples of subjects that involve a progressive sequence of subject matter. Sometimes the lapse of time between one course and another may be considerable, as, for example, when a graduate student needs to refer to notes he made in undergraduate courses. Thus, notes often have value long after they were made.

Notes should be properly identified (labeled) and stored in a suitable and accessible place, preferably, not far from the place where one studies. The notes should be arranged according to the subjects to which they pertain.

FOR DISCUSSION AND PARTICIPATION

1. Three criteria for measuring the difference between good notes and poor ones are selectivity, pertinence, and organization. Discuss each of these criteria fully.

2. Give several reasons why notes should be reviewed promptly.

3. Everyone should review his notes at least twice. When should these minimum reviews take place?

4. Describe the process of reviewing actively.

5. What are derived notes? In what circumstances might they be used most effectively?

6. Give reasons why notes should be saved. Describe your plan for filing notes or one that you would recommend for notes on note cards and on note paper.

PRACTICAL TIPS AND SUGGESTIONS FOR NOTEMAKING

INDEX YOUR NOTES

The careful student may want to make an index to his notebooks. Sometimes a partial table of contents, showing the more important items, will be as useful as an index and it has the advantage of being quicker and easier to make. A helpful table of contents may be made during the making of the notes — even with lecture notes.

If you plan to have a table of contents or an index for your notes, leave a few blank pages at the beginning of each subject. As the course proceeds, you will gradually establish some headings in the table of contents or index on these blank pages. If it is to be a partial index, you will want to spread the entries out to permit the insertion of subheadings under the main headings and to permit the addition of new main headings in alphabetical order.

For instance, if the course is on the Elizabethan period of English history, your index would have main headings for Essex, Burleigh, Drake, and so on (as illustrated on page 234). As important facts about any of these people appear in the lectures, appropriate subheadings would be added. During the lecture you might have time only to insert the page number on which the material appears in the notes, leaving the remainder of the line blank in the index, to be filled in later. Usually, however, there will be time for a hasty Gregg Notehand indication of the nature of the material on the page indicated. For example, under the main heading *Essex* the last entry might be simply the page number and one word in Gregg Notehand, "execution."

With the help of even the simplest index of this kind, you could find in a matter of seconds your notes on the execution of Essex even though you had a hundred pages of notes. Otherwise, you might have to spend five or ten minutes rummaging through the notes.

A table of contents is even less trouble to prepare, although it is somewhat less helpful than the simplest index. For the table of contents you need only put the date of each lecture and the page reference on the next blank line of the page left for that purpose at the beginning of your notebook. Then during or after the lecture you can write a brief note in Gregg Notehand under the date. Then, instead of rummaging through many pages of notes, you need only run quickly through the table of contents to find the reference to the numbered page in the body of the notes.

MOST-USED GREGG NOTEHAND FORMS

Here is another group of ten most frequently used words to be added to your card. At this stage in your study of Gregg Notehand, no doubt most of them are already old friends.

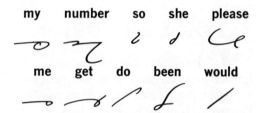

| my | number | so | she | please |
| me | get | do | been | would |

PUTTING GREGG NOTEHAND INTO PRACTICE

Study the table of contents and index on pages 233 and 234, and make a copy of them. The key for these pages is on 311.

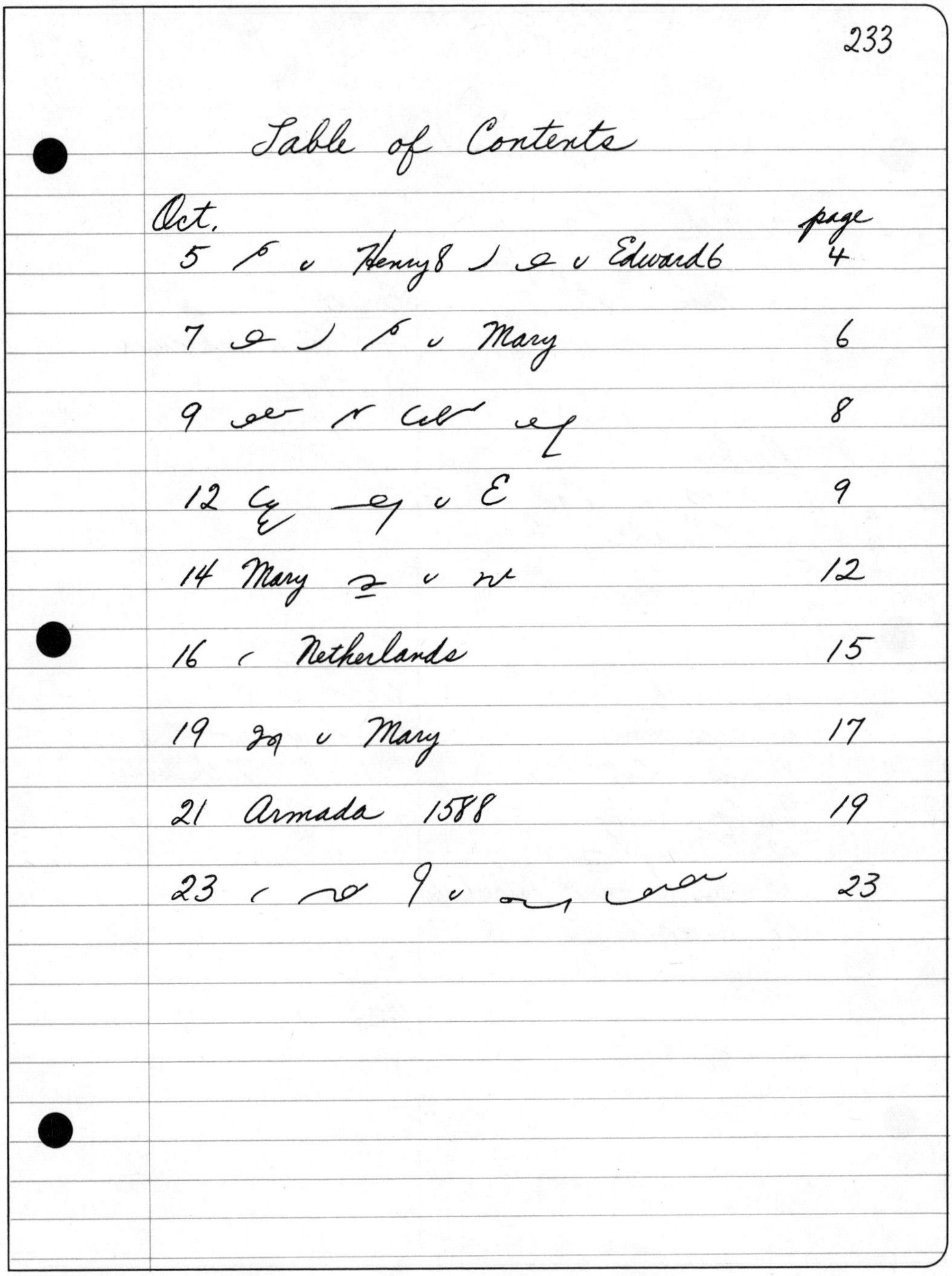

This is a table of contents for a series of college lectures on Elizabethan history, with lectures three times a week.

Index

Burleigh
8 *[shorthand notes]*
    Mary's

Essex
24 Irish expedition
29 *[shorthand]*

Drake
18 *[shorthand]* Cadiz
20 Armada

Elizabeth
6 accession
8 *[shorthand]*
9 *[shorthand]*
12 *[shorthand]* Mary *[shorthand]*
15 *[shorthand]* Netherlands
19 Armada

Leicester
9 *[shorthand]*
18 *[shorthand]*
    Netherlands

Mary *[shorthand]* Eng
5 *[shorthand]*

This is the first page of a running index for the same course in Elizabethan history for which the table of contents on the preceding page was made. If the next entry were for Frobisher's search for the Northwest Passage, the entry would be made between the present entry for Essex and Leicester, to preserve the alphabetical order.

UNIT 58

149.   **Word Beginnings**

Ex-

1

Com-

2

Trans-

3

Sub-

4

KEY

1. Expulsion, explanation, exercise, expiration, examine, exceeded, exciting.
2. Completely, compare, complaint, complains, compel, compose.
3. Transfer, transmit, transmitted, transform, translate, translation.
4. Subscription, subscribe, submit, submission, submitted, substantially, subway.

150.   **READING AND WRITING PRACTICE**

The Fifty-First Dragon

In the next six units you will enjoy the trials and tribulations of Gawaine, The Dragon Killer, one of the most delightful tales ever written by Heywood Broun.

"I cannot

"Would any

In the afternoon

(Continued in Paragraph 152)

UNIT 59

151. Word Endings

-ment

1 *[shorthand outlines]*

-ly

2 *[shorthand outlines]*

-tion

3 *[shorthand outlines]*

-ble

4 *[shorthand outlines]*

-ure

5 *[shorthand outlines]*

KEY

1. Moment, treatment, accomplishment, compliment, statement.
2. Sincerely, humanly, possibly, probably, partly, smartly, greatly.
3. Fashion, nation, creation, extension, expression, relation, contemplation.
4. Terrible, cable, invisible, imaginable, payable, honorable, comfortable, legible.
5. Nature, natural, feature, picture, lecture, stature, ventured.

152. READING AND WRITING PRACTICE

The Fifty-First Dragon (Continued)

[shorthand outlines]

"They say ... 500 ... !"

"But the size ... 200 ... 100

239

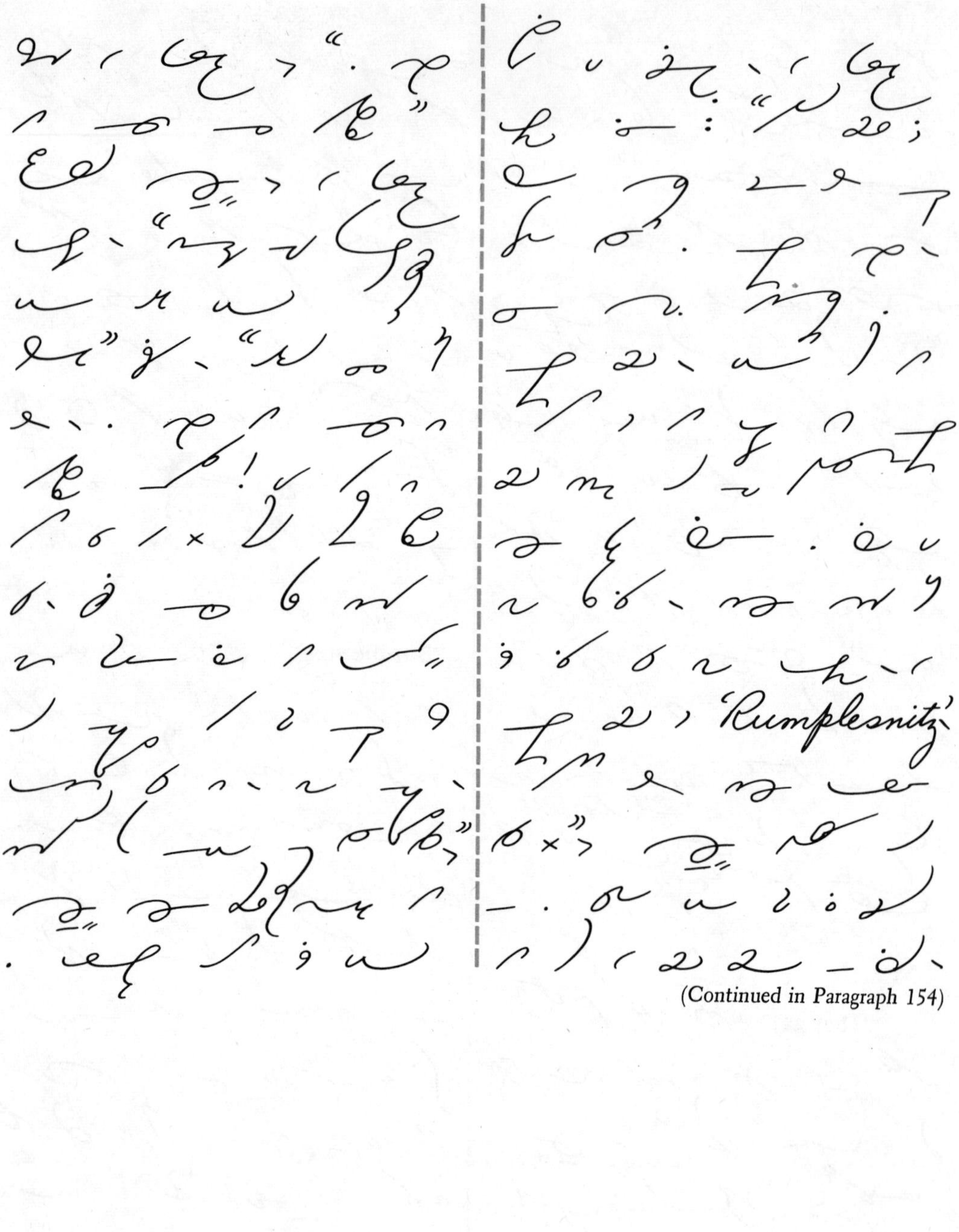

(Continued in Paragraph 154)

UNIT 60

✓ **153.** **Blends**

Rd

1 [shorthand symbols]

Ld

2 [shorthand symbols]

Ses

3 [shorthand symbols]

Md, Mt

4 [shorthand symbols]

Ded

5 [shorthand symbols]

KEY

1. Toward, hovered, wondered, record, assured, reassured, stored, bored.
2. Spelled, failed, mailed, bold, gold, fold.
3. Insisting, consist, resist, assist, persist, faces, vases, ceases, fixes.
4. Claimed, named, blamed, prompt, promptly, empty.
5. Decided, graded, traded, needed, guided, added, deduct.

✓ **154.** **READING AND WRITING PRACTICE**

The Fifty-First Dragon (Continued)

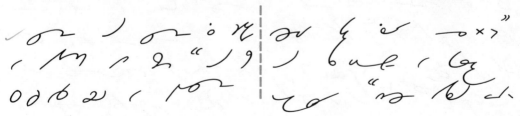

About a mile

As he said it,

Few good days

As Gawaine's record

(Continued in Paragraph 156)

155. Word Families

-dent

1 *[shorthand outlines]*

-less

2 *[shorthand outlines]*

-ver

3 *[shorthand outlines]*

-use

4 *[shorthand outlines]*

-bled

5 *[shorthand outlines]*

KEY

1. Confident, resident, student, president, incident, accident, evidently.
2. Helpless, needless, careless, harmless, thoughtless.
3. Ever, never, clever, sever, cover, discover, silver, river.
4. Use, fuse, confuse, abuse, accuse, refuse, refuses, refusal, refused.
5. Trembled, cabled, rambled, stumbled, resembled, scribbled.

156. READING AND WRITING PRACTICE

The Fifty-First Dragon (Continued)

[shorthand outlines]

"I've forgotten

Much to the

245

With the suggestion ⌣ .

(Continued in Paragraph 158)

157. Vowel Omission

Omission of E in -ious, -eous

1 *[shorthand outlines]*

Omission of Vowel Preceding -tion

2 *[shorthand outlines]*

Omission of Short U

3 *[shorthand outlines]*

Omission of E in U

4 *[shorthand outlines]*

Omission of Minor Vowel

5 *[shorthand outlines]*

KEY

1. Various, serious, obvious, previous, tedious, studious, courteous, erroneous.
2. Explanation, nomination, addition, admission, commission, notation, station.
3. Come, become, some, fumble, lumber, column.
4. News, dues, duty, renew, renewal, reduce, produced.
5. Terrific, classic, magic, tragic, topic, literal.

158. READING AND WRITING PRACTICE

The Fifty-First Dragon (Continued)

[shorthand outlines]

Again and again

Gawaine frowned.

Gawaine surprised

(Concluded in Paragraph 160)

UNIT 63

√ 159.   Brief-Form Derivatives

Over-

1   *[shorthand outlines]*

Under-

2   *[shorthand outlines]*

In-

3   *[shorthand outlines]*

Be-

4   *[shorthand outlines]*

For-

5   *[shorthand outlines]*

KEY

1. Over, overhead, overcome, overcoat, oversupply, overturn, overpaid, overrate.
2. Under, underpaid, underground, understand, understood, underneath, under-
   nourished, undergone.
3. In, income, inscription, inside, increase, intense, incomplete.
4. Be, because, believe, become, before, behind, beyond, below, betray.
5. For, force, forgive, forget, forgot, inform, informed, foreman.

160.   READING AND WRITING PRACTICE

The Fifty-First Dragon (Concluded)

[shorthand outlines]

The assistant professor

50

Accordingly,

50

— Heywood Broun

Fair Deal

— Callisthenes

How to Make Notes in Discussions, Meetings, and Conferences

Most class meetings include discussions during which class members exchange facts, ideas, and opinions about the subject under consideration. Many advanced courses are in the form of seminars or workshops in which there is no formal lecture. Instead, the class consists entirely of a free exchange of information and opinions gathered from reading, observation, and research.

In class discussions your primary concern is to pay close attention to what is going on and to *participate actively* in the discussion. In addition to participating, you should also make notes on the major points covered.

MAKING NOTES OF CLASS DISCUSSIONS

Participation is so important that if you find it impossible to make notes and take part in the discussion at the same time, you should let the notes go. Actually, however, if you are fairly skillful in Gregg Notehand and observe the rules for good notemaking, you won't find it too difficult to do both.

When you are participating in a general discussion and making notes at the same time, your notes will usually be of two types: (1) notes about what others are saying and (2) notes to yourself. For example, someone may make a statement that you do not agree with, that you believe to be in-

correct, or that you wish to enlarge on later. While you are making notes from the participant's remarks, you are also making brief notes to yourself to remind you what you want to say when he has finished. Suppose you are engaged in a discussion of Federal aid to education. On page 254 is an example of how your notes might appear.

Notice in the example that the note-maker has allowed a very wide left margin for notes to himself. For such notes you might use a different color from that of your regular notes, as in the illustration.

The notes in the illustration are summary statements of the remarks of the participants. In a typical class discussion it is

Executives attend many meetings and have frequent opportunities for notemaking.

Ewing Galloway

Joan D:

Hank J:

John H:

Bill J:

Mary L:
①
②
③
④

(Key appears on page 315.)

difficult, if not impossible, to make your notes in true outline form, since the subjects, points of view, and the appropriateness of the remarks vary widely. It is best, therefore, to organize your notes according to the identity of the participants, as in the illustration. Of course, sometimes their remarks may lend themselves to an outline form. Observe in the illustration, for example, the notes made from Mary L's remarks.

If you will study carefully the notes illustrated, you will see that some of the most important aspects of the subject of Federal aid to education are covered. Ideas do not have to come from textbooks or from a lecture to be important!

This is only one form, of course, in which discussion notes may be made. The form isn't too important. What is important is that notes of some type be made.

USING YOUR NOTES

You should review notes made from discussions as promptly as possible after the discussion, especially in view of the difficulty of organizing your notes as you make them. If you wait too long, you may not be able to make sense out of your fragmentary jottings, particularly if you are trying to write and participate at the same time. Reorganize your notes as you review, putting them in a form that will be most helpful and usable. Of course, the reorganization should tie in as closely as possible with the notes you have made from lectures or reading to which the class discussion is related. Reorganizing discussion notes is a valuable learning experience in itself. Your reorganized notes on the discussion of Federal aid to education might appear as follows:

FEDERAL AID TO EDUCATION

ADVANTAGES

    1. Would provide more nearly equal opportunity for all pupils,
       regardless of individual community wealth
    2. Would probably result in better education
          a. Better facilities
          b. Better teaching
                (1) Higher salaries for teachers
                (2) More rigid teaching requirements
          c. Standardized courses for pupils as well as for teacher
             training
             (Questionable as an advantage)
    3. Probably get more for each dollar spent

DISADVANTAGES

    1. Individual communities might lose interest ("let the
       Government do it")
    2. Government control encourages bureaucracy -- "red tape"
    3. Might become "political football" (System of checks and
       balances might prevent this)

OTHER TYPES OF MEETINGS AND DISCUSSIONS

In addition to class discussions, you will attend many other types of meetings in which you can use notemaking to good advantage. If you belong to a club or organization that holds regular meetings, there are frequent discussions of important ideas, suggestions, and business matters. In business, you will perhaps be a member of one or more permanent committees — the advertising committee, the research committee, the forms control committee, and so on. Teachers, engineers, doctors, lawyers, and others attend many conferences and committee meetings related to their professions. As an ordinary citizen, you will attend meetings of civic organizations, church groups, parents' committees, and social clubs. Good notemaking skill comes in handy in such meetings and conferences, and the suggestions offered earlier in this unit apply here.

If you are recording secretary of any of these groups, in which case your notes must be converted into "minutes," notemaking becomes a "must."

MAKING NOTES AS A RECORDER

Notes that will result in official records of your group must accurately interpret the proceedings, sifting the unimportant from the important. Some suggestions for making notes as a recorder are given in the following paragraphs.

Identify the Participants. It is usually essential for the recorder to identify the participants in a discussion, because in the minutes they are often given credit for their ideas and proposals. Correctly identifying all the participants in a discussion group is simple if the group is small and you know all the members. You can identify each

Hays from Monkmeyer
Graduate students often meet in a seminar where discussion among participants is the primary activity.

speaker merely by using his initials. If the meeting consists primarily of a report from each individual, you may place his initials at the top of your notes, recording his comments directly underneath, like this:

Key: 1. Quantity of questionnaire returns not so important as quality. 2. Questionnaire forms should leave plenty of room for personal comments — not merely checking off objective statements.

If, on the other hand, it is a free-for-all discussion where you never know who is going to speak next and when he is going to be interrupted, it is better to place the initials at the side (such as in the example on page 254), as is done in identifying the characters in the script of a play.

Make Verbatim Notes for Motions and Resolutions Only. Except for motions, resolutions, and similar formal statements, the notemaker should not attempt to record verbatim what is said in discussion meetings. His responsibility is to record the major ideas and proposals discussed. Gregg Notehand is not designed for verbatim recording where ideas fly thick and fast. But it does provide the recorder with an excellent means for noting essential points.

Make Use of the Agenda. In some cases, an agenda (list of the topics to be discussed) is prepared and distributed to the members a few days before the meeting. This agenda will be an important guide to your notemaking. If the items in the agenda are numbered, your notes can merely refer to the number rather than repeat the subject.

Discussions and reports at school and club meetings are often written up in the form of minutes.

H. Armstrong Roberts

Some meetings are tightly run, never deviating from the agenda, and the problem of identifying the subject is solved for the notemaker. But in other meetings, the agenda is used only as a point of departure and the meeting is allowed to develop into free-for-all discussions ranging far and wide. In this case, it is best to repeat the subject matter you are reporting even though it may appear on the agenda.

Indicate Time, Place, and Other Details. Be sure to record the date, time, and place of the meeting. Also, indicate who presided, who was present, who was absent, correct name and title of the speaker (if any), and so on. These details will be needed when you are ready to type up your notes in the form of minutes.

Verify Important Points. Sometimes the recorder is given an opportunity at the time, or later, to verify the wording of a particular resolution or motion; if not, he should check his notes with one or more of the other officers after the meeting is over, since he must record such items verbatim.

WRITING THE MINUTES

The notes of a meeting should be written up as promptly as possible after the meeting ends. The longer you wait the more difficult it is to make corrections or to decide what is meant by a passage that is difficult to interpret. Read through all your notes carefully before proceeding to type them; you may even find it desirable to make an outline before you begin to write. Check for any additional facts that are needed for making the report — information that was to be obtained or things that were to be done. Then make a rough draft of your report, using Gregg Notehand (see Unit 43). Finally, type it in final form and distribute it to all those who should receive copies.

Do not destroy your notes until the

minutes have been approved. This approval is usually given at the next meeting at which the minutes are read.

An illustration of minutes of a meeting is shown on page 259. Some minutes are much longer, depending on the amount of business transacted. It is a good idea, however, to keep your minutes as short as possible — recording only the essential points and no more.

FOR DISCUSSION AND PARTICIPATION

1. Why is it more important that you participate actively in class discussions than make notes if you can't do both?

2. What is the value of open discussion from the viewpoint of the teacher? of the participants?

3. Why should notes made at open discussions be reviewed as quickly as possible after the discussion? What is the value of reviewing these notes?

4. What would you suggest that professional people use to make their notes in? Discuss.

5. In a formal meeting, where minutes are kept, why is it important to identify each participant?

6. "Those who try to record everything said at a meeting usually turn out to be poor notemakers." Do you agree with this statement? Discuss.

PRACTICAL TIPS AND SUGGESTIONS FOR NOTEMAKING

USE SIGNALS OF IMPORTANCE

In the process of making notes, some points will impress you as being of more than ordinary importance. Or perhaps the lecturer may indicate that some points should be emphasized or remembered. You can make these points stand out in your notes if you will mark them distinctively with some type of "signals of importance." These signals will be of value when you review your notes in preparation for an examination.

Perhaps the simplest and quickest signals of importance are vertical lines placed to the left of an item. This type of signal can be used to indicate degrees of importance. One vertical line can be used to indicate something of moderate importance; two vertical lines, something of considerable importance; three vertical lines, something of great importance.

USE UNDERSCORES FOR EMPHASIS

To make a single word or phrase stand out in your notes you can place a wavy underscore below the item to be emphasized. If you use red for underscoring, such items will stand out even more.

If the item to be emphasized runs more than a line, you will save time by using the vertical line signal rather than the underscore.

USE SPACE TO INDICATE COMMAS

Ordinarily, the Gregg Notehand writer will use the familiar longhand mark for the comma, encircling it in order to avoid any possibility of hesitation in reading. In most

POLITICAL SCIENCE CLUB

MINUTES OF MEETING, APRIL 3, 19--

Time and
Place

The regular meeting of the Political Science Club was called to order by the President, John Updyke, on Wednesday, April 3, 19--, in the Chinese Room of the Student Union Building. All 32 members were present.

Minutes

The minutes of the March meeting were read by the Secretary, Mary Jo Juleson, and were approved.

The report of the Nominating Committee was given by the Chairman, Pauline Glass. A slate of nominees for next year's offices is to be presented at the May meeting.

Committee
Reports

The report of the Education Committee was given by the Chairman, Price Logan. News articles about the activities of the club have appeared in three recent issues of the Aggie Daily and the January issue of "Aggievator." The club has been invited to continue its 15-minute radio program next year over WAGI on "Our Political Heritage." This program has received wide attention and has generated a great deal of interest among students in the club's activities.

Old
Business

The question of whether dues to the club should be increased was brought up for further discussion. It was moved, seconded, and passed THAT DUES FOR THE COMING YEAR REMAIN THE SAME AS THE CURRENT YEAR AND THAT A SPECIAL ASSESSMENT BE PERMITTED IF NECESSARY.

New
Business

After a discussion about the possibility of having a picnic in place of the June meeting (the last of the year), a committee consisting of Harry Longman, Eileen Warren, and Jim Pogue was appointed to report at the next meeting.

The following resolution was presented and approved:

WHEREAS, Professor Ralph Thomassen has, for the past three years, been faculty sponsor of the Political Science Club, and whereas Professor Thomassen is leaving to accept an important administrative position in another college, this club desires to incorporate the following resolution in the minutes:

Resolution

RESOLVED, That we recognize the excellent, energetic, and intelligent leadership and service that Professor Thomassen has rendered to the Political Science Club. We feel that the accomplishments of the club have been attained largely because of his earnest efforts and untiring devotion.

RESOLVED FURTHER, that in recognition of his service to the club, Professor Thomassen be elected Honorary Lifetime Member of the Political Science Club of Midwestern College.

Respectfully submitted,

Mary Jo Juleson

Mary Jo Juleson, Secretary

[shorthand notes]

Key: The great Finnish runner, Nurmi, set many athletic records.

notemaking, however, space, instead of the written comma, may be used to indicate a comma. This device is not only timesaving but it also provides further emphasis because often, as in the example above, the word set off with commas is a proper name. The extra space on each side indicates commas and at the same time makes the name stand out on the page.

MOST-USED GREGG NOTEHAND FORMS

Here is the final group of ten most frequently used words.

glad   know, no   give   go   wish

[shorthand notes]

got   good   day   may   or

[shorthand notes]

On the back end paper of this book you will find a chart of 100 frequently used words. From this point on turn to the chart occasionally and read through those words as rapidly as you can.

PUTTING GREGG NOTEHAND INTO PRACTICE

Read, study, and make a copy of the lecture notes on page 261. Observe how the notemaking suggestions presented in this unit are applied.

The key to these notes appears on page 315.

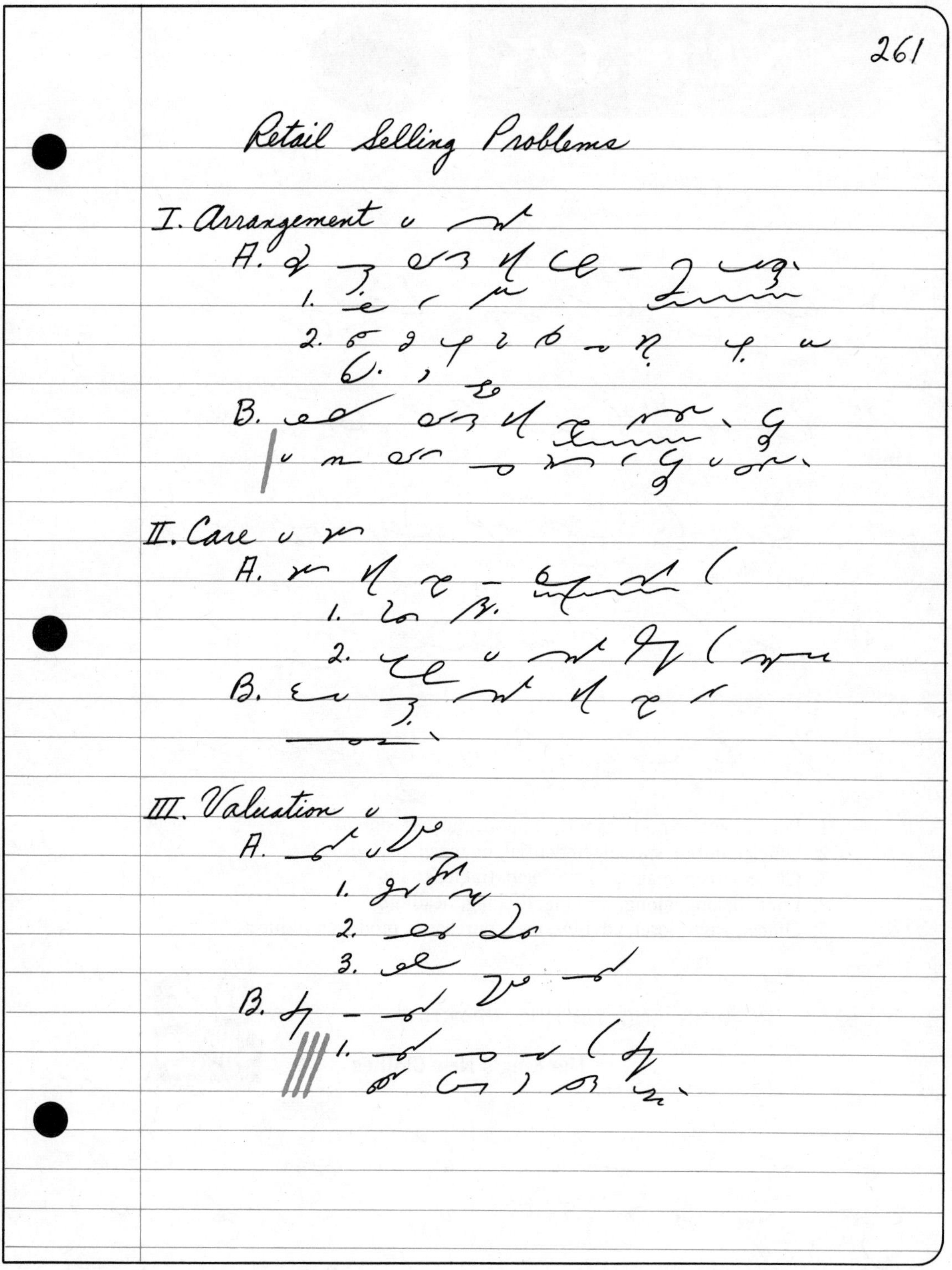
261
Retail Selling Problems
I. Arrangement
A.
1.
2.
B.
II. Care
A.
1.
2.
B.
III. Valuation
A.
1.
2.
3.
B.
1.

UNIT 65

161. Word Families

-port

1 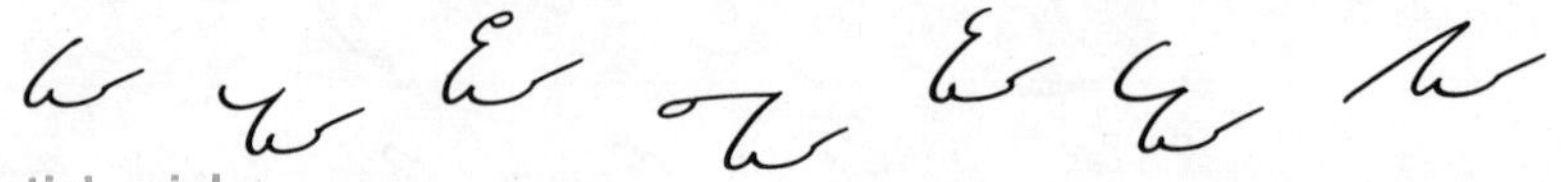

-tial, -cial

2 

-ic

3 

-long

4 

-ser, -cer

5 

KEY

1. Port, report, export, import, support, purport, deport.
2. Official, initial, special, credential, financial, partial.
3. Classic, basic, magic, tragic, logic, traffic, graphic.
4. Long, belong, along, prolong, lifelong, headlong.
5. Officer, wiser, loser, advisers, user, purchaser, producer, reducer.

162. READING AND WRITING PRACTICE

The King's New Clothes

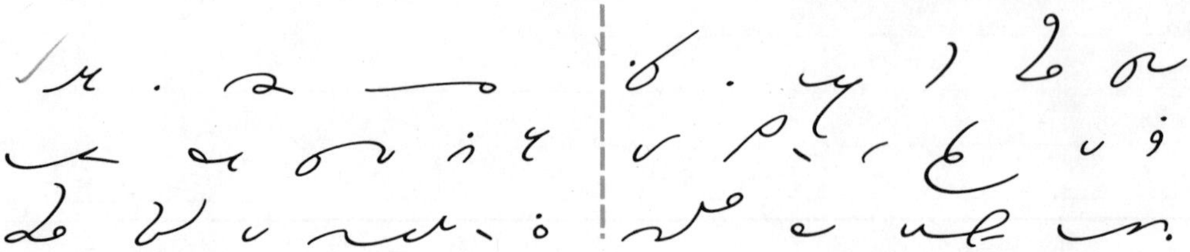

"That is just

One morning

They pretended

(Concluded in Paragraph 164)

163. Word Families

-claimed

1 *(shorthand outlines)*

Pro-

2 *(shorthand outlines)*

-vl

3 *(shorthand outlines)*

-ary, -ery, -ory

4 *(shorthand outlines)*

-rer, -ror

5 *(shorthand outlines)*

KEY

1. Claimed, exclaimed, proclaimed, reclaimed, acclaimed.
2. Procession, promote, provide, proceed, propose, professor, proper, property.
3. Civil, marveling, novel, approval, rival, naval, travel.
4. Primary, necessary, imaginary, finery, machinery, memory.
5. Clearer, nearer, dearer, laborer, lecturer, mirror.

164. READING AND WRITING PRACTICE

The King's New Clothes (Concluded)

(shorthand outlines)

And they returned

"Well,

Of course,

UNIT 67

✓ 165. **Theory Review**

OO Hook

1 *[shorthand outlines]*

W

2 *[shorthand outlines]*

Sw

3 *[shorthand outlines]*

Wh

4 *[shorthand outlines]*

W Dash

5 *[shorthand outlines]*

KEY
1. Who, to, do, whom, broom, room, rule, rude.
2. Weaken, window, worth, walk, waited, waste, women, well.
3. Swim, swelling, swear, sway, swift, switch, swallow, Swedish, sweetly.
4. Why, whether, while, wheat, white, wheel, whip, whisper.
5. Quickly, equipped, equipment, twice, quite, quietly, qualify, quotation.

166. **READING AND WRITING PRACTICE**

Tessie the Mannequin

[shorthand outlines]

268 \\\

$59.95.

✓ "It doesn't

"

$10

$59.95!"

"

✓ "Your what?"

"

"

"

So Mr. Smith

(Concluded in Paragraph 168)

UNIT 68

Blends

Ld

1 *[shorthand outlines]*

Rd

2 *[shorthand outlines]*

Ted

3 *[shorthand outlines]*

Nt

4 *[shorthand outlines]*

Ten

5 *[shorthand outlines]*

KEY

1. Hailed, riddled, shoulder, hold, gold, fold.
2. Discovered, inspired, appeared, blizzard, recovered, inquired, stored.
3. Dominated, started, treated, toasted, tested, listed.
4. Couldn't, shouldn't, wouldn't, didn't, isn't, aren't, wasn't, doesn't.
5. Stand, understand, hesitantly, maintain, contained, retained, sustained.

168. READING AND WRITING PRACTICE

Tessie the Mannequin (Concluded)

[shorthand outlines]

/// **271**

Mr. Smith

The finished

$114.35

Mr. Smith

10

"Over my

19.

– Weare Holbrook

UNIT 69

✓169. **Word Families**

Per-

1 *(shorthand outlines)*

Post-

2 *(shorthand outlines)*

-tance

3 *(shorthand outlines)*

-cy

4 *(shorthand outlines)*

-ction

5 *(shorthand outlines)*

KEY

1. Perhaps, perform, permission, persuade, personal, persistent.
2. Postage, postal, postpone, postponed, postmaster, postman, post office.
3. Remittance, distance, assistance, substance, acceptance, resistance, instance.
4. Policy, accuracy, vacancy, literacy, agency, tendency, efficiency.
5. Collection, selection, election, reflection, correction, direction.

170. **READING AND WRITING PRACTICE**

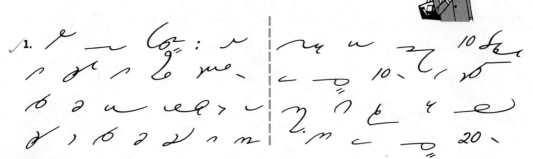

4. ... $38.90 ...

5. ...

$15.21 ...

✓ **171.** **Word Families**

-ance

1 *[shorthand outline]*

-ness

2 *[shorthand outline]*

-mission

3 *[shorthand outline]*

-let

4 *[shorthand outline]*

Man-

5 *[shorthand outline]*

KEY

1. Appearance, insurance, assurance, reassurance, ignorance, clearance.
2. Sickness, illness, fairness, darkness, thoughtlessness, helpfulness.
3. Commission, permission, submission, admission, omission, transmission, intermission.
4. Let, booklet, leaflet, pamphlet, bracelet.
5. Man, manpower, mankind, manage, manual.

172. **READING AND WRITING PRACTICE**

1. *[shorthand outlines]*

2.

3.

$450.

$250.

$200

$300.

$5

$10,000

$200

4.

Key to Gregg Notehand

(The number of words is indicated at the end of each group or article.)

PART 1

UNIT 2

3. The letters that would not be written in Notehand because they are not pronounced are: y in *day*; a in *mean*; a in *eat*; e in *save*; i in *main*; a in *steam*.

15. Reading and Writing Practice

1. Dave made the Navy team.
2. Dean made the Navy team the same day.
3. Dave may see me on May 10.
4. Meet me on East Main.
5. Amy made me stay home.
6. May I see your vase?
7. Dave may stay all day.
8. Fay made tea for me.
9. Amy saved the fee.
10. The date is May 12. (41)

UNIT 3

22. Reading and Writing Practice

1. Ray wrote me he leaves for Rome late in May.
2. Is the date May 26 or May 27?
3. I am twenty-one; I may vote.
4. Dear Lee: Monday is a free day for me. I have no classes. May I see you for an hour or so? Ray
5. I am free Friday. Is Ray free?
6. Dave's train is late.
7. I need more seed for the lawn.
8. I made a note to see Lee if he is free.
9. I have made no plans for May.
10. Mary drove me to Dave's store on East Main Street. (74)

UNIT 4

25. Reading and Writing Practice

1. Ray is staying home. He is feeling ill.
2. I need a heater for my store. I may buy a heater later.
3. I am a dealer in motor cars.

4. Ray Taylor made a date with me for Sunday.
5. Dave's train is thirty minutes late.
6. I have purchased a mail meter for our State Street retail store.
7. Do me a favor; leave a note for Lee to phone me Saturday evening at eight.
8. Ray is a home owner. He bought a home Friday.
9. I hear Lee is leaving Saturday for a rest. He may stay for a week or more.
10. Even though it is snowing, I feel I have to leave for home. (97)

UNIT 5

26. Reading and Writing Practice

1. He eats most meals at home.
2. Ray Macy owns four retail stores on Main Street.
3. Most of the main state roads need paving.
4. Ray fears he may have to leave college.
5. Rose Stevens is sailing for Rome in ten days.
6. I have known Rose for more than a year.
7. I have four seats for Saturday's meet. (46)

27. Reading and Writing Practice

1. Peter paid Mary's plane fare. Please pay him $120.
2. I am postponing our opening meeting for a day or so. I am feeling the heat.
3. Please leave the papers in a safe place.
4. Ray's reading speed is low.
5. I am opening a store for men.
6. Please see that he pays for the papers. He owes me for 20 papers.
7. He is preparing a paper for a sales meeting. (67)

28. Reading and Writing Practice

1. Ray Bates plays first base. He is a fair player.
2. I am opening a boating store on Main

Street on Saturday.

3. He placed an order for 1,500 labels, 1,200 post cards, 100 reams of plain paper.

4. Peter's neighbor, Lee Bates, is a paper dealer.

5. Peter's neighbor owns a sailboat. He is a born sailor.

6. He is preparing a brief for me.

7. He is an able labor leader. (72)

UNIT 6

30. Reading and Writing Practice

Group A

1. Most of our players are in shape for the opening of the polo season. It will open May 25.

2. I will trade in our car at the end of the Easter season. The dealer will pay me $450 for it.

3. He is promoting the sale of our mail meters in the East. Our mail meters are retailing for $50.

4. He will pay me $50 for preparing the brief. (71)

Group B

5. I hope most of the people will vote in the election for mayor. I will vote for Lee for mayor.

6. Our phone number is Main 4-1414.

7. Peter is in favor of trading in our car. It is old.

8. The least our neighbor will take for the vase is $10. He feels it is worth more. (51)

Group C

9. He bought a stove for our home. He will pay for it later.

10. Our motorboat is for sale.

11. He wrote me that he will place the deed in our safe. Most of our papers are in the safe.

12. Peter will leave for Spain the end of May. I will see Peter off. (41)

UNIT 7

31. Recall Chart

1. Save, saves, saved, stay, stays, stayed.

2. Free, freeing, freed, place, placing, placed.

3. Trade, trades, trading, open, opens, opening.

4. Deal, dealing, dealer, see, sees, seeing.

5. Heat, heating, heater, face, faced, facing.

6. Read, reading, reader, snow, snows, snowing.

7. Note, notes, noting, vote, votes, voting.

8. Know, knows, knowing, near, nears, nearer.

9. Hope, hopes, hoped, need, needs, needing.

10. Blame, blames, blaming, labor, labors, laborer.

11. Boat, boats, boating, prepare, prepares, preparing.

12. Mail, mails, mailing, mean, means, meaning.

13. Feel, feels, feeling, lease, leased, leasing.

14. Rate, rates, rating, motor, motors, motoring.

15. Is, a-an, for, have, I, am.

16. It, in, of, the, are-our, will.

17. I have, I am, I will, in the, in it, in our.

18. For it, for the, for our, of the, of our, it is.

32. Reading and Writing Practice

Group A

1. Please place the deeds in the safe.

2. The name of our neighbor is Lee Bates.

3. He drives a 1960 roadster.

4. Please leave the mail here.

5. He bought the heater for me wholesale. He saved me $50. (33)

Group B

6. Even though it snowed Monday, the main roads are open.

7. He paid me $100 for the boat. I am pleased.

8. Peter will have to meet me later in the day.

9. The phone is in the living room.

10. I hear he stayed home Saturday. (39)

Group C

11. He made me feel at home.

12. I am in favor of having the meeting later in May.

13. I have a feeling Mary is to blame for the error.

14. Ray will pay the note in 60 days.

15. He wrote me he needs more paper. (37)

Group D

16. The motorboat is for sale for $180. I feel $180 is a fair price.

17. Is he able to sail the boat? Sailing a boat

is an easy job for me.

18. Peter is training for the relay race.

19. I will have the phone placed near the rear door.

20. I will read the mail in the morning. (54)

UNIT 8

April 7

Spent the day sailing with Lee in Ray's boat. It was a good sailing day, but the breeze died down in the evening. I brought the boat in on the motor.

Had a note from Peter saying he will be home Friday for Easter. I have a job for him for the week in our Mailing Department. It will pay Peter $50 or $60. He needs the money.

Finished reading "A Tale of Two Cities."

Made phone call to Dad. He is fine.

April 8

Stayed home most of the day preparing for meeting of Sea Scouts this evening. Sea Scouts are hoping to raise $600 by May 15 for a new motorboat. It will not be easy.

Had a brief chat with our new neighbor. He is in the wholesale paper business. He is also a sailor. He was in the Navy for more than ten years.

Went bowling in the evening.

UNIT 9

33. Reading and Writing Practice

1. Our neighbor's pool is two feet deep.

2. Whom do I see to have our roof repaired?

3. I am moving to Maine soon.

4. Please remove Ray Blue's name from the payroll. It is true that he is leaving.

5. To whom do I have to pay the fee? Do I pay it to Lee, or do I pay it to Ray?

6. Judy will have to leave soon to catch the train.

7. I am leaving soon for a two-day meeting of retail food dealers in the Blue Room of the Hotel Drew. It is a routine meeting. (76)

34. Reading and Writing Practice

1. He will take the claim to court.

2. Our decreasing sales in the East make it hard to raise his pay.

3. He came to speak to the meeting of retail food dealers as a favor to me.

4. He makes a clear case for raising salaries.

5. Please keep our file of local dealers up to date.

6. I will take care of the brakes on our car.

7. In case I am late, please take care of the mail. (61)

35. Reading and Writing Practice

1. He gave me the brief two days ago.

2. The girl is making low grades in the course.

3. If he goes to the game Saturday, he will take me, too. He is the owner of two box seats.

4. Mary Gray is leaving in May. I know an able girl for the vacancy.

5. Please place Miss Gray's name on the payroll.

6. Grace is having two keys made for our safe. (57)

UNIT 10

36. Reading and Writing Practice

1. She showed me a pair of shoes she bought.

2. She gave me five shares of stock for Christmas.

3. Please show Mrs. Baker our line of shades. She will visit our store soon.

4. She will sell 20 shares of steel stock to raise cash to take care of the legal fees.

5. He made it clear that the shoe sale closed on May 10.

6. By making 10,000 sheets of note paper, she will save a great deal. (61)

37. Reading and Writing Practice

1. Mary Chambers teaches a speech course each evening from seven to nine. She wrote a book on the teaching of speech.

2. The chief feels we will reach our sales goal for May.

3. She came to the store for an easy chair. The easy chairs are on sale.

4. The chief chose Ray Bates to take care of the details of the meeting.

5. I hear the police chief made a speech at the grade school. (60)

38. Reading and Writing Practice

1. The agency is preparing a story for the evening paper.

2. James made two changes in the lease. He made a note of the errors on page 4.

3. She gave her age as twenty-six. She seems at least forty.

4. James Baker owns an agency for Jones Ranges in the East.

5. Please read page 2 of the deed with care. I made a change on page 2.

6. James will leave for Erie in June. (64)

39. Reading and Writing Practice

1. The light in my library is poor.

2. I have tried four times to reach Mary on the phone. Is Mary in town?

3. James Price likes to drive at night. He drove 50 miles two nights ago. Night driving tires most people.

4. I need a file for my private library. May I have a file soon?

5. Please sign my name to the note.

6. Mary's style of writing is like mine.

7. She sells a fine line of dry goods. The price is low. (68)

UNIT 11

40. Reading and Writing Practice

1. He said he enclosed several checks in the letter. The letter and checks will reach you next Friday night.

2. Needless to say, he is very pleased to have the checks.

3. She tells me she is in debt.

4. Ned Price will never settle the case. He feels he has a real grievance.

5. My memory is poor.

6. He made a perfect score on the engineering test.

7. Perry Page takes a test in French next Monday.

8. I am very pleased Mary came home for Easter. (74)

41. Reading and Writing Practice

1. Bill bid $1,500 for the business. His bid is low. I know he will get the business.

2. Jim Rivers is very busy. His business leaves him no time for fishing.

3. I shipped a special gift to him Friday. Did he get it?

4. James Mix set July 16 as the date for the meeting of our group. Please mail each member of the group a notice of the meeting.

5. The food bill is very big.

6. His grades in history are very low. If he fails, he will have to take the course again. (84)

42. Reading and Writing Practice

1. Miss Gray's firm gave her ten days' pay before letting her go.

2. The firm will close the 1st of July.

3. He urged her to enroll in the special course for clerks. She is an earnest girl.

4. The date set for the first teachers' meeting is September 8.

5. The June *Journal of Nursing* will reach her Monday.

6. Dear Dave: I hurt my leg hurrying to the train Wednesday night. My surgeon tells me I will have to stay in bed for five or six days.

Please take care of my mail in my absence. Ted Ellis (81)

43. Reading and Writing Practice

1. He showed me the letter he typed to the mayor of the city.

2. I urged her to visit me the next time she came to New York.

3. Mary baked a cake for James.

4. If the desk is shipped via freight, he will get it Monday.

5. Helen served tea in her home.

6. I searched every room in my home for the missing papers. I did not locate the papers.

7. The teacher checked the test papers with great care. (65)

UNIT 12

45. Reading and Writing Practice

1. Dear Mary: Would you like to have two seats to the July 15 game? When I purchased the tickets, I did not know my folks were going to visit me.

If you would like to have the tickets, phone or write me by July 12. Jim (39)

2. Dear James: Would it be of help to you when you write the minutes of our June meeting if I were to let you have the notes I made? If so, phone me; I shall be pleased to mail the notes to you. Fred (33)

3. Dear Henry: Will you be able to see Mary Green when she gets to New York Friday? She would like a little help with a term paper she is writing.

If I were here, I would help her myself; but I shall be in Erie Friday for a business meeting. James (45)

4. Dear Dad: I know you will be pleased to see the enclosed list of my mid-semester grades. You will notice I made two A's and two B's. I have a B in French, a course I felt I would fail.

You will remember you said you would mail me a check for $10 if my mid-semester grades were high. Did I earn the $10? Mary (57)

UNIT 13

46. No Business Runs Itself

Every businessman knows that no business can run itself. The day any business, any factory, any store, is left to run itself, it has passed its prime.

Every business needs a brain back of it, a brain to supply a rapid stream of plans. A business that is left to take care of itself will soon die. (55)

47. Reading and Writing Practice

Dear Mark: I am having a large party on Saturday, March 10, in my barn for Harry Star. Perhaps you know he has a ten-day leave from the Army starting March 5.

If you can make it, will you drive to the farm? If you do drive, would you pick up Harvey Green, who lives at 415 Parker Road.

Please let me know: (1) if you plan to be at the party, (2) if you will be able to pick up Harvey. Jerry (71)

48. Saving with a Purpose

Saving for no special goal can be very dull. It is true that a miser will save dollars so that he can admire them. Most people, though, need more specific goals than that. They have to save for a trip or a car or a home.

Do you have any special goals that you are striving to achieve through saving? If you do,

you are in for a real thrill when you achieve those goals. (64)

UNIT 14

49. Recall Chart

1. Who, whom, to, do, night, nights.
2. School, schools, schooling, check, checked, checking.
3. Keep, keeps, kept, tell, tells, teller.
4. Clear, clearer, clears, bill, bills, billing.
5. Go, goes, going, next, fixed, mixed.
6. Grade, grades, grading, urge, urged, urging.
7. Share, shares, sharing, hurry, hurrying, hurried.
8. Shape, shapes, shaped, agree, agreed, agrees.
9. Throw, throws, throwing, mark, marked, marks.
10. Bath, baths, bathing, part, parts, party.
11. Cheer, cheers, cheering, close, closing, closed.
12. Change, changes, changed, take, takes, taken.
13. Leave, leaving, left, grow, grows, growing.
14. Try, tries, tried, gain, gains, gaining.
15. Shall, be-by, you, when, would, were.
16. I shall, I shall have, by the, I would, he would, you would.
17. You are, you will, you will be, I would be, he would be, you would be.
18. For you, to you, have you, you may, he may, I may.

50. Plans for Annual Sales Meeting

Time: It would seem that the best time for our sales meeting is May 10 to May 20. It is a slow season in most territories. Please let me know, though, if you feel a later date would be better for you.

Place: The staff will meet each day from nine to five in the large room on the first floor. If a change of meeting place has to be made, I will post a notice near the elevator. Please try to get to each day's meeting on time.

Expenses: Each man will, of course, be paid his railroad or plane fare. He will be paid $15 a day to take care of his meals and hotel. The members of the staff will be my guests for a night game and a show.

Agenda: Each man will prepare in writing a list of sales helps that he would like for his territory. These lists will be a guide to me in planning our next major sales campaign.

Speakers: Every day we shall have a guest speaker for our morning meeting. After each speaker has finished his speech, you will be at liberty to ask him any questions that you feel relate to the selling of our line of fine papers.

Special Visits: On May 12 the staff will visit our paper mill in James River. You will have a chance to learn how our paper is made. I have arranged for three cars to take the staff to James River. (219)

UNIT 15

Making a Speech

Appearance
Select your clothing with care. Be sure you look "right." The feeling that you are well dressed promotes self-confidence.

Posture
Place your weight evenly on both feet and lean forward a little. Let your arms hang loosely from the shoulders. For a "change of pace" occasionally place your hands in back of you or put one hand in your pocket.

Platform Manners
As you wait your turn to speak, give your attention to any speakers who may precede you. Do not exceed the time that has been allotted to you. At the end of your speech thank your audience.

Delivery
Adopt the same tone you would use when speaking to friends. Be sure that everyone can hear you. Look at your audience. Do not look at the ceiling or on the floor.

UNIT 16

51. The Tonic of Praise

I know an official of a large firm who will not often praise a member of his staff for doing a fine job. He is afraid that he will be asked for a raise. The man who adopts that policy is not an asset to any business. He fails to realize a very vital factor — no man lives by bread alone.

Often a man will stay on a low-paying job if he has a boss who makes him feel that he is part of the team. That boss never hesitates to say, "Fine job, Fred," when Fred turns in a fine job. Every man likes praise from his boss even though it is not followed by a raise in salary.

The next time you see a man doing a fine job, pat him on the back! (119)

52. You Can Do It

The head of a large law firm bought a small sign for his desk that read, "You can do it." When he sees himself getting lost in an absorbing problem that he cannot solve, he will glance at his sign. The sign encourages him to try again. More often than not, he will get the answer to his problem from that "one more try."

All sorts of problems are facing our people in these trying times. To help solve these problems, we need more people who will not give up trying. (79)

53. Four Ways to Be a Happier Person

1. Learn early in life to smile readily. The happy man is he who can smile even though things are going badly. The man who can smile only when all is going smoothly is not likely to go far in business or in social life.

2. Have faith in your fellow man. Do not admit even remotely that any man will not treat you fairly, honestly, and sincerely.

3. Do not play favorites. Treat all people alike.

4. Finally, accept setbacks in good spirit. Remember that you cannot be on top all the time. (93)

UNIT 17

55. Tom

In a freshman college class, the teacher was trying to impress on the scholars the need for a large vocabulary. He said, "If you use a word five times, it will be yours for life." Soon I heard the girl in back of me start to mumble. With her eyes closed, this is what she was saying: "Tom, Tom, Tom, Tom, Tom." (53)

Proof

George, it seems, was not happy. About

thirty days ago he had let his neighbor have $500 as a loan. He made a mistake, though, by not asking his neighbor for a note or a letter acknowledging this loan. What is more, his neighbor gave no sign that he owed George the $500. Therefore, George was at a loss to know what to do.

Finally, he spoke with his father about the matter.

"That is easy, George," said the father. "This is what you are to do. Write him that you need the $1,000 today."

"You mean the $500," George said.

"No, I do not mean the $500. Write him that you need the $1,000. He will write back to you that he owes you only $500. Then you will have it in writing!" (133)

56. The Apple Eater

A boy is a born apple eater. At almost any time of the day he can be seen thoroughly enjoying the meat of an apple. A boy's eating of apples has no bearing on the state of his appetite. It matters not that at noon he may have had a thick, choice slice of roast beef—he still enjoys his apple. A farm boy eats apples all day. He has nests of choice apples mellowing in the barn. An apple is indeed the fruit of a boy.

As a boy ages, he enjoys apples less. If a man would rather die than be caught eating an apple in the street, if he can enjoy a chilly night by the fireside and not crave the meat of an apple, he has ceased to be a boy both at heart and in years. (124)

57. Reading and Writing Practice

Dear Roy: I will take care of securing the furniture for a lecture hall for our May 15 meeting. So far, I have not been able to procure the right type of projector so that John can show the pictures he made in China. Naturally, I am still trying.

He may have to postpone showing his pictures till the next meeting.

Please let me know if there is any more I can do. Sam (69)

58. Reading and Writing Practice

Dear Samuel: I had a note from John this morning saying that his schedule has been changed; hence, he cannot show his pictures at our annual meeting. Though I would not say it to him, I am actually greatly relieved. After seeing the pictures myself, I feel that they would bore the boys stiff; so lose no more sleep about a projector. Roy (61)

59. Vacation

If you have not made any provision for your annual vacation, plan to take at least a portion of it in the state of Maine. In Maine, the vacationer can enjoy fishing in the ocean. If he prefers a pretty lake in a natural location for a camping site, Maine offers him a large selection.

After you have been in Maine for even a brief vacation, you will realize that it is a perfect vacation state. (78)

60. Five Principles of Selling

The salesman who hopes to succeed must keep the following five principles ever before him:

1. He will be jealous of his firm's name.

2. He will learn all the selling features of his product.

3. He will not be too unhappy if he occasionally does not succeed in making a sale, but he will keep trying.

4. He will not speak ill of the other fellow's product; but, rather, he will plug the merits of his own.

5. He will follow up every lead he gets. (83)

61. Spare-Time Learners

Spare-time learners are often good learners. Their learning is helped by the fact that they are eager learners.

As an illustration, a boy by the name of Ed Burchell took a job as a full-time janitor in a hospital. He actually did not have a great deal of time for study. He did his cleaning in the lecture halls as the professors gave their lectures. It looked as though he were only cleaning, but as a matter of fact he took in the full lecture. At night, he would write in his notebook the meat of the lecture. Picking up his learning in bits, Burchell made himself a specialist on the structure of the head. Surgeons from all parts of the state looked to him for advice before they tried to do puzzling brain operations.

Burchell is a good illustration of a spare-time learner. (140)

UNIT 20

62. Be Calm

Honest Abe, with all his worries, was a master at keeping calm. When he was faced with a trying problem, he weighed all the facts first; then he took action. The following story illustrates why he was such a great man.

While the war was in its early weeks, no one in the Capitol had the whole story on the way the war was actually going.

Honest Abe took one of his cabinet members with him to visit the man who would have the facts—the general in charge of the armies. When the two of them arrived, the general was not at home. They had no choice but to wait. When the general finally arrived, they naturally thought that he would see them at once. But the general just walked past his waiting visitors, going right to his suite on the top floor. (135) (Concluded in Paragraph 63)

63. Be Calm (Concluded)

The visitors kept on waiting. The cabinet member, who had a quick temper, was quite annoyed. He asked the general's aide to tell the general that he had guests.

The man came back quite embarrassed. The general was already in bed; he would gladly see his visitors the following day. The cabinet member was a picture of rage. He tried to persuade Honest Abe to fire the general at once, but he did not succeed in persuading him.

Honest Abe said to him: "Let us not fret about the general's bad manners. I will be glad to watch the general's horse for him if he will win victories for us!" Honest Abe always thought twice before he took action. (118)

64. Memory

"I am sorry that I did not recall the name of that man who just left. I used to know him when I was in charge of a unit in Mexico City." That was the view that Robert E. Lee took when a man whom he had met once, ages ago, came in to see him.

Lee's memory for names was quite unusual. Once he saw a human face, he would always remember it. That trait was of great value to him while he was an Army general.

Lee's unique memory won the admiration of his enemies as well as of his allies.

Few will argue with the fact that Robert E. Lee was a great man. Those who were close to him agreed that a part of his greatness might be traced to his unique memory. (125)

UNIT 21

65. Recall Chart

1. Cross, crossed, crossing, cut, cuts, cutting.

2. Shop, shops, shopped, rough, roughly, rougher.

3. Broad, broadly, broader, full, fully, fuller.

4. Talk, talked, talks, book, books, booked.

5. Rarely, fairly, really, swim, swims, swimmer.

6. Annoy, annoyed, annoying, wheel, wheels, wheeling.

7. Toy, toil, soil, equip, equipped, equips.

8. Secure, securely, secures, thick, thicker, thickly.

9. Nature, natural, naturally, human, humans, humanly.

10. Equal, equals, equally, view, viewed, views.

11. Schedule, schedules, scheduling, square, squares, squarely.

12. Ration, rations, rationed, weigh, weight, weighed.

13. Motion, motions, motioned, win, winning, winner.

14. Caution, cautions, cautioned, thrill, thrills, thrilling.

15. What, with, there-their, was, this, about.

16. What is, what are, what will, there is, there are, there will.

17. With the, with these, with this, it was, I was, he was.

18. About it, about that, about this, in this, on this, for this.

66. Follow the Leader

Whether he likes it or not, whether he knows it or not, every man in business is playing the game of "follow the leader." In all that he does, he is either following or leading.

If you look about you, you can quickly tell those who lead from those who follow. If the leader puts up a modern factory, its special features will be copied by others. If each season he dreams up unique ways of improving his business, other firms will have copied his plans before the season is past.

There are firms that follow all their lives; there are others that always lead.

It may be much easier to follow, but it is actually more thrilling to lead. The man who follows has the easier time. He need not take any risks; he need only adopt methods when their value has already been proved. He need not take the risk of giving vital jobs to members of his staff; he can fill those jobs with people who have proved their capacity on the staff of another firm.

But for all this, who would follow if he might be a leader? People who enjoy life look for more than an easy time — they look for a thrill from life. Only the small man with no real ambition will be happy to adopt what others have tried for him. (215)

The Miser

One day a miser who never stopped worrying about the safety of his possessions thought he would sell them all. With the money his possessions brought him, he bought a large piece of silver that he buried next to a wall near his home.

Each day he would dig up the piece of silver to admire it. He dug it up so often that a thief noticed the miser's actions. One day the thief followed the miser to see what he was doing. Of course, he saw the great treasure. Late that night he stole it.

The next day the poor miser saw that his piece of silver had been removed — stolen! He did so much screaming that a number of his neighbors came to see what the noise was all about. After learning the cause, a neighbor said, "Enough of that screaming! Place a stone in the hole; then imagine that it is the piece of silver. It will serve the same purpose as the silver!" The moral of the tale is: The true value of money is not in its possession but in its use. — *Adapted from Aesop's Fables* (166)

UNIT 22

Woodrow Wilson

Education
1. Early education in the South.
2. Entered Princeton University in 1875.
3. Good debater but not great scholar.
4. Served as professor and later as president of Princeton University.

Politics
1. Democrats elected Wilson Governor of New Jersey in 1910.
2. Democrats elected Wilson President in 1912. His election was made possible by split in Republican Party.

Domestic Policy
1. Democratic campaign called for lower tariff. Wilson proposed and Congress passed Underwood Tariff Act.
2. Wilson proposed and Congress passed Federal Reserve Act.

Foreign Policy
1. Wilson asked for neutrality at start of war in 1914.
2. Wilson's policy approved by people who elected him for second term in 1916 by narrow margin.

UNIT 23

68. Easy Profit

The following is the story of a great senator who was known for his thrift. He never gave his clothes a thought; therefore, he was often shabby in appearance, which annoyed his daughter, who undertook to take care of him. What is more, she never could get him to buy any clothes.

One day, though, she did get him to a clothing store, in which he tried on a few overcoats. The senator liked one of the overcoats very much; in fact, he even asked the price. "$125," said the clerk. The senator dropped the overcoat as though it had been a hot potato.

"I never saw an overcoat in my life for which I would pay that price," he snapped. With that, he left the store.

A little later his daughter came back.

"Here is $90," she said to the clerk. "Please put that overcoat aside. Then in ten days call my father on the phone. Tell him the store is having a sale. Tell him the overcoat he liked is selling for $35. If I know him, he should be here in a hurry!"

The clerk agreed. In ten days he got the senator on the phone. The senator came in on schedule, said it was high time that they charged a fair price for the overcoat, paid the $35, and left.

Back at the nation's Capitol, the overcoat was the natural object of the admiring eyes of his fellow senators.

"That is a mighty fine coat you have there, Jim," said one senator. "It is my size, too."

"I should say it is a fine coat. I bought it at a sale. It was originally $125, but I had an opportunity to get it for $35."

"I'll give you $50 for it," said the senator.

Jim, who could never pass up the opportunity to make a quick dollar, said, "It's a deal." Paying Jim the $50, the senator left with the overcoat under his arm.

It was four or five months before the senator's daughter had the courage to tell her father that his easy profit of $15 had really cost them $75! (359)

69. Temper

My cousin had without a doubt the worst temper of any girl in our town. In her youth she could always have her own way.

When she married a timid Army officer, we all thought that he would soon be a very henpecked spouse. We were surprised, though, when after several months she was as meek as a mouse. We had an opportunity to ask her about it one day. Blushing a little, she said: "One day after the wedding, there was a pair of trousers over a chair in our bedroom. I was ready to put them in the closet when Joe said, 'Put them on, dear.'

"'But why should I put them on, honey?' I asked. The trousers were about a foot too big at the waist. He was so firm, though, that I put them on.

"'Do they fit?' he asked.

"'Now, sweetheart, of course they do not fit.' I said. As he sat me down on his knee, he said without so much as a smile on his face,

'Then remember which one of us wears the trousers in our house!'" (159)

70. A Boy

I have a great love for young boys. A boy is a man in cocoon. One cannot tell how he will turn out. He may make or unmake kings, write books, be a famous lawyer or a great singer.

Of one thing you may be sure — every man was once a young boy!

It would be thrilling to turn back the clock on the young, hungry Corsican lad who was such a problem in his youth. At 26, he was master of every phase of warfare. When he saw that the treasury of France was in bad shape, he said in a strong voice, "Leave it to me; I will arrange things." That young man, with a singleness of purpose, actually changed the course of history. (111) (Concluded in Paragraph 71)

71. A Boy (Concluded)

Then there was a boy by the name of Abraham Lincoln, who at the age of twelve had never worn a pair of shoes. This lank, lean, frank boy lived a life that was not easy. To make a living in his youth, he split logs. When he was a young man, he ran a grocery store that was soon bankrupt.

I also cannot help thinking of a thin, anxious boy who was born on the wrong side of the tracks in our town. He used to pick up coal along the tracks so that the house in which he lived could be warm. The other day I stopped at the bank to make a loan. That same boy was treasurer of the bank. He passed on the loan that helped me carry on my business.

Have patience when you are dealing with a young boy. Be frank with him. There may be a day when he will make a deep impression on the future. (135)

72. Dither

The cashier of the paper in which the famous writer Henry Watterson ran a column for some time was always in a dither, for each day his cash drawer was out of balance. Whenever Watterson felt the need, he would fill his pockets from the till without telling a soul. One fine day, the treasurer, with the cashier in tow, came to see Watterson. "Frankly, it is not that we object to your taking whatever you need — you are welcome to it. But it would help us a great deal it in the future you would jot down on a piece of paper the sum you take. If you will leave that paper in the cash drawer, it will help us keep our books straight." Watterson said that it would be done, though he was not happy about it.

The next morning, just before lunch, the treasurer saw Watterson coming to the cashier's cage. After helping himself from the till, Watterson made a few scratches on a piece of paper. When that was done, he placed the paper in the drawer. As soon as he left the cage, the treasurer made a dash for the cash drawer. In the drawer from which the cash had been taken was a note which said, "I took it all. H. W." (196)

UNIT 25

73. The Lark and Her Young Ones

A lark who had her nest of young ones on a wheat farm had to leave them each day to go out to find food for them. As the wheat ripened, the mother warned her young larks to tell her all they learned while she was gone.

One day the man who owned the farm came down to look at the crops. "It is high time," he said to his son, "that the grain should be cut. Tell all our kind friends to come early in the morning to lend us a hand with the reaping."

When the mother lark returned, her young ones anxiously asked her to move them at once to a place of safety. "There is lots of time," she said. "If the farmer waits for his kind friends to help him, there will be no harvesting in the morning."

The following day the farmer came over again. Finding the wheat ripening rapidly, he said to his son, "There is not a second to be lost. We cannot rely on our friends; therefore, we must call in our relatives. Tell them all to be here in the morning to help us with the harvesting." (164) *(Concluded in Paragraph 74)*

74. The Lark and Her Young Ones *(Concluded)*

The larks again asked their mother to move

them. "If that is all, don't worry. We have plenty of time. Relatives have their own interests to look after. But I want you to keep listening when I am absent." Eventually, the farmer came back again. Finding the grain almost fully ripe, he said to his son: "We can't wait any longer for our friends or relatives. We must harvest the crop ourselves in the morning." When the mother learned of this, she said: "Then it is high time to be off. If the master has now made up his mind to do the job himself, then the grain will really be cut." So the mother moved her nest to the country. The following morning, the farmer came with his sickle to cut the wheat.

Moral: If you want a task done well, do it yourself. — *Adapted from Aesop's Fables* (134)

75. Study

On finishing college, two boys — one named Brown, the other named Smith — took jobs in business. Both promptly showed that they were going places in business. At twenty-five, both were earning fine salaries. It seemed that both were on their way to the top.

Smith did reach the top. At forty, he had climbed to the position of treasurer of his firm. Brown seemed to mark time when he reached thirty. Why had Smith climbed to the top so rapidly while Brown stood still? The answer is this: Smith never stopped studying. He welcomed every opportunity to better himself through reading or studying.

Brown, on the other hand, claimed that he didn't have time to read or study.

When a person stops studying, it is time to be alarmed. (124)

UNIT 26

77. Fast Shrinkage

An important businessman we know was overweight, and his wife was alarmed about his health. She suggested that he try to bring his weight down while on his farm. He took the suggestion; and a short time later he walked over to the general store, where he promptly picked out a pair of overalls in which he would take workouts.

As the clerk was wrapping the overalls, the man thought of a fact of importance that he had overlooked. "Wait a bit," he said. "Those overalls fit me now, but shortly I hope to work off a lot of weight. Perhaps I ought to buy a smaller pair."

The clerk shook his head and frowned. "Brother, if you can shrink as fast as these overalls can, you will be doing pretty well!" he said, and went on with the wrapping of the overalls. (131)

The Measure of a Man

I suggest that the place to take the true measure of a man is by his fireside, where he puts aside his mask so that you can soon learn what type of man he is. I do not care how important he is in business or what his work may be; I do not care whether people think he is a hero or a villain. If his young ones shrink from him when he gets home at night and if his wife cringes every time she has to ask him for a $5 bill, he is a fraud.

But if his young ones rush up to the door to meet him at night and if love can be seen on the face of his wife every time she hears his footsteps, you can be sure he is pure.

I can overlook much in that man who would rather make a fellow man swear than a woman weep. I cannot but honor a man who cherishes a smile from his wife more than he fears the frown of all his neighbors. — W. C. Brann (149)

78. Surprise

A doctor out of school just a short time hung up his shingle in a small town, but it was some time before a patient stepped inside his office.

When a man finally came in, the doctor thought it wise to impress him with his importance. Therefore, he picked up the phone and barked, "I have 20 patients on my list today, and I don't believe I can get to the hospital to perform that brain operation before six in the evening." Then he hung up and turned to his visitor with a smile. "Now, what seems to be paining you, my good man?"

"Nothing is paining me," his surprised visitor informed him. "I am here to hook up your phone, sir." (112)

79. Loyalty

In a city located on the West Coast, there lived a noted lawyer who had a Chinese servant by the name of Sam. The two had lived together for a long time and had great affection for each other.

But one morning, as Sam greeted his master, he hesitated a little and then informed him, "Next week I must leave you. Before I go, I will hire for you a better man." The lawyer waited, thinking that Sam would say more; but Sam just stood silently.

"So you are going to leave me; I do not pay you enough. That Doctor Sanders who visited us last week — he knows what a treasure you are. Don't be a fool, Sam. Your pay will be adjusted. Say no more." The noted lawyer thought that that would end the matter. Instead, Sam indicated that he was in earnest. "Next week I leave you — I go to China," he said. (144) (Continued in Paragraph 80)

80. Loyalty (Continued)

"I see," added the lawyer. "You are going back for a wife. All right, bring her home. You can return in two months. I will see that she is provided for. I will also get the papers that are needed." He thought he had Sam persuaded, but he was wrong.

"I go to China next week; no papers are needed. I will never come back," Sam said.

"By heaven, you shall not go!" said the strong-headed lawyer.

"By heaven, I will!" said Sam heatedly.

It was the first time that Sam had spoken that way to his master.

The lawyer pushed his chair back and then added, "Sam, you must forgive me. I spoke without thinking. I do not own you. But," he pleaded, "what have I done? Why do you leave me? You know I need you more than I ever needed you before." (127) (Continued in Paragraph 81)

81. Loyalty (Continued)

"I am going to China to die!"

"Nonsense. You can die here. I promised you many months ago that I would ship your body back to China if you die before I do. I meant it."

"I will die in four weeks, two days."

"What!"

"Many weeks ago my brother was tried for a tremendous crime. He is now in prison. He must die. He has a wife who is going to have a baby before many days. In China," he added, "they accept a brother to die in his place. I will go to China. I will give my money to my brother. He will live; I will die."

The lawyer started to speak again but stopped. He thought he understood men, but it took him a long time to grasp the immensity of Sam's sacrifice. (124) *(Concluded in Paragraph 82)*

82. Loyalty *(Concluded)*

The following day, with a minimum of fuss, another Chinese boy by the name of Joe arrived to administer the lawyer's affairs. After some preliminary instructions from Sam, Joe took over. He was just like Sam in many ways. Sam terminated his service to his master without saying good-by. He went to China, where he was beheaded four weeks and two days almost to the minute from the time he had spoken to his master. His brother was set free after Sam's death and returned to his wife.

The lawyer's house goes along about as usual, save that the master calls for Sam when he should say "Joe." At such times there comes to him a kind of clutch at his heart, but he keeps his thoughts to himself. — *Adapted from Elbert Hubbard's Notebook* (126)

UNIT 28

83. Recall Chart

1. Vow, vowed, vows, run, runs, runner.
2. Sing, singing, singer, long, longed, longer.
3. Bank, banks, banker, friend, friends, friendly.
4. Come, comes, coming, deduct, deducts, deduction.
5. Bind, binds, bindery, meant, mental, mentally.
6. Hand, hands, handle, minute, minutes, minimum.
7. Name, names, named, guide, guides, guided.
8. Prompt, promptly, promptness, smooth, smoothly, smoother.
9. Start, starts, started, unite, unites, united.
10. Under, over, should, and, suggest, work.
11. Could, opportunity, which, important-importance, short, where.
12. Underneath, undergo, undertake, overcome, oversee, overpaid.
13. Increase, insert, forget, foreclose, begin, below.
14. Under the, under that, under these, over the, over them, over my.
15. I should, he should, you should, I could be, he could be, you could be.
16. Which is, in which, for which, I could see, he could see, you could see.

84. Green Dye

It seems that young Tom Murphy was swimming in the Hudson River. Before he went swimming, Tom had black hair, black eyebrows, and black eyelashes.

When Tom had his fill of swimming in the waters of the Hudson, he put on his overalls and went home. When Mama Murphy saw him, she fainted, for there was her little boy with green hair, green eyebrows, and green eyelashes. All his hair had turned green from the dyes that had been dumped in the river by the blanket firm that had its plant nearby.

As soon as she realized what had happened, she grabbed Tom by the ear and marched him off to the bathroom, where she scrubbed him almost down to the bone, but to no avail. She was very angry and finally wrote a scathing letter to the blanket firm. "If you don't get that stuff off, I will take the matter up with my lawyer," she wrote.

The letter was given to the head chemist to answer. He promptly wrote Mama Murphy the following letter:

Dear Madam: I am sorry that your son Tom came home with green hair after swimming in the Hudson River below our mills; but, as the river is posted, we cannot be blamed for his color.

We have a perfectly legal right to make green blankets at our plant, and we also have a permit to dump the surplus dyestuffs in the river.

I might mention that we have been brought to court about this matter before, madam; but we have always won. Only last spring a man came to us with a purple goatee because he had fallen out of a boat one day when we were making a large batch of babies blankets. We did all we could to please this man and even agreed to have him dry cleaned without cost to him; but he took the case to court, where he lost.

If you will bring Tom over to the plant, we shall be glad to soak him for a few minutes in our vat No. 8 in the hope that we can bring back the natural color of his hair. I am sorry to say, though, that we use fast dyes in our blankets and guarantee them against running or fading.

The only other suggestion that I can make is that we dip Tom in a boiler of black dye, which will be a less offensive shade than green. I will call you the next time we have a run of black lap robes.

As a matter of fact, madam, you ought to be glad that your boy didn't have a mustache when he swam in the river; or matters might have been worse if we had been emptying the overflow from a run of striped woolen mufflers.

I will grant you that green hair is not a very popular shade; but at least his hair and eyebrows do not clash, as we say in the wool industry. Sincerely yours, Chief Chemist (459)

UNIT 29

Stages in Personality Development

1. Stage of Dependence. Everyone starts life completely dependent on others. A few are never weaned entirely from this stage and always lean on others.

2. Stage of Comfort and Eating. A child's interests during the first couple of years of life are bodily comfort and food.

3. Show-Off Stage. Shortly after he learns to walk, the child likes to get attention by showing off the things he can do. "Watch me" is a phrase he uses very often.

4. Stage of Low-Boiling Point. About the time he is three, his parents start to worry about the mischief he gets into. They are always stopping him just as he is doing the most important things. He doesn't like being stopped and gets angry and screams and bites.

5. Gang Stage. Toward the end of grade school, boys begin to form boys' clubs and girls form girls' clubs. They start to work as groups.

UNIT 30

85. Brief-Form Review

1. A-an, is, for, have, am, I.
2. It, in, of, the, are-our, will.
3. Shall, be-by, you, when, would, were.
4. What, with, their-there, was, this, about.
5. Under, over, should, could, opportunity, which.
6. And, suggest, work, importance-important, short, where.

87. Ten Signs of a Mature Man

1. He can say "no" to himself, even on difficult questions, and make it stick.

2. He can take suggestions in good spirit and profit by them. They do not send him into a rage. He knows that suggestions will probably help him to grow.

3. He has close friends among men and women. His friendships are long-lasting.

4. He can look into a question or a problem with care and thought and make up his mind on what course to follow; but he does not act on impulse alone.

5. He promptly admits a weakness, but at the same time he can realize his strong points without being vain about them.

6. He can put aside his failures of yesterday and look to the future. (117) (Concluded in Paragraph 88)

88. Ten Signs of a Mature Man (Concluded)

7. He is tolerant. The immature man, who will find success difficult, often criticizes those who do not believe as he does.

8. He thinks for himself. He analyzes. He raises many questions. He does not follow fads or buy on impulse. It is necessary to sell him.

9. He is calm. When necessary, he faces a crisis on an even keel. If the other fellow insists on arguing — probably even loses his temper — he smoothes things out.

10. He follows a long-range plan. He arranges his finances so that he can pay for what he needs. He does not get into debt if he can avoid it. He faces the future; he does not live in the past. (121)

UNIT 31

89. Strictly the Truth

The captain of a certain vessel once wrote the following sentence in his log: "The mate was drunk tonight." When the mate became normal and the sentence was brought to his attention, he was very angry. He pleaded with the captain to scratch out the sentence. He said that he had never been drunk before, and he never intended to be drunk again. But the captain insisted that the entry must stand. "In this log we write the whole truth," he said.

The following week the mate kept the log; and in it he wrote, "The captain was sober tonight." (94)

90. Time to Forget

Very often we can remember better by remembering less. Some of us have a tendency to try to remember too much.

Suppose that you have to go to the dentist or attend a meeting or a dinner. Make a note in your date book of the time you are to see the dentist or attend the meeting or dinner. Don't try to keep these facts in the front of your mind all day.

Use good sense in what you remember. It is evident that there is no use in trying to remember a phone number you may never call again. It is also evident that there is no use in remembering all the bus or train schedules. Just the part you will use is worth remembering. For your guidance, keep these two facts in mind:

1. Remember that which you will use over and over again.

2. Forget that which you will not use in the near future. (146)

91. Big Business and Small Business

The person who maintains for a moment that our country can survive without small business is lacking in good judgment. Every fact of our economic life tends to prove that big business cannot get along without small business. It is an elementary fact that you cannot add to the stature of a dwarf by cutting off the legs of the big fellow. Our entire business structure is a unit just like a machine. It is made up of an assortment of big parts and little parts; and each part, large or small, does a fundamental job.

Big business needs small business; small business needs big business.—*Abraham Lincoln* (106)

UNIT 32

92. Hard Work

A hard-working farmer was getting tired and made up his mind to get a hired man to help him. When the hired man came, he set him to work in the garden chopping wood. Toward the middle of the morning, the farmer went down to see how the hired man was getting along. To his amazement, he found the wood in the garden all chopped.

The following day, the farmer asked the hired hand to get the wood stored in the shed. This was a hard job that required a lot of lifting, and the farmer figured that the job would keep the man busy a long time. But by noon the man had the job done and was ready for another task. (106) (*Concluded in Paragraph 93*)

93. Hard Work (*Concluded*)

On the third day, the old farmer, thinking that the hired hand was entitled to a light assignment for a change, called him over and told him to sort out the potatoes in the bin.

"Put the good ones in one pile, those that you are not sure about in another, and throw out the spoiled ones." An hour later the old farmer went back to see how the job was coming. Suddenly he found the hired man stretched out cold in the field, with almost nothing done.

After throwing cold water on the man's face and bringing him to, the old farmer wanted to know what had happened. "The thing that killed me was figuring out which pile each potato should be put in!" answered the hired man. (114)

94. Boiling Water

One day, a capable and reliable young doctor was asked if all those pots of boiling water that the country doctors always seem to call for in the movies are necessary.

"I wondered about that, because it is a lot of trouble; and all the doctor has to have available is one pot in which to boil a needle," he said. "But one of my old professors in school gave a plausible and acceptable answer. He said: 'If you have to bring a baby into the world in the home, the thing that will give you the most trouble is the father. He will make it impossible for you to work efficiently; therefore, it is advisable to keep him busy. Tell him that it is possible for him to help by getting all the pots obtainable and boiling lots of hot water. Many farmhouses have coal or wood stoves, and keeping the fire hot and the water boiling will get the father out of the way. After it is over and you have patted him on the back, you have part of the ingredients for steaming hot coffee.'" (184)

UNIT 33

95. Wasted Time

Every morning you are handed 24 beautiful hours. They are one of the few useful things in life you get free of charge, whether you want them or not. Your schooling must be paid for, and even your health costs money to achieve or regain. But these 24 wonderful hours do not cost you a penny. If you were the most powerful man in the world, it would not be possible for you to buy another hour. If you were the poorest beggar, not a single minute could be taken from you.

What do you do with this wonderful treasure? Do you use it gainfully? Remember, you must use it at once; you cannot save it up for your old age.

Wasted time is a greater tragedy than wasted money or wasted health. Either of these you may regain with thoughtful effort, but time wasted is gone for good.

Be grateful for the time that is given to you. (151)

96. On the Alert

Waiting in the conference room of a steamship office to be interviewed for a job as a wireless operator, a number of applicants filled the room with such a confusion of conversation that they were not conscious of the constant flow of dots and dashes that were coming over a loudspeaker. About that time, another man entered and was content to sit by himself in one corner. All of a sudden he snapped to attention, walked confidently into the private office of the president, and soon came out with a cheerful smile on his face.

"Say," one of the group called out, "how did you get in before us? We were here first."

"One of you would have had the job if you had been concerned with the announcement coming over the loudspeaker."

"Concerned with what announcement?" they asked in confusion.

"Why, the code," the stranger answered. "It said, 'The man I need must constantly be on the alert. The first man who gets this message and comes into my private office will get a contract as an operator on one of my ships.'" (181)

97. Hearing Aid

An old but competent gentleman often complained about his deafness. He had completed a long and successful business career and had amassed considerable wealth. His physician had tried for a long time to compel him to get a commercial hearing aid, but without success.

The old man learned, though, that our company had just completed a comfortable hearing aid that combined the good features of all the others on the market; and he made up his mind to try it.

Two weeks later he returned to tell us that he could hear conversations with comparative ease, even in the next room. "Your friends and relatives must be happy that you now hear so well," I said.

"I haven't told them," he confessed with a chuckle. "I have been sitting around listening — and do you know what? I have already changed my will twice!" (145)

98. A Little Late

In the offices of the Memphis Transportation Company, there worked a young, reliable secretary who was quite an efficient transcriber and who would consistently turn out fine transcripts of whatever was dictated to her.

But she was in the habit of coming a few minutes late every day. Her boss had warned her many times and even threatened to have her transferred, but to no avail.

One day, he reached his wit's end and told

her that he was going to suspend her for one day without pay and asked her when she wanted to take that day.

She thought it over carefully and then transmitted the following message to him, "If it is all right with you, I think I should like to use it up by coming in a little late every day." (134)

UNIT 34

99. A Tooth for a Tooth

Some time ago, a number of business companies made it a practice to mail a person expensive goods that he had not ordered and then bill him for them.

One day, a doctor in Buffalo got such a package with the following letter of transmittal: "We are taking the liberty of sending you three exceptional ties. Because these excellent ties have the approval of thousands of professional men and business executives who are careful dressers, we know that you will like them. Please send us $10."

As you might expect, the doctor was considerably annoyed. He answered: "I am taking the liberty of sending you $10 worth of extra-fine pills. These excellent pills have helped thousands of professional men and business executives, and I am sure that they will help you. Please accept them in payment of the exceptional ties that you sent me." (156)

100. Shock

One morning, a couple that had been married for only a few days had a delightful surprise delivered to them by the mailman — two complimentary tickets to the best show in town. It developed, though, that the donor neglected to give his name.

All day long the couple wondered, "Who could have sent those desirable tickets?" After considerable debate, they decided to use the tickets.

They enjoyed the show, but on their return home they experienced a definite shock. All their wedding presents had been stolen. There was a note fastened directly to one of the pillows in the bedroom that read, "Now you know!" (111)

101. No Smoking!

I have always had a definite sympathy for those who have the tobacco habit. That is, I have always had it the last nine days since I reformed and gave up smoking myself. The result is that my head has recently been cleared of fumes and my blood of nicotine; therefore, I have been able to review and reflect on the entire problem of smoking. I am happy to report here the results of my reflections and researches.

The average smoker spends $127.50 in twelve months on his habit — enough to buy some 45 good books or a comfortable chair or a restful holiday at some resort. All of this goes up in smoke.

Figuring still further, I uncovered the revealing fact that, if I had never started smoking, I would have saved $3,800 — enough for an excellent car or a transcontinental trip or a first payment on a desirable residence. (169) (Concluded in Paragraph 102)

102. No Smoking! (Concluded)

I have heard the financial problems of our times discussed and described and explained in many different ways, but I think I have discovered their real cause. In short, if there were no tobacco, the average home would have more than $20 a month extra at its disposal for groceries, rent, or furniture. Our financial troubles would be completely dissolved, dismissed, disposed of!

After nine days of refraining from smoking, I have discovered that civilization is not dying of poverty or war but of tobacco. How can we dispose of our larger problems and transact our business when our eyes are constantly blinded with smoke?

As I say, it is nine days since I discovered my mistake. Aside from the fact that I have been miserable the whole time, these have been the happiest days of my life. I am free at last; and as I swore off for one month, I still have twenty-one days of freedom left before I am plunged back into slavery again. I am counting those days! (176)

103. Recall Chart

1. Attend, attends, attendance, consider, considered, considerable.

2. Threaten, threatens, threatened, complete, completely, completed.

3. Chances, ounces, notices, informed, conformed, performed.

4. Fixes, mixes, gases, transmit, transmits, transmitted.

5. Spend, depend, expend, examine, examines, examined.

6. Procure, procures, procured, excel, excelled, excellent.

7. Hard, harder, hardly, depress, depressed, depression.

8. Bold, bolder, boldly, deserve, deserves, deserving.

9. Equal, equals, equally, repay, repaid, repayment.

10. Equip, equipped, equipment, receipt, receipts, receipted.

11. Ship, shipped, shipment, displace, displaced, displacement.

12. Reason, reasons, reasonable, disappoint, disappointed, disappointment.

13. Desire, desirable, compute, computed, waste, wasted.

14. Thought, thoughtful, sing, sink, transfer, transferred.

15. Question, yesterday, send, probable, difficult, into.

16. Questions, questioning, questioned, questionable, unquestioned, improbable.

17. Probably, sends, sending, sender, difficulty, difficulties.

104. Medicine Cabinet

Recently a young couple invited me to their home for a weekend. The morning after the weekend, they got up and started for work; but I didn't get up until noon. I had my face completely soaped for shaving when I cut my ear with the razor.

More angry than hurt, I pulled open the medicine cabinet to see if I could find a styptic pencil; and out from the top shelf fell a little paper packet containing nine needles. The packet fell into the soapy water in the bowl, where it fell apart, leaving nine needles at large in the bowl.

I was, of course, not in the best shape to recover nine needles from a bowl. For a minute or two I groped around in the bowl and soon was successful in getting four of the needles in the palm of one hand and three in the palm of the other. Two of them, I could not find. If I had given some careful thought to the matter, I wouldn't have done that. A man with lather on his face and whose ear is bleeding and who has four needles in one hand and three in the other may be said to have reached what is probably the lowest-known point of human efficienecy.

I attempted to shift the needles in my right hand to the palm of my left hand, but I couldn't get them off my right hand. Wet needles cling to you. In the end, I wiped the needles off on a bath towel. Hunting for seven needles in a bath towel is the hardest job in which I have ever engaged. I found five of them.

Grave thoughts came to me of what might transpire if a person used the towel.

I sat down on the edge of the tub; and, after considerable thought, I made up my mind that the thing to do was to wrap the towel in paper and take it with me. I also decided to leave a note for my friends, explaining the whole thing to them. I looked in every nook and cranny of the house, but I could not find a pencil.

I then had a sudden inspiration — I could write a message with a lipstick. The wife might have one lying around; and, if so, it might be in the medicine cabinet. I discovered what looked like the metal tip of one, and I got two fingers around it and began to pull — it was under a lot of things. Every item in the medicine cabinet began to slide. Bottles broke in the bowl and on the floor. Red, green, and white liquids spurted over me. It took me about thirty-five minutes to get the mess all together in the middle of the bathroom floor.

I made no attempt to put things back in the cabinet. I felt it would take a steadier hand than mine. Before I got out (with but one side of my face shaved), I left a note saying that I was afraid there were needles in the bathtub and in the bowl and that I had taken their towel and that I would call up and tell them all about it—I wrote it in shoe polish with the end of a toothbrush.

I did not keep my promise. I have not had the courage. I guess my friends believe that I messed up their bathroom and stole their towel on purpose. I don't know for sure, because they did not call me up either! — *James Thurber* (536)

UNIT 36

Essentials of a Good Savings Program

I. Have a definite plan
   A. A plan will tell you where your money is going.
   B. Without a plan, you will often neglect providing for emergencies.
II. Be sure your money is safe
   A. Some people put money in a hole in the ground.
   B. There are many safe places:
      1. Savings banks
         a. No checks but you get interest.
         b. You may take out money at any time without loss of interest.
         c. Savings are protected by government.
      2. Government Savings Bonds, Series E
III. Put your savings where they will earn interest
   A. In a checking account you have convenience in making checks but receive no interest.
   B. There are two types of interest:
      1. Simple
      2. Compound
         a. Most banks pay compound interest.
         b. Interest is usually compounded quarterly.

UNIT 37

105. Table Conversation

There is one extremely important detail of conduct at dinners or anniversary parties that I have never seen discussed satisfactorily in etiquette books — what to do when you inconveniently find both the person on your left and the person on your right busily engaged in conversation with somebody else.

You have perhaps turned briefly from Mrs. Jones on your right to take care of some minor matter; and when you turned back, you found her already engaged in conversation with Mr. Smith on her other side.

So you quickly wheel about to your left, only to find yourself confronted by the back of Mrs. Brown. Consequently, you are left looking directly in front of you with a roll in one hand and nothing in particular to do with your face. Should you sit and cry softly to yourself or should you start playing with your knife and fork? (154) *(Continued in Paragraph 106)*

106. Table Conversation *(Continued)*

Of course, the main thing is to be careful not to let your hostess notice that you are not engaged in conversation. If she spots you seemingly looking into space, she will either think that you have insulted Mrs. Jones on your right and Mrs. Brown on your left, or she will feel responsible for you personally and accordingly will start a long-distance conversation that has no particular basis except that of emergency. Consequently, you must spend your time acting convincingly as though you actually are very busy.

You can always make believe that you are engaged in an exceedingly interesting discussion with the person opposite, occasionally changing the expression on your face and laughingly nodding your head knowingly. This may fool your hostess in case her glance happens to fall your way, and it will surely confuse the person sitting opposite you if he happens to catch you in the act. (169) *(Concluded in Paragraph 107)*

107. Table Conversation *(Concluded)*

If you have thought to bring along a bit of charcoal, you can make little drawings on the back on either side of you. These proceedings would, at least, get one of your partners to turn around, even though reluctantly!

As time wears on, you can start juggling your cutlery. If the other guests have any feelings, this ought to attract their attention.

Of course, there is always one last resort; and that is to slide under the table, where you can either crawl about collecting slippers that have been kicked off, growling frighteningly like a dog and scaring the more timid guests, or you might collect your bearings and crawl out from the other side and go home. Perhaps this last would be the best—it would end your evening's difficulties.—*Robert Benchley* (126)

UNIT 38

108. The Value of Reading

Before Morris Fishbein, the brilliant doctor, decided to transfer to a school of medicine, he took a course in shorthand to speed up his notetaking. He was a brilliant scholar, who added to his brilliance by adopting exceedingly efficient working methods. When he was a young doctor, his association made him editor of its magazine, a post he held for more than a decade. He was constantly presenting creative and workable ideas, many of which were the result of his readings in all areas of medicine.

When he retired, the association had to appoint four people to do the work that this speedy reader had been doing alone. (122) (*Continued in Paragraph 109*)

109. The Value of Reading (*Continued*)

Thomas Edison, that quiet man of science who did so much for society, did not have much schooling; but his wide reading made him one of the best-informed men in the country. While his deafness was a great trial to him, he says in his diary that it enabled him to concentrate on reading. In his laboratory he built up one of the finest scientific libraries of his time.

"When I want to invent an appliance," he said, "I begin by reading up on all that has been done in that area in prior days. Frankly, that is what all these books are for. I use these books to prevent the waste of time and money in the future by not doing again the things that have already been done and tried out by others." (131) (*Continued in Paragraph 110*)

110. The Value of Reading (*Continued*)

Henry Ford got the idea for his first car from a magazine — *The Science of the World* — which he read while he was away visiting a friend. He laid awake all night reading the magazine and sketching his plan for a gas engine that was far ahead of his time. We are aware, of course, that Ford was a man of ac-tion; but the reading that made him a successful man should not be overlooked. Describing his early days, he said, "I devoted every second I could spare to the reading of scientific books." (92) (*Concluded in Paragraph 111*)

111. The Value of Reading (*Concluded*)

Our fast-moving world requires more and more thoughtful reading if we hope to keep up with it. There are hundreds of magazines in the area of business and office methods. Last year there were more than a hundred papers and magazines for farmers on the market. Nearly ten thousand books are published in the United States yearly. Yet, as few people are aware, reading is a recent accomplishment. One hundred fifty years ago not half the people in the country could actually read. Those who could read had been taught by trial-and-error methods that made their reading inefficient. They read too slowly and did not gain enough from their reading. Many older persons are still poor readers.

Yes, extensive reading will yield big dividends. (132)

UNIT 39

112. The Traits of Successful People

What combination of traits will you find in the person who has risen to a high station in life? An examination of the traits of 100 people in many different areas who have earned a fine reputation for themselves in recent years reveals that they possess these traits:

1. They are not afraid of hard work. They attack a difficult task without hesitation and stay with it until, in their estimation, the job has been done well. They are self-reliant.

2. They have the patience to sit down and think. Most people find thinking a painful process.

3. They always have a pleasant smile on their faces. In addition, they are aware of the importance of getting along with people in all stations of life.

4. They have the habit of study. They are always eager for information on any and every topic. (150)

113. The Art of Saying "No"

Last year a friend of mine submitted to a feature magazine to which I subscribe a paper he had written on a subject in which he had done substantial research. The editor subsequently returned the paper together with a letter of explanation saying that the paper did not meet the needs of the magazine.

Usually, getting back a paper that had been submitted for publication is a discouraging experience; but it was not in this instance. The letter that accompanied the returned paper was so gracious and so complimentary of the author's handling of the subject that the author said he would almost rather have it than a substantial check.

The "no" he had received was given in the right manner and was taken in the right manner—which goes to show that we can say "no" and still leave a good taste in the mouth of the person to whom we say it. (161) (Continued in Paragraph 114)

114. The Art of Saying "No" (Continued)

In the typical business concern, the employer must periodically say "no"—and the person who has learned to say it so that it will be accepted in the right spirit has a practical asset indeed.

A man I know has charge of a "suggestion" committee in a large medical, surgical, and chemical supply firm. He says that, when a suggestion is made that is not practical or logical, he does not promptly turn it down. He considers the employee's feelings. He takes the trouble to meet with the person who submitted the suggestion, and the two of them analyze the suggestion critically. The one in charge of suggestions may actually think highly of the other fellow's idea but still know that technically it will not work. By analyzing and then discussing the suggestion critically, the person who made the suggestion can be brought to see it in the same way and accordingly be satisfied to take "no" for an answer. (176) (Continued in Paragraph 115)

115. The Art of Saying "No" (Continued)

In business there is always the awkward matter of salary increases. When a person approaches an employer about an increase that cannot be granted, the employer can compliment the man's work and still point out the reasons why he cannot reward the employee further at the present time. The employer can assure the employee, though, that he can look forward to an upward revision of his salary just as soon as conditions permit.

When an employee understands the logical reasons why he cannot have an increase in salary, he holds no grudge afterwards. (106) (Continued in Paragraph 116)

116. The Art of Saying "No" (Continued)

A very successful and forward-looking personnel man in a transportation company in my locality tries not to say "no" when he is angry or when he is in a hurry. He also has the faculty of facing each problem squarely. He believes in the desirability of dealing with each problem at once to the best of his ability, so that the person with whom he is dealing knows exactly where he stands. It is his belief that the employee who is left in doubt about a matter will not perform so well as the one who may have been told "no" but who, at least, knows without any possibility of misunderstanding where he stands. The members of the staff appreciate this quality in him and give him their loyalty. (137) (Concluded in Paragraph 117)

117. The Art of Saying "No" (Concluded)

People in authority must often take the responsibility of saying "no" — and this is especially true of parents. The majority of parents must say "no" many times before their children reach maturity. The chances are that long afterwards the child will remember how the "no" was said—whether the parents explained their refusals with sincerity.

Perhaps no person gets told "no" with greater regularity than a salesman. In his case, he must learn to take that answer in good spirit, whether it is given nicely or not; but he does not forget how it was said.

The majority of us have to say "no" many times in life. If we are to enjoy popularity and prosperity, we must learn how to say "no" with tact and with sincerity. (139)

118. Dominoes

George Bernard Shaw was having a serious discussion about various matters of importance with a colleague of his at dinner in a restaurant. The orchestra struck up a particularly noisy and tedious piece. When, after the briefest pause, it launched into an even noisier piece, Shaw was obviously annoyed. He called the headwaiter and courteously asked, "Does this orchestra play anything on request?"

"Oh, yes," said the headwaiter with sincerity.

"Excellent," said Shaw seriously. "Kindly tell them to play dominoes!" (99)

119. Press the Button

Three men stood on the third floor of the new Fifth Avenue Music Building, with briefcases under their arms, waiting for an elevator. In due time the elevator came down, passing their floor without stopping. All obviously had failed to press the button. Each thought one of the others had pressed it.

Many things in life are never done because each of us thinks the other fellow will press the button that produces action. Numerous good plans never see the light of day because each of us is expecting the other fellow to put them into action.

Don't wait for the other fellow; it is your duty to press the button yourself. The world needs more button pressers. (119)

UNIT 41

120. Revenge

One Sunday morning a school teacher was issued a ticket for driving through a stop light. She was told to appear in court the following Monday. She went before the judge and explained that school had already started the first week of September and that she had to teach on that Monday; therefore, she wanted her case disposed of at once.

"So you are a school teacher," said the judge seriously. "Madam, your presence here fulfills a long-standing ambition of mine. You sit right down at that table and write, 'On Sunday I went through a stop light' 500 times!" (97)

121. He Liked Everybody

"When I die," Will Rogers once said, "my epitaph, or whatever you call those things on gravestones, is going to read: 'I joked about every big man of my time; however, I never met anybody that I didn't like.' I am so proud of that I can hardly wait to die so that it can be carved on my stone. When you come around to my grave, you will probably find me there proudly reading it."

When they built the memorial to Will Rogers some years ago, someone remembered his wish. Below the bronze bust of the famous humorist appear these words: "I never met anybody I didn't like."

Will Rogers lived up to his epitaph. He met everybody with an open hand and an open heart. (126)

122. Reading and Writing Practice

Mr. Gray: The school board has decided to hold its monthly meeting on Saturday, April 16, in the Chamber of Commerce Building. The meeting will begin at 11 a.m. and run through until about 1 p.m.

I should like to discuss with you something that I plan to bring up before the school board on April 16. Would it be convenient for you to stop at my office on Friday, April 1, about 10 a.m.? The matter I wish to discuss with you will take only a few minutes. John H. Green (91)

UNIT 42

123. Recall Chart

1. Convenient, conveniently, inconvenient, a.m., p.m., chamber of commerce.

2. Exceed, exceeded, exceedingly, long, longer, longingly.

3. Build, builder, buildings, shame, shames, shamed.

4. Begin, beginner, beginnings, chair, chairman, chairmen.

5. Diet, diets, dieted, actual, actually, actuality.

6. Apply, appliance, appliances, figure, figures, figured.

7. Create, created, creation, youth, youths, youthful.

8. Appreciate, appreciated, appreciates, repel, compel, dispel.

9. Awake, awaken, awakened, announce, announces, announcement.

10. Yell, yells, yellow, contain, contained, container.

11. Submit, submission, submitted, transform, transformation, transformed.

12. Chemical, chemicals, chemically, think, thinks, thinking.

13. Forward, backward, outward, dispute, disputes, disputed.

14. Studious, envious, serious, depend, depends, dependable.

15. New, renew, renewed, oil, soil, boil.

16. Majority, minority, sincerity, win, winner, winnings.

17. Possibility, ability, reliability, despair, despairs, despairingly.

18. January, February, September, technical, radical, particle.

124. Never Satisfied!

I met a man yesterday who was once on a large ocean liner that sank. When the ship took her final plunge, my friend felt himself go down into the waters. When he eventually came to the surface, a great joy possessed his soul. He was alive!

Then there came to him the thought that he could swim for only a little while. The water was very cold. About a hundred feet away, he saw a floating spar; and he felt that if he could only reach that spar it would indeed be paradise. After considerable effort, he reached it, tediously drew himself up, and sat on it. Once more he was grateful. He was alive! But the wind was cold, and he knew he could not physically hold on much longer. Just then he saw a lifeboat about five hundred feet from him. He yelled, and the boat came forward to pick him up. Again, he felt he was in paradise.

Some time later the people in the lifeboat saw a great form, with many lights, off in the distance. The great ship came nearer and nearer, and my friend uttered a great prayer that he might climb the side of the ship and lie on the deck. His prayer was soon answered.

He realized, though, that his strength had been substantially spent; and he prayed that he be placed in the most miserable room in the steerage, just so that he had a bed and could be covered with blankets. Some of the mothers and children in the crowded steerage willingly made room for him; and when he was in the bunk, he said with sincerity, "This is paradise." But after an hour or two, the crying of the children began to depress him; so he asked a petty officer if there was any possibility that he might have a cabin. A bunk was conveniently found for him in a cabin, and he was happy and he thought, "This is paradise indeed." He slept well that night, but the next morning he realized that the cabin was not too comfortable; and so he asked the sailor who came to wait on him if there was not a berth in a cabin on the upper deck. The sailor explained that every bunk was full except in the captain's cabin. And so my friend wrote a letter to the captain of the ship. Here is the letter:

"Dear Sir: The cabin in which I am located is right over the engines. Also, it is very small and not very well ventilated. I understand that you have a vacant bunk in your cabin on the upper deck. I should appreciate it if you would let me know whether I may occupy your cabin with you. Sincerely,"

No answer or explanation came from the captain. But the moral of this story is this: nobody is ever happy with a thing after he gets it. (466)

PART 2

UNIT 43

Courage in Business

The foreman in any company is a VIP. The person who is to be a good foreman must, of course, have tact and diplomacy. But being a good foreman requires more than tact and diplomacy; it requires a great deal of courage — determination to see that the job is done well. Tact is important, but it is not a substitute for firmness.

A foreman is supposed to organize, to instruct, and to correct other people's mistakes. It is his job to see that people who work for him do a good job. That is how he earns his pay.

The things that a foreman must insist on

are not always popular; but unless he insists on them, people will lose respect for him.

UNIT 44

126. Reading and Writing Practice

1. Dear Mr. Dyer: Upon making the customary room inspection after a guest's departure, our maid reported that two woolen blankets, replacement value $8 each, were missing from the room you occupied on Saturday, September 30, and Sunday, October 1.

May we ask that, should you discover these blankets upon unpacking your luggage, you return them to us. Very often, in their haste to catch a train, guests unknowingly pack such items in their bags and, of course, return them when they discover them in unpacking. Very sincerely yours, (101)

2. Dear Mr. Roy: I am desolated to learn, after reading your letter of October 3, that you actually have guests in your hotel who, when packing their neckties, are so careless as to check out and take such slight souvenirs as woolen blankets. By the same token, I suppose that the passengers on some railroads are apt to carry off a locomotive or a few hundred feet of rails when getting off the train on reaching their destination. Or a visitor to a city zoo might conceivably take away an elephant or a rhinoceros, concealing same in a sack of peanuts — after removing the peanuts.

In this particular case, though, I may be able to assist you in running down your blankets. As I had a substantial amount of luggage with me, I needed all the space you so thoughtfully provide in each room. The blankets in question occupied the second drawer of the dresser. I wanted to place a few white shirts (replacement value $4 each) in that drawer; so I lifted out the blankets and placed them on a chair.

Later, the maid came in, and I handed the blankets (same blankets and same replacement value) to her, telling her in nice, polite language to get them out of the room. If you count all the blankets in your establishment, you will find that there is not a blanket missing. Very truly yours, P. S. Have you counted your elevators lately? (250)

3. Dear Mr. Dyer: I wish to thank you for one of the most delightful letters it has been my pleasure to read in my entire career. With all sincerity, I offer you my congratulations.

Yes, it is essential that we do a lot of counting around here. I have counted the elevators, and they are where they should be and are operating — every one of them. What I want to count now is more important to me. I want to continue counting you as a friend of this hotel.

Twenty-five thousand dollars' worth of our finest silver (by actual auditor's replacement value) is carried away annually by our guests. A similar total (in replacement value) in linens is cherished by sentimental guests who like souvenirs of their visit.

And so it goes.

We are sorry indeed that you were annoyed as a result of the maid's mistake.

As the song goes, "Let's call the whole thing off." And there is another song I should like to mention: "Can't we be friends?" Very sincerely yours, (180)

UNIT 45

128. Your Vocabulary

Would you like to increase your mastery of words? If you would, here are five steps that will help you:

1. Read. You cannot build a vocabulary without reading. You cannot make friends if you never meet anybody and stay at home by yourself all the time. In the same way, you cannot build a vocabulary if you never meet any new words. To meet new words, you must read. The more you read, the better. A book a week is good; a book every other day is even better.

Keep on reading. Keep on meeting unfamiliar words on printed pages.

2. Look up an unfamiliar word in the dictionary. Read carefully everything the dictionary says about the word. Study the way it is pronounced, where it comes from, what it means, and what other words are connected with it. Be sure you find the meaning that fits exactly to the sentence in which you found the word. Remember that meaning. Remember the way it was used in the sentence. Compare the word with the words you would have used if you had written the sentence.

Looking up a word in the dictionary, though, won't get you anywhere if you don't remember what you found. If you really want to do something about your vocabulary, keep a notebook, jotting down the words you didn't understand and everything in the dictionary that will help you remember what those words mean.

3. Say the word. Get used to the way it is pronounced. Say the word aloud often enough to be sure you won't stumble over it when you use it the first time.

4. Use the word. Reading, looking up, and pronouncing is not enough. To add a word to your vocabulary, you have to use it. The first time you get a chance to work it into a conversation, do so. This is the most important step. Use the word in conversation as if it had always been yours. Never mind whether your friends will think you are showing off. Neither should you worry about not using the word entirely appropriately.

5. Keep in touch with your vocabulary. Knowing words is like knowing people. If you don't keep in touch with them, you lose them. After a while, you may even forget their names. Watch out for words that you have recently acquired. Look them up again in the dictionary if necessary. Keep saying them and using them. That is easy. In fact, you will find that the words you have just added to your vocabulary will keep cropping up in your reading and in your speech.

Vocabulary building is fun. It is fun to find out where words come from. It is even more fun to take a new word and use it to say exactly what you mean to say. (461)

130. Mixer

The failure of many men to make a success of their business can often be traced to the lack of proper records, especially records that show the amount and source of profits and expenses incurred in obtaining these profits. If a certain store around which we are now going to spin a tale ever fails and its creditors devour it to its last chandelier, "lack of proper records" will most surely be a substantial contributing factor to its downfall!

It seems that a young mother decided to try some cooking suggestions she had found in her cookbook. Before she started, she went into a big city department store and bought one electric mixer, priced $15. All went well until one day she thought it would be nice if she surprised her family with the lemon meringue pie described in her cookbook.

As instructed in her cookbook, she put the whites of three eggs, some lemon sauce, and a pinch of salt — or whatever one puts in a meringue pie—into the mixer bowl and turned the switch. The mixer mixed for a minute or two, but then it heaved a sigh and expired with the ingredients only slightly mixed.

So she called the store and told them that they had better come and repair it (the mixer — the pie was beyond repair!)

A man from the store came quickly; but after examining the mixer, he confessed: (1) that he could do nothing with it; (2) that he would have to ship it to the factory; (3) that the cost of repairs would be $3; (4) that it would take about two weeks to do the repairing.

So the whites of three eggs, the lemon sauce, and the pinch of salt were dumped into the sink; and the mixer went to the factory for overhauling.

Two weeks went by and no mixer was returned; then three weeks; and four weeks. Finally, the young mother called the store and asked what had happened to her mixer. The store investigated but could find no trace of the mixer. They said, though, that they would replace the broken mixer with a brand-new one for the $3 they had quoted for repairs. The next day a truck appeared, bringing two mixers — the old one and the new one that was to replace it. The young mother packed up the new one and sent it back. A week later the store wrote acknowledging receipt of the mixer and enclosing a check for $15, the cost of the new mixer!

We understand that she cashed the check because she was sure that, if she sent it back, the store would send her another mixer! So you can see why we feel that, if the store fails some day, it will be the "lack of proper records" that will bring about its ruin. (451)

132. Miracle

Children are not merely people; they are the only really living people who have been left to us in a weary world. To them, every hour of the day is a perfect miracle.

There is good reason to believe, though, that the enthusiasms of a small boy will outrun those of his sister, although some will want to argue that point.

He is an early riser and is inclined to be a noisy one. His zeal for getting up does not extend to immediate dressing and preparation for school. He must be driven to this action.

He may, if he feels any early morning weakness, sneak to the kitchen and fix himself a bowl of cereal to dull the edge of his appetite; but soon he is back in his room again, ready to start a varied routine of activity that will not stop until he is pushed into bed again at night.

By the time the boy sits down at the breakfast table, he will have reduced to new chaos his room, which he was forced to straighten before retiring. He will also have listened to a few programs on his radio.

His enthusiasms do not extend to brushing his teeth, washing his face, and combing his hair; and his mother is likely to be in a state of exhaustion before the day is well begun by the time she has put him into rubbers, a coat of the proper weight, and a cap to start the trip to school.

Only a teacher would be able to pay proper tribute to the endless energies of a young boy in the schoolroom, but enough of the tale is carried home to fill in the picture. This may entail some spitball throwing; a battle in the closet, in which a front tooth is broken off; a disciplinary trip to the principal's office to discuss the right approach to learning; and finally wind up with a street fight on the way home.

It is amazing how weariness settles down like a storm cloud on the small boy when he finds himself up against the duty of a half hour of practice at the piano. Headaches set in and the stomach grows sick; and only the strong parent who has seen this happen again and again and noted the time of its occurrence will heartlessly drive this poor lad to his musical exercises. Yet, once they are done, the recovery is so rapid as to be miraculous.

Weariness will show itself without fail again when a bath is proposed; but immediately afterward, children will once again be the only really living people in this otherwise weary world.

Somehow it seems absurd to drive them to bed at 8:30, still wide-eyed at the miracles around them and needing sleep less than anybody in the house. But either they go to bed or their parents must, from utter exhaustion. (483)

134. The Little Things

Most of us forget the fact that it is the little things that count. We have heard often enough that this is true; but because we feel that the big things are more important, we fail to appreciate the value of little things.

The baseball player who bats .250 earns an average salary of perhaps $7,000 a season. The player who bats .350 earns $30,000 or more. The difference is only one more safe hit in every 10 times at bat; and 7 times out of 10, the batter is safe or out at first base by as narrow a margin as 6 inches. Little things make the big difference, and the player must be on the alert to capitalize on them.

How far you climb on the ladder of success depends on how much attention you give to little things. (146)

Yesterday and Tomorrow

There are two days in every week about which we should not worry — two days that should be kept free from any fear or apprehension. One of these days is Yesterday with its mistakes and cares, its aches and pains, its faults and blunders. Yesterday has passed forever beyond our control. All the money in the world cannot bring back Yesterday. We cannot undo a single act we performed. We cannot erase a single word we said. We cannot correct a single mistake. Yesterday has passed beyond our control. Let it go.

The other day we should not worry about is Tomorrow. Tomorrow is also beyond our control. Tomorrow's sun will rise, either in splendor or behind a mass of clouds — but it will rise. Until it does, we have no stake in Tomorrow, because it has not yet arrived.

That leaves us only one day — Today! And every man can fight the battles of just one day! (157)

An Educated Man

An educated man is not one whose memory is trained to carry a few dates in history. He is one who can accomplish things. A man who cannot think is not an educated man, no matter how many college degrees he may have acquired. Thinking is the hardest work anyone can do, which is probably why we have so few thinkers.

There are two extremes to avoid. One is the feeling of contempt for education; the other is the assumption that going through a college is a sure cure for ignorance. You cannot learn in any school what the world is going to do next year, but you can learn some of the things that the world has tried to do in the past and where it has failed and where it has succeeded. If education succeeded in warning the young student away from some of the false theories on which men have tried to build so that he may be saved the loss of time in finding out by bitter experience, its value would be unquestioned. — *Henry Ford* (171)

UNIT 49

136. A Dissertation Upon Roast Pig

Mankind, we are told, for the first 70,000 years, ate its meat raw. It seems that the art of roasting was hit upon by accident in the following strange manner:

The Chinese farmer Ho-ti one day left his cottage in the charge of his son, who was very fond of playing with fire. While the son was building a fire, some of the sparks escaped into a pile of straw; and soon the entire cottage had burned down.

The son reached down to feel one of the pigs to see whether there were any signs of life in it. He burned his fingers; and to cool them off, he put them into his mouth.

Some of the crumbs of the burnt skin stuck to his fingers — and for the first time man had tasted crackling! Again he felt the pig. It did not burn so much now; still he licked his fingers from a sort of habit.

The truth broke into a slow understanding that it was the pig that tasted so wonderful — and he tore whole handfuls of the skin with the flesh next to it.

While he was thus enjoying himself, his father entered, armed with a big stick. When he found how affairs stood, he gave the boy a terrible beating; but he could not beat him from his pig until he had almost made an end to it.

The son raked out another pig and pushed it into his father's hands, shouting, "Eat, Father, eat the pig."

The father trembled at every joint as he held that awful pig; but then he, too, put his fingers in his mouth. He then tasted some of the burnt pig's flavor, which was not at all unpleasant to him. The upshot was that both father and son raked out the remaining pigs and never left the spot until they had eaten every bit of them.

The father warned his son not to let the secret escape, but strange stories got about. It was noticed that the father's cottage was now on fire more often than ever.

At length, father and son were watched; and the terrible truth was uncovered. Father and son were brought before the court and the evidence produced. The jury was about to announce its decision when the foreman of the jury asked that some of the burnt pig be handed to the jury. He handled it and they all handled it, burning their fingers as the father and son had done before them. They put their fingers into their mouths — and, against all the evidence, they brought in a verdict of not guilty without leaving the courtroom.

The judge, who was a shrewd fellow, winked at the decision; and when court was over, he went and bought up all the pigs that could be had for love or money. In a few days the judge's town house was seen to be on fire. Soon there were fires in every part of town.

Thus this custom was carried on until, in the course of time, some wise man found out that the flesh of pigs or any other animal might be cooked ("burnt," as they called it) without the necessity of burning a whole house to dress it! — *Charles Lamb* (489)

Grant — first term

Weak President. Judgment of men was poor. He was often attracted by wealthy and polished people. Many of his associates were dishonest — Jay Gould, for example.

He rewarded friends and relatives.

Graft and corruption brought morale of government to a new low.

Lorant, The Presidency, page 303.

Grant — second term

Marked by more scandals such as "Whiskey Ring" and graft in Indian affairs. Felt that his friends were being persecuted and made things difficult for investigators. Those friends who were tried and convicted he pardoned. Viewed the investigations of corruption in his administration as political propaganda.

Faulkner, American Political and Social History, page 421.

Grant — the man

Grant probably excellent example of a true extrovert. Rejoiced in his friends and his family. Both he and Mrs. Grant loved to entertain and did so lavishly (30-course dinners!)

Mrs. Grant dressed expensively and led the social season dynamically. Probably the entire family loved the good things too much. Had little concern, it seems, for public opinion.

Me

Illustration of footnote

In most states a corporation comes into existence when a certificate of incorporation is prepared by the persons* who wish to form the corporation.

---

*Three or more persons usually are required as incorporators to form a stock corporation.

The document is signed by each of the incorporators and is sent to the Secretary of State for filing.

Stoppage in Transit

Sometimes a seller learns that the buyer to whom he has shipped goods is insolvent.*

*Failure on the part of the buyer to meet a payment is considered to be sufficient evidence of his insolvency to justify the exercise of the right of stoppage in transit by the seller.

He may notify the common carrier that the goods should not be delivered. That is known as stoppage of goods in transit. This occurs only while goods are in the hands of the common carrier.

The seller should keep this in mind, however: He may be held liable for damages if he stops goods in transit without just cause. That liability exists if the buyer is assumed to be insolvent on the basis of information that is not correct.

138. Just-a-Little-Late Club

When I was a commuter, I sometimes went to the station early to watch the other commuters running for the trains. I came to know many of them by sight. There were ladies and old men, occasional visitors to the city, who arrived long before train time. There were businessmen who arrived one minute ahead. And just as the gate was about to slam, there would come piling across the station the members of the Just-a-Little-Late Club.

I used to sympathize with them at first, supposing them to be unfortunates who had missed the bus or had lost their watches; but after two years of watching, I understood the difficulty. They were members of the Just-a-Little-Late Club. The members of the Just-a-Little-Late Club do not change from day to day. Membership is not an accident. I submit that it is a habit, and one of the most annoying in the world.

"Never be on time," Mark Twain said. "You waste too much time waiting for the other fellow." He had in mind the members of the Just-a-Little-Late Club.

I was lunching with a friend the other day when a "captain of industry" passed me. "A wonderful fellow," said my friend. "Last year I had a long series of technical meetings with him about the formation of a new company in this locality. It was necessary for us to meet almost every day for nearly three months. In all that time he was late for the proceedings but twice, and then only a few minutes. Each time he sent word to me, telling me that he would be late."

Lord Nelson said, "I owe all my success in life to having been a quarter of an hour before my time."

I hold up these records in the hope that they may do some good. Yet, with all sincerity, I believe the hope is very faint. The habit of being late is tenacious.

If I am fortunate enough to be inside when the pearly gates are closed on Judgment Day, I shall know what to expect. Five minutes later, there will be a terrific battering. Saint Peter will be surprised, but I shall not.

When the gates swing outward again, there they will be, some of the most lovable and exasperating people who ever lived — panting and apologetic to the last. — *Bruce Barton* (386)

UNIT 52

140. Mr. Murphy's Chickens

It was some years ago when the Methodists were in the habit of moving their ministers every three years or less. On one occasion, when appointments were handed out, a young minister drew a small town that provided a nice home with a good-sized garden in the rear. The man who was there before him said, "That's a fine garden, John, but you won't be able to use it. The Murphys' chickens from next door won't let you."

"Oh, I don't think I will let a few chickens bother me," said our friend.

Just as the minister's friend warned, the Murphys did have a big flock of chickens that were permitted to run at will; and the new minister had no more than planted his seeds when the hens came over. No amount of driving them away had any effect; and that night the new minister went over to see his neighbor, Mr. Murphy.

Yes, the chickens were Mr. Murphy's; but there wasn't any law against letting them run. What is more, when they were shut up, they quit laying. No, there wasn't anything he could do about it. He had to have those eggs.

A few days later, without telling his wife,

the minister slipped away to town and bought several dozen eggs. That night he planted them in the grass, in the bushes, and in the hedge bordering his garden. Early in the morning he was to be seen carefully replanting his garden seeds. Soon Mr. Murphy let his chickens out. They headed as usual for the new garden. Suddenly, though, the minister called excitedly to his wife. "Mary, bring a pan. I've just found a nest of eggs." So his wife brought out a small pan. "This is too small," he called out loudly. "There are a lot more here." By this time, he had an interested visitor, Mr. Murphy.

"What's that you've got there?" he wanted to know.

"Why, I found some eggs," the minister said.

"I guess those must be my eggs," said Mr. Murphy.

"Oh, I think not," replied the minister. "I found them all on my lot."

"But you haven't got any hens," said Mr. Murphy. "Those must have come from my hens."

"But they are on my property," said the minister. "It looks as if the good Lord knew the Church was a little behind on my pay and is helping me out. No, there is nothing I can do about it, Mr. Murphy. Maybe the Lord figures we will do better on eggs than on the produce of the garden anyway."

Mr. Murphy did not stop to hear any more. He was busily rounding up his astonished hens. They did not appear in the garden again. Mr. Murphy, you see, had to have those eggs! (436)

UNIT 53

142. Open Door

For some reason, women who go to college to prepare for a career in business or industry seem to prefer every other field to that in which opportunities are greatest. They study psychology, economics, history, and everything under the sun except the one subject that is their open door to the world of business.

Take Helen, for example, who applied for a position with our organization. Helen completed a four-year college course with honors. She had been President of her sorority and

Vice-President of the Student Council. She was an alert, charming girl looking for a chance to get started at $200 a month or less.

We did not hire Helen, even though we had a number of vacancies with a starting salary of $275 a month. Helen could have had her choice of a job in the engineering, purchasing, or sales departments if only she could take dictation and transcribe.

Many young women, especially in the glamour jobs in advertising or television or publishing, find their work so time consuming that they often have little time for outside interests. A secretary has leisure hours for fun and self-improvement. The job of a secretary is a big one.

The critical shortage of engineers has received national attention in recent years. Yet today it is easier to hire an engineer than it is to find a secretary with a college degree.

It is not my purpose to comment on the relative merits of a liberal arts education and vocational preparation, except to say that they need not be mutually exclusive. I do not suggest that every woman in college (or planning to go to college) take her degree in Secretarial Science, but I sincerely and earnestly urge that every college woman who is hoping for a business career become really proficient in shorthand and typewriting. Let her take her major in one of the sciences or arts but take her electives from the business courses. Then, when she starts looking for a job, she will have a skill to offer as well as a liberal education.

The way in and the way up is a secretarial job, whether the final aim is fashion designer, editor, or personnel manager. If her goal is Vice-President, let her start as a secretary. — H. M. Overley (439)

UNIT 54

144. Profit

A schoolboy, disturbed by the current fashion of speaking disparagingly of the profit system that has formed the basis of our way of life, wrote to his grandfather, asking him to "Explain just how there can be a profit that is not taken from the work of someone else." The grandfather replied:

My dear Grandson: I will answer your question as simply as I can.

Profit is the result of enterprise that builds for others as well as for the enterpriser. Let us consider the operation of this fact in a primitive village of perhaps 100 persons who obtain the mere necessities of life by working hard all day long.

Our primitive village, located at the foot of a mountain, must have water. There is no water except at a spring near the top of the mountain. It takes the people one hour to go up, and they do this until at last one of them notices that the water from the spring runs down inside the mountain in the same direction that he goes when he comes down. He conceives the idea of digging a trough in the side of the mountain all the way down to the place where he has his home. He goes to work to build a trough.

Then one day this 100th man turns a small part of the water from the spring into his trough, and it runs down the mountain into a basin he has made at the bottom. He then says to the other 99 people that, if they will give him the daily production of 10 minutes of their time, he will give them water from his basin. He will then receive 990 minutes of the time of the other people each day, which will make it unnecessary for him to work 16 hours a day in order to provide for his necessities. He is making a great profit—but his enterprise has given each of the 99 other people 50 additional minutes each day for himself.

The enterpriser, now having 16 hours a day at his disposal, and being naturally curious, spends part of his time watching the water run down the mountain. He sees that it pushes along stones and pieces of wood. So, he develops a water wheel. Then he notices that it has power and finally makes the water wheel run a mill to grind his corn.

This 100th man then realizes that he has enough power to grind corn for the other 99. He says to them, "I will permit you to grind your corn in my mill if you will give me onetenth of the time you save." They agree, and so the enterpriser now makes an additional profit. He uses the time paid him by the other 99 to build a better house for himself. (465)

(Concluded in Paragraph 146)

146. Profit (Concluded)

This 100th man's time finally becomes all his own to use as he sees fit. He does not have to work unless he chooses to. His food and shelter and clothing are provided by others. His mind, however, is constantly working; and the other 99 are constantly having more time to themselves because of his thinking and planning.

For instance, he notices that one man of the 99 makes better shoes than the others do. He arranges for this man to spend all his time making shoes, because he can feed him and clothe him and arrange for his shelter from profits.

The other 98 do not have to make their own shoes. They are charged one-tenth of the time they save. The 99th man is also able to work shorter hours, because some of the time that is paid by each of the 98 is allotted to him by the 100th man.

So it goes on as this 100th man constantly finds ways to save the 99 the total expenditure of their time — one-tenth of which he asks of them in payment for his enterprise.

But suppose that, when the 100th man had completed his trough down the mountain, the people had turned on him and said: "We are 99 and you are only one. We will take what water we want. You cannot prevent us, and we will give you nothing." What would have happened then?

You can see that the incentive of the most curious mind would have been destroyed. He would have seen that he could gain nothing by solving problems if he still had to use every waking hour to provide his living. There could have been no advancement in the village. The primitive state that first existed would have remained. Life would have continued to be difficult for everyone, with opportunity to do no more than work all day just for a bare living.

Need we say more to prove that there can be profit from enterprise without taking anything from others; that such enterprise adds to the ease of living for everyone?

These principles are as active in a great nation such as ours as in our imaginary village. Laws that kill incentive and cripple the honest enterpriser hold back progress. True profit is not something to be feared, because it works to the benefit of all.

We must try to build rather than tear down what others have built.

We must be fair to other men, or the world cannot be fair to us. Sincerely, Grandfather (420)

148. Silly Advice

A man who was not feeling well stopped in to see his doctor, a grouchy old fellow.

The doctor asked, "Have you been to see any other doctor before you came to see me?"

"No, sir," replied the meek patient. "I went to a druggist."

"You went to a druggist?" exclaimed the doctor. "That shows how much sense you have! And what silly advice did the druggist give you?"

"He told me to come and see you," replied the patient. (71)

Long Life

People who wish they were "as strong as a horse" or "as contented as a cow" may be surprised to learn which mammal actually lives the longest. It is not the horse nor the cow nor the durable elephant. The longest-living mammal today is woman. The average girl can expect to live fully 71 years. The mighty elephant, once ranked as the longest-living mammal, now lags far behind with its 60-year life span. The horse has a life expectancy of 25 years; and the cow averages from 9 to 15 years. Even men live longer than elephants these days; they have an expectancy of 65 years.

The turtle, which is not a mammal, lives at least a century longer than human beings. But the turtle can't brag about its advanced age, and women probably won't; so we men are safe. — *Charles Adams* (148)

Office Hours

A girl entered the office of a personnel manager to apply for a job. When she was asked whether she had any particular talents, she stated that she had won several prizes in crossword puzzle and advertising slogan contests.

"That sounds good," the manager told her. "But we want somebody who will be smart during office hours."

"Oh," she exclaimed brightly, "this was during office hours!" (71)

Solution

Two women in a train argued long and loud about the opening or closing of a window. The argument became so heated that finally one of the women called the conductor. "If this window is open," she cried, "I shall catch pneumonia and probably die."

"If the window is shut," the other said, "I shall suffocate."

The poor conductor was at a loss to know what to do. Finally, a man sitting nearby who had listened with growing impatience to the bickering of the two women said to the conductor:

"I have a solution. First, open the window. That will kill one. Then, shut the window. That will kill the other. Then we can have some peace on this train!" (119)

Darkness

"Mary," said the mother severely to her eight-year-old daughter, "there were two pieces of cake in the pantry this morning and now there is only one. How did this happen?"

"I don't know," said the little girl sadly. "It must have been so dark in the pantry that I didn't see the other piece." (51)

UNIT 57

Table of Contents

Index

UNIT 58

150. The Fifty-First Dragon

Of all the students in the School for Knights, Gawaine was among the least promising — he lacked spirit. He would hide in the woods when the jousting class was called, although his classmates and members of the faculty tried to appeal to his better nature by shouting to him to come out and break his neck like a man; but Gawaine would not respond.

The principal and the assistant professor were discussing the case one spring day, and the assistant professor could see no remedy but expulsion.

"I cannot subscribe to expulsion," said the principal. "I think I will transfer him to the dragon-slaying division."

"He might be killed," said the assistant professor.

"So he might," replied the principal, "but," he added soberly, "we must consider the greater good. We are responsible for the formation of this lad's character."

"Are the dragons bad this year?" asked the professor.

"I have never known them to be worse," replied the principal. "Up in the hills to the south last week they killed a number of peasants, two cows, and a prize pig. If this dry spell holds, there is no telling when they may start a forest fire simply by breathing indiscriminately."

"Would any refund of the tuition fee be necessary in case of an accident to Gawaine?"

"No," the principal answered. "That is completely covered in the contract. But, as a matter of fact, he won't be killed. Before I send him up in the hills, I am going to give him a magic word."

"That's a good idea," said the professor. "Sometimes a magic word works wonders."

From that day on Gawaine specialized in dragons. The course included both theory and practice. In the morning there were lectures on the history and manners of dragons. Gawaine did not do too well in these studies. He had a gift for forgetting things.

In the afternoon he showed to better advantage, for then he would go down to the south meadow and practice with a battle-ax. In this exercise he was impressive, for he had great strength as well as speed and grace. Old alumni say that it was a thrilling sight to see Gawaine charge across the field toward a dummy paper dragon that had been set up for his practice. It never took him more than one stroke to cut off the head of the toughest of these dummies, which had no terrors for Gawaine. One sweep of the ax did the business.

By the end of June the principal thought that it was time for the test. Only the night before a dragon had come close to the school grounds and had eaten some of the lettuce from the garden. (440) *(Continued in Paragraph 152)*

152. The Fifty-First Dragon (Continued)

The faculty decided that Gawaine was ready. They gave him a diploma and a new battle-ax, and the principal called him to a private conference. "Sit down," said the principal. "You are no longer a boy. You are a man. Tomorrow you will go out into the world, the great world of accomplishment.

"Here you have learned the theories of life; but, after all, life is not a matter of theories. Life is a matter of facts. It calls on the young and the old alike to face these facts even though they are hard and sometimes unpleasant. Your problem, for example, is to slay dragons."

"They say that those dragons down in the south wood are 500 feet long," ventured Gawaine timidly.

"Stuff and nonsense!" said the principal. "One of the members of the faculty saw a dragon last week sunning himself in the valley. The professor did not have an opportunity to look at him very long because he felt it was his duty to hurry back to make a report to me. He said the dragon — or should I say, 'big lizard' — was not an inch over 200 feet.

"But the size has nothing at all to do with it. You will find the big ones even easier than the little ones. They are far slower on their feet and don't have so much fight, I am told. What is more, before you go I am going to equip you in such a fashion that you need have no fear of all the dragons in the world."

"I should like a magic cap," said Gawaine.

"What's that?" asked the principal.

"A cap to make me disappear," explained Gawaine.

The principal laughed. "You must not believe all those old wives' tales," he said. "There isn't any such thing. A cap to make you disappear, indeed! What would you do with it? You haven't even appeared yet. Why, my boy, you could walk from here to London and nobody would so much as look at you. You're nobody. You couldn't be more invisible than that."

Gawaine came very close to a relapse into his old habit of whimpering. The principal reassured him: "Don't worry; I will give you something much better than a magic cap. I am going to give you a magic word. All you have to do is to repeat this magic word once, and no dragon can possibly harm a hair of your head. You can cut off his head at your leisure. The magic word is 'Rumplesnitz.' Do you think you can learn that?"

Gawaine tried, and in an hour or so he seemed to have the word well in hand. (417) *(Continued in Paragraph 154)*

154. The Fifty-First Dragon (Continued)

Again and again he stopped the discussion to ask, "And if I say that word, the dragon cannot possibly hurt me?"

And always the principal replied, "You can depend on it. If you only say, 'Rumplesnitz,' you are perfectly safe."

Toward morning Gawaine was resigned to his career. At dawn the principal saw him to the edge of the forest and pointed him in the direction in which he should proceed.

About a mile away to the south, a cloud of steam hovered over an open meadow in the woods; and the principal assured Gawaine that under the steam he would find a dragon. Gawaine went forward slowly. He wondered whether it would be best to approach the dragon on the run, shouting "Rumplesnitz" all the way.

The problem was decided for him. No sooner had he come to the meadow than the dragon spied him and began to charge. It was a large dragon, and it seemed very much inclined to fight in spite of the principal's statement to the contrary. As the dragon charged, it released clouds of steam through its nostrils. It was as if a large teapot had suddenly gone mad. The dragon came forward so fast and Gawaine was so frightened that he had time to say, "Rumplesnitz" only once.

As he said it, he swung his battle-ax and off popped the head of the dragon. Gawaine had to admit that it was even easier to kill a real dragon than a paper one, if only you said, "Rumplesnitz."

Gawaine brought the ears home and a small section of the tail. His schoolmates and the faculty made much of him, but the principal wisely kept him from being spoiled by insisting that he go on with his work. Every clear day Gawaine rose at dawn and went out to kill dragons. The principal kept him home when it rained, because he said the woods were damp and unhealthy at such times and he didn't want the boy to run needless risks.

Few good days passed in which Gawaine failed to get a dragon. On one particularly fortunate day he killed three, a husband and wife and a visiting relative. Gradually he developed a technique. Students who sometimes watched him from the hilltops a long way off claimed that he often allowed the dragon to come within a few feet before he said, "Rumplesnitz." He came to say it with a mocking sneer. Occasionally he did stunts. Once, when a party from London was watching him, he went into action with his right hand tied behind his back. The dragon's head came off just as easily.

As Gawaine's record of killings mounted higher and higher, the principal found it impossible to keep him completely in hand. He fell into the habit of stealing out at night and engaging in long drinking bouts in the village inn. It was after such an event that he rose a little before dawn one fine August morning and started out after his fiftieth dragon. (494) *(Continued in Paragraph 156)*

156. The Fifty-First Dragon (Continued)

Gawaine's head was heavy and his mind sluggish. He was heavy in other respects as well, for he had adopted the practice of wearing his medals and ribbons when he went out dragon hunting. The decorations began on his chest and ran all the way down to his abdomen. They must have weighed at least eight pounds.

Gawaine found a dragon in the same meadow where he had killed his first one. It was a fair-sized dragon, but evidently an old one. Its face was wrinkled, and Gawaine thought he had never seen such an ugly creature.

Much to the lad's disgust, the dragon refused to charge. He whistled as he went. The dragon looked at him hopelessly. Of course, it had heard of Gawaine. Even when the lad raised his battle-ax, the dragon made no move. It knew that there was no salvation in the quickest thrust of the head, for it had been informed that this hunter was protected by a charm. Gawaine raised his battle-ax and suddenly lowered it again. He had grown very pale and trembled violently. The dragon was expecting some clever trick. "What is the matter?" it asked, with false solicitude.

"I've forgotten the magic word," Gawaine stammered.

"So that was the secret. It doesn't seem

quite sporting to me, all this magic stuff, you know," said the dragon.

Gawaine was so helpless with terror that the dragon's confidence rose, and it could not resist a temptation to show off a bit.

"Could I possibly be of any assistance?" it asked. "What is the first letter of the magic word?"

"It begins with r," said Gawaine weakly.

"Could it be 'reactionary'?"

Gawaine shook his head.

"Well, then," said the dragon, "we had better get down to business. Will you surrender?"

With the suggestion of a compromise, Gawaine mustered up all his courage to speak. "What will you do if I surrender?" he asked.

"Why, I will eat you," said the dragon.

"And if I don't surrender?"

"I will eat you just the same."

With that, the dragon drew back his head and struck. In that second there flashed into the mind of Gawaine the magic word "Rumplesnitz." But there was no time to say it. (358) *(Continued in Paragraph 158)*

UNIT 62

158. The Fifty-First Dragon *(Continued)*

There was time only to strike, and without a word Gawaine met the charge of the dragon with a full swing. He put all his back and shoulders into it. The impact was terrific, and the head of the dragon flew away almost 100 yards and landed in a thicket.

Gawaine did not remain frightened long after the death of the dragon. His mood was one of wonder. He was puzzled. He cut off the ears of the dragon almost in a trance.

Again and again he thought to himself, "I didn't say, 'Rumplesnitz.'" He was sure of that, and yet there was no question that he had killed the dragon. In fact, he had never killed one so utterly. Never before had he driven a head for anything like the same distance. Twenty-five yards was perhaps his best previous record. All the way back to the knight school he kept seeking an explanation for what had occurred. He went to the principal at once; and after closing the door, told him the news. "I didn't say, 'Rumplesnitz,'" he explained.

The principal laughed. "I'm glad you have found out the truth," he said. "It makes you ever so much more a hero. Don't you see that? Now you know that it was you who killed those dragons and not that foolish little word."

Gawaine frowned. "Then it was not a magic word after all?" he asked.

"Of course not," said the principal. "There isn't any such thing as a magic word."

"But you told me it was magic, and now you say it isn't."

"It wasn't magic in a literal sense," answered the principal, "but it was much more wonderful than that. The word gave you confidence. It took away your fears. If I hadn't told you that it was a magic word, you might have been killed the very first time. It was your battle-ax that did the trick."

Gawaine surprised the principal by his attitude. He was obviously distressed by the explanation. "You mean, if I hadn't hit them all mighty hard and fast, anyone of them might have crushed me like a—" he fumbled for a word.

"Egg shell," suggested the principal.

"Like an egg shell," agreed Gawaine, and he said it many times.

All through the evening meal people who sat near him heard him muttering, "Like an egg shell." (370) *(Concluded in Paragraph 160)*

UNIT 63

160. The Fifty-First Dragon *(Concluded)*

The next day was clear, but Gawaine did not get up at dawn. Indeed it was almost noon when the principal found him cowering in bed with the covers pulled over his head. The principal called the assistant professor, and together they forced the boy into the forest.

"I believe he will be all right as soon as he gets a couple of more dragons under his belt," explained the principal.

The assistant professor agreed. "It would be a shame to stop such a fine run," he said. "Why, counting the one yesterday, he has killed fifty dragons."

They pushed the boy into a thicket above which hung a meager cloud of steam. It was obviously quite a small dragon. But Gawaine did not come back that night or the next. In fact, he never came back. Some weeks after, the braver ones of the school explored the thicket. They could find nothing to remind them of Gawaine except the metal parts of his medals. Even the ribbons had been devoured.

The principal and the professor agreed that it would be just as well not to inform the school how Gawaine had achieved his record and still less how he came to die. They held that it might have a bad effect on school spirit.

Accordingly, Gawaine has lived in the memory of the school as its greatest hero; and no visitor succeeds in leaving the building today without seeing a great shield which hangs on the wall of the dining room. Fifty pairs of dragon ears are mounted upon the shield; and underneath in gold letters is "Gawaine," followed by the simple inscription, "He killed 50 dragons." — *Heywood Broun* (270)

Fair Deal

If people are to run their fastest in any race, they must be sure that the prize is to be given to the winner. If it were to be found that the prizes were given not in accordance with speed but sometimes because a competitor was a friend of the judges, there soon would be a decline in speed and in the number of competitors. The necessary condition for a full effort is a fair deal.

This is as true of business as of the race track. It is idle to expect full effort from the men and women in a firm where there is favoritism. Men and women do not like to work in an atmosphere of injustice, no matter how much they are paid. — *Callisthenes* (119)

UNIT 64

Notes on Class Discussion

Joan D: Not important whether state or federal government provides the funds for education.

Hank T: Yes, it is. Control should be local. Federal government has too much power now. (*How local?*)

John H: Local governments influenced by local pressures. European democracies make central government control work for them.

(*Which ones? Works how? Educational opportunities restricted?*)

Bill T: Contributions to various governments could act like federal government's system of checks and balances.

Mary L: Biggest advantages:

1. Better teaching because of more rigid requirements for teachers, higher salaries
2. Better buildings and equipment
3. Wider variety of courses
4. Standard courses

Retail Selling Problems

I. Arrangement of goods
   A. Fast-moving articles should be placed in convenient locations.
      1. Near the door
      2. Within easy reach so that no stooping, reaching, or bending is necessary
   B. Related articles should be kept together. Purchase of one article may suggest the purchase of another.
II. Care of stock
   A. Stock should be kept in saleable condition by
      1. Frequent dusting
      2. Replacement of goods damaged by customers
   B. Slow-moving goods should be kept to the minimum.
III. Valuation of inventory
   A. Methods of computation
      1. Exact cost
      2. Market value
      3. Retail inventory method
   B. Change in method
      1. Method may not be changed without permission for tax reasons.

UNIT 65

162. The King's New Clothes

There was a king many long years ago who was very fond of clothes. He had a robe for every hour of the day. The people of his country were always looking for new silks and new styles and new colors for him.

One day two strangers came to the palace and said they could weave the finest garments anyone could imagine. But their cloth would not be ordinary cloth, they said; theirs would be a magic cloth. If a stupid man looked at it, he would not be able to see it at all.

"That is just what I want," said the king. "Make me robes of that magic cloth, and then I shall see which of my advisers are unfit to hold office."

So the king gave the weavers much money and sent them the finest silk, and they set up two looms for their weaving. They appeared to work hard every day and far into the night; but if you had been there, you would have said the looms were empty. You could have seen no cloth at all.

One morning the king, wanting to know how the work was getting along, decided to send an official of the palace to see. "But," said he to himself, "if the man I send is stupid, he will not be able to see the stuff. How then could he tell me what the magic cloth is like?" So the king sent his honest, wise old Minister of State. The good man entered the room where the weaving was going on and suddenly stopped — startled! He saw two looms, but there was not a thread of material on them! The weavers — who were rogues — pretended to point out the fine patterns of the stuff.

They pretended to hold up great pieces of cloth for his inspection, but the poor old man could see only their empty hands moving in the air. But he didn't say so, for that would have showed that he was stupid and unfit for his office. So he only said, "Charming — very charming indeed. I shall tell the king you are going along very well."

From time to time, the king sent others to report. They could see nothing, but not one of them dared say so. All the time the two rogues asked for more and more rich materials and more gold, which they did not use but kept for themselves.

All the people in the city were talking excitedly of the wonderful magic qualities of those robes, and all were eagerly waiting to see the king wear them in public. (390) (Concluded in Paragraph 164)

164. The King's New Clothes (Concluded)

At last the day came when the two rogues announced that the weaving was finished, and the king with all his court went to see it. And the king could see nothing. "This is terrible," he said to himself. "Am I stupid? Am I unfit to be king?" But his officials, who couldn't see anything either, exclaimed how wonderful it all was; and so the king said, "It is wonderful; indeed it is. Excellent! I approve it highly."

And they returned to the palace wondering, for tomorrow the king was to wear the new robes in a public procession.

Morning came and the king went forth for his robes; and the two rogues pretended to be handling very precious cloth, holding up this garment to be admired and then that garment, with all the nobles vowing how fine they were, though none of them could see so much as a patch of cloth. They took off the king's clothes and then pretended to dress him in his new ones. The king stood before the mirror, turning himself this way and that, as if to admire his new finery — but all he could see was himself only partly dressed.

"Well, I am ready," he said, and bravely went out to the procession. His attendants stooped down, pretending to lift the train of the royal robes; and all the people stood on the sidewalks marveling and saying how beautiful the king's clothes were, until a little girl cried out, "Why, he has nothing on but his shirt!" And then all the people said, "He has nothing on but his shirt!" And the king said to himself, "The child is right. There isn't any magic cloth at all!" But he went through the parade just the same; and the attendants carried the imaginary train with great dignity, just as if it were a real one.

Of course, you could tell the story the other way around. You could tell of a king who promised to clothe all his *people* in magical robes. On a certain day he declared that he had clothed all his people in magical robes; and all the people stood around not daring to contradict, because everyone thought that everyone else thought the thing was actually true. Finally one plain person said, "Why he hasn't clothed us at all"; and then everybody said, "Why, he has deceived us all."

One simple word of truth — and another bubble was burst, for both these things have happened in this world. (394)

166. Tessie the Mannequin

It may come as a surprise to many a man that women's dresses need not be bought in a dress shop. They can be made right at home with no more equipment than it would take to launch a small battleship.

One day last summer, Mrs. Smith took her husband out on a window-shopping expedition, primarily to look at a dress that one of the local stores was offering for $59.95. "It is a bargain," she said.

"It doesn't look like any bargain to me," Mr. Smith remarked. "Why, I will bet there isn't $10 worth of material in it — and they have the nerve to ask $59.95!"

"But you have to consider that this dress isn't something that is just turned out by machinery. It is an exclusive model. It has as much personality as if I had made it myself."

Mr. Smith was struck with an inspiration — an inspiration that he estimated quickly might represent a saving of about $50. "Why don't you make it yourself?" he suggested.

Mrs. Smith's determination to buy the dress was weakening; and by the following morning, the store had lost a potential customer. She called her husband at his office and asked him sweetly whether he would mind stopping at Johnson's to get her form.

"Your what?" inquired Mr. Smith.

"My dress form," she explained. "I went there a few hours ago and picked it out, but it was too big for me to carry; so I told them you would call for it. I need it this evening."

That was Mr. Smith's first contact with Tessie the Mannequin, a creature with no head or arms and a single adjustable leg equipped with casters. Mr. Smith picked up Tessie and started out the door. At the door, though, he was forced to pause. The door was a revolving one, and there was not room for both himself and Tessie in the same compartment.

So Mr. Smith conceived the bright idea of setting Tessie up on her casters in one compartment and then getting into the next one and trundling her out. The only drawback to this was that, when he got outside, Tessie was back in the store again. Re-entering his compartment, Mr. Smith made three round trips in the revolving door, gaining speed on each trip. Then he darted out to the sidewalk and waited panting for Tessie to roll by. He missed her on the first try — the door was spinning too fast. But on her next appearance, he was able to snatch her out of her compartment and drag her into the street.

Mr. Smith picked up Tessie and hurried her down the street. Tessie was not heavy, but she was hard to handle. Walking along the street with his arm around her waist seemed so intimate somehow. (466) *(Concluded in Paragraph 168)*

168. Tessie the Mannequin *(Concluded)*

Hoisting Tessie up on his shoulder was no better; it made him feel like an adagio dancer.

Finally, Mr. Smith hailed a taxi. And when the driver inquired, "Where to, buddy?" he was tempted to whisper hoarsely, "To the river!" But he didn't; he took Tessie straight home, as a chivalrous escort should.

From that time on, Tessie dominated the Smith household. The dining room — where there was a large table and a good north light — became her sanctum.

Mr. Smith, meanwhile, had his meals in the kitchen, standing up. This was not merely a posture inspired by self-pity; there were chairs on which he might have sat. But there were pins, too — hundreds of them.

Dressmaking, Mr. Smith discovered, called for much more pinwork than needlework. For one needle that was dropped, a dozen pins found their way to the floor. They also found their way to the chairs, sofa, bed, and bathroom.

After two weeks of industrious effort, Mrs. Smith appeared before her husband in a costume made up of slabs of white muslin loosely threaded together at the edges. "Well, how do you think it looks?"

"I think it looks like a collapsible shroud," he replied hesitantly.

"You don't understand. This is just the muslin pattern," she explained. "I haven't even begun the dress itself."

The finished garment, which emerged some six weeks later from a blizzard of pins, was really quite attractive. Mrs. Smith displayed it proudly on Tessie.

"That is fine! I knew you would be able to do it," he exclaimed. "Frankly, I couldn't tell it from the one in the store window. How much did it come to?"

"Let me see. There was the material, the muslin for the pattern, three pairs of scissors, and the dress form. The whole thing adds up to $114.35."

Mr. Smith reeled and then recovered himself. "Well, anyhow, you got a dress out of it."

"Yes," agreed Mrs. Smith hesitantly, "except that it doesn't fit. As long as it is on the dress form, it is perfectly stunning; but when I put it on, it just hangs. Of course, the fact that I have lost about 10 pounds since I started making it may have something to do with it. So I thought the next time I would get a smaller form —"

"Do you mean to say you are going to start making another dress?"

"Why, yes. With all this equipment —"

"Over my pin-riddled body you are!" muttered Mr. Smith. He sat down at the writing desk and scribbled a blank check payable to the department store. "Here," he said, "Go and buy yourself a dress!"

But Tessie still wears Mrs. Smith's initial creation, and everyone agrees that it fits her as if it had been made for her — which, as a matter of fact, it was! — *Weare Holbrook* (459)

UNIT 69

170. Reading and Writing Practice

1. Dear Mr. Brown: There are two sides to every story. That we all realize.

Our side is that we sent you one gross of our No. 10 pencils on May 10. The statement covering this shipment was mailed to you on May 20. Since then, we have mailed you several notices that your payment was overdue. So far, we have had no word from you.

That is our side of the story. Would you mind turning this letter over and, on the reverse side, telling us your side. Then I am sure we can get together. Very sincerely yours, (93)

2. Dear Mr. Graham: Very likely you have a good reason for not having paid anything on your account since last August. In fact, I am sure of that.

However, you haven't told us what that reason is — whether something is wrong or whether you may have been too busy.

If there is anything wrong, I am sure we can quickly straighten it out.

Whether you send a check now or later, I do hope you will write and let us know. Yours truly, (77)

3. Dear Friend: Your unpaid account with us is now several months overdue. Our auditors will soon be checking our records and will find your good name among our "unpaid accounts" unless we hear from you promptly.

The enclosed blank is attached for your convenience. Why not fill it in, sign it, and mail it promptly in the enclosed postage-paid envelope. This action will save us both a great deal of embarrassment and will maintain your good credit record.

Won't you please fill it out now and mail it today before you forget. Yours very sincerely, (95)

4. Dear Mrs. Gray: We wish to call your attention to an amount of $38.90 that is still due on a purchase you made last March. Perhaps there is some reason for your nonpayment; and, if this is the case, would you be good enough to let us know what adjustment we can make?

On the other hand, if your account has merely been overlooked, please send us your check.

We know we can count on your co-operation. Very truly yours, (79)

5. Dear Mrs. Ward: As you know, your account with us shows a balance of $15.21. Perhaps you have overlooked your last statement. In these days, when there is so much to do, it is understandable that such a small amount might escape your attention.

According to our established credit terms, accounts are payable by the tenth of the month. Your interests are best served by a prompt payment policy. Our constant low prices are made possible only by prompt settlement and the elimination of unnecessary collection expenses.

We know you will appreciate this reminder

and will send us a remittance soon. Sincerely yours, (119)

UNIT 70

172. Reading and Writing Practice

1. Dear Mr. Mix: As you probably know, the amount of insurance to which you are entitled under your company's group life insurance plan is governed by your annual salary. Your last salary increase moved you to a higher insurance bracket. I am, therefore, enclosing a form that shows the new amount for which you are now covered. This form should be attached to the policy you received when you originally enrolled in our insurance plan. Yours truly, (85)

2. Dear Friend: A man may be down because of sickness or accident, but he doesn't have to be out; he can protect himself with insurance. He must do it, however, before he is out.

Plan now to protect yourself in case you should someday be down. Make sure that you have the cash necessary to take care of yourself in case of emergency.

The National Insurance Company has a new income-protection plan that pays you up to $300 a month for as long as you are sick or hurt — for the rest of your life, if necessary.

For complete details on how you can be down and yet not out, mail the enclosed card today. You will incur no obligation. Yours truly, (121)

3. Dear Mr. Smith: If your wife had to support your two children herself, her expenses would be about $450 a month. The amount she would receive from Social Security would be $250 a month. Where will the extra $200 come from? It can come from the National Insurance Company if you act today and take advantage of our family-income insurance plan.

Under this plan the cost for your family will run about $5 a week. If something should happen to you, your family will receive $10,000 immediately, and then $200 a month until your children are capable of supporting themselves.

Our agent can show you in a matter of minutes how this plan works. Why not return the enclosed card and let him know when he may call. Very truly yours, (152)

4. Dear Mr. Jones: There is one man who is constantly working for you. Yet, you pay him no commission; you pay him no salary. He is constantly working to protect you from loss. This man provides safe protection for your business, for your home, and for your property. He is your local insurance agent. He is your friend.

Often he must work long hours analyzing your peculiar problem and planning the right insurance coverage for you. Consult him today and let him give you the benefit of his specialized knowledge of insurance. Yours truly, (99)

KEY TO CHARTS ON BACK LEFT END PAPER

Brief Forms of Gregg Notehand in Alphabetic Order

1. A-an, about, am, and, are-our, be-by, could.

2. Difficult, for, have, I, importance-important, in, into.

3. Is, it, of, opportunity, over, probable, question.

4. Send, shall, short, should, suggest, the, there-their.

5. This, under, was, were, what, when, where.

6. Which, will, with, work, would, yesterday, you.

100 Frequently Used Words in Alphabetic Order

1. A-an, about, after, all, also, am, and.

2. Any, are-our, as, at, be-by, been, before.

3. But, can, come, could, date, day, did.

4. Do, find, for, from, get, give, glad.

5. Go, good, had, has, have, he, her-here.

6. Him, his, hope, how, I, if, in.

7. Is, it, just, know, made, make, matter.

8. May, me, more, much, must, my, not.

9. Now, of, on, only, or, other, out.

10. Over, please, same, say, see, send, sent.

11. Shall, she, should, so, some, take, that.

12. The, them, there-their, they, this, time, to.

13. Up, us, very, was, we, well, were.

14. What, when, which, will, wish, with, would.

15. You, your.

INDEX TO GREGG NOTEHAND

The first figure refers to the unit; the second refers to the paragraph.

BRIEF FORMS OF GREGG NOTEHAND
IN ALPHABETIC ORDER

	A	B	C	D	E	F	G
1							
2							
3							
4							
5							
6							

100 FREQUENTLY USED WORDS
IN ALPHABETIC ORDER

	A	B	C	D	E	F	G
1							
2							
3							
4							
5							
6							
7							
8							
9							
10							
11							
12							
13							
14							
15							

NOTE: The key to the above charts appears on page 319.